The Assault
on Reason

The Assault on Reason

Al Gore

BLOOMSBURY

First published in Great Britain 2007
This paperback edition published 2008

Copyright © Al Gore, 2007

The right of Al Gore to be identified as the author of this work has been asserted by him
in accordance with the Copyright, Designs and Patents Act 1988

Bloomsbury Publishing Plc
36 Soho Square
London W1D 3QY

www.bloomsbury.com

Bloomsbury Publishing, London, New York and Berlin

A CIP catalogue record for this book is available from the British Library

ISBN 978 0 7475 9334 8
10 9 8 7 6 5 4 3 2

Printed in Great Britain by Clays Limited, St Ives plc

All papers used by Bloomsbury Publishing are natural,
recyclable products made from wood grown in well-managed forests.
The manufacturing processes conform to the
environmental regulations of the counrty of origin.

To my father,
Senator Albert Gore Sr.,
1907–1998

Contents

The Assault
on Reason

Introduction

Not long before our nation launched the invasion of Iraq, our longest-serving senator, Robert Byrd of West Virginia, stood on the Senate floor and said: "This Chamber is, for the most part, silent—ominously, dreadfully silent. There is no debate, no discussion, no attempt to lay out for the nation the pros and cons of this particular war. There is nothing. We stand passively mute in the United States Senate."

Why was the Senate silent?

In describing the empty chamber the way he did, Byrd invited a specific version of the same general question millions of us have been asking: "Why do reason, logic, and truth seem to play a sharply diminished role in the way America now makes important decisions?"

The persistent and sustained reliance on falsehoods as the basis of policy, even in the face of massive and well-understood evidence to the contrary, seems to many Americans to have reached levels that were previously unimaginable.

A large and growing number of Americans are asking out loud: "What has happened to our country?" More and more people are trying to figure out what has gone wrong in our democracy, and how we can fix it.

To take another example, for the first time in American history, the executive branch of our government has not only condoned but actively promoted the treatment of captives in wartime that clearly involves torture, thus overturning a prohibition established by General George Washington during the Revolutionary War.

It is too easy—and too partisan—to simply place the blame on the policies of President George W. Bush. We are all responsible for the decisions our country makes. We have a Congress. We have an independent judiciary. We have checks and balances. We are a nation of laws. We have free speech. We have a free press. Have they all failed us?

In the immediate aftermath of Hurricane Katrina, there was for a very short time a quality of vividness and clarity of focus in our public discourse that reminded some Americans—including some journalists—that vividness and clarity used to be more common in the way we talk with one another about the problems and the choices that we face. But then, like a passing summer storm, the moment faded.

It was not always this way. Why has America's public discourse become less focused and clear, less *reasoned*? Faith in the power of reason—the belief that free citizens can govern themselves wisely and fairly by resorting to logical debate on the basis of the best evidence available, instead of raw power—was and remains the central premise of American democracy. This premise is now under assault.

We often tend to romanticize the past, of course, and there was never a golden age when reason reigned supreme, banishing falsehood and demagoguery from the deliberations of American self-government. But for all of America's shortcomings in the past, we did usually strive to honor truth and reason. Our greatest president, Abraham Lincoln, said in 1838, when he and the United States were both very young, "Reason—cold, calculating, unimpassioned reason—must furnish all materials for our future support and defence. Let those materials be moulded into general intelligence, sound morality, and in particular, a reverence for the Constitution and laws."

The truth is that American democracy is now in danger—not from any one set of ideas, but from unprecedented changes in the environment within which ideas either live and spread, or wither and die. I do not mean the physical environment; I mean what is called the public sphere, or the marketplace of ideas.

It is simply no longer possible to ignore the strangeness of our public discourse. I know I am not alone in feeling that something has gone fundamentally wrong. In 2001, I had hoped it was an aberration when polls showed that three-quarters of Americans believed that Saddam Hussein was responsible for attacking us on September 11. More than five years later, however, nearly half of the American public still believes Saddam was connected to the attack.

At first I thought the exhaustive, nonstop coverage of the O. J. Simpson trial was just an unfortunate excess—an unwelcome departure from the normal good sense and judgment of our television news media. Now we know that it was merely an early example of a new pattern of serial obsessions that periodically take over the airwaves for weeks at a time.

Late in the summer of 2006, American news coverage was saturated with the bizarre false confession of a man who claimed to have been present at the death of JonBenét Ramsey—the six-year-old beauty queen whose unsolved murder eleven years before was responsible for another long-running obsession. A few months prior to John Mark Karr's arrest in Bangkok, the disappearance of a high school senior in Aruba and the intensive search for her body and her presumed murderer consumed thousands of hours of television news coverage. Both cases remain unsolved as of this writing, and neither had any appreciable impact on the fate of the Republic.

Like JonBenét Ramsey, O.J. has recently been back at the center of another fit of obsessive-compulsive news, when his hypothetical non-confession wasn't published and his interview on television wasn't aired. This particular explosion of "news" was truncated only when a former television sitcom star used racial insults in a comedy club. And before that we focused on the "Runaway Bride" in Georgia. And before that there was the Michael Jackson trial and the Robert Blake trial, the Laci Peterson tragedy and the Chandra Levy tragedy. And of course we can't forget Britney and KFed, and Lindsay and Paris and Nicole. Tom Cruise jumped on Oprah's couch and married Katie Holmes, who gave birth to Suri. And Russell Crowe apparently threw a telephone at a hotel concierge.

In early 2007, the wall-to-wall coverage of Anna Nicole Smith's death, embalming, and funeral plans, and the legal wrangling over the paternity and custody of her child and disposition of her estate, served as yet another particularly bizarre example of the new priorities in America's news coverage.

And while American television watchers were collectively devoting a hundred million hours of their lives each week to these and other similar stories, our nation was in the process of more quietly making what future historians will certainly describe as a series of catastrophically mistaken decisions on issues of war and peace, the global climate and human survival, freedom and barbarity, justice and fairness.

For example, hardly anyone now disagrees that the choice to invade Iraq was a grievous mistake. In late 2005, the former head of the National Security Agency, retired lieutenant general William Odom, said, "The invasion of Iraq, I believe, will turn out to be the greatest strategic disaster in U.S. history." Yet, incredibly, all of the evidence and arguments necessary to have made the *right* decision were available at the time and in hindsight are glaringly obvious.

Whether you agree with General Odom's assessment or not, Senator Byrd's point before the invasion was that, in America, we are supposed to have a full and vigorous debate about questions as important as the choice between war and peace. So why didn't we? If we had engaged in such a debate, instead of impulsively invading a country that did not attack or imminently threaten us, we might well have avoided the tragic problems created by that war and its aftermath.

Those of us who have served in the U.S. Senate and watched it change over time could volunteer a response to Senator Byrd's incisive description of the Senate prior to the invasion: The chamber was empty because the senators were somewhere else. Many of them were at fund-raising events they now feel compelled to attend almost constantly in order to collect money—much of it from special interests—to buy thirty-second TV commercials for their next reelection campaign.

The Senate was silent on the eve of war because senators don't feel that what they say on the floor of the Senate really matters that much anymore—not to the other senators, who are almost never present when their colleagues speak, and certainly not to the voters, because the news media seldom report on Senate speeches anymore.

Our Founders' faith in the viability of representative democracy rested on their trust in the wisdom of a well-informed citizenry, their ingenious design for checks and balances, and their belief that the rule of reason is the natural sovereign of a free people. As Thomas Paine put it, "For as in absolute governments the king is law, so in free countries the law ought to be king and there ought to be no other."

Our Founders knew all about the Roman forum, and the agora in ancient Athens. They also understood quite well that in America, our public forum would be an ongoing conversation about democracy in which individual citizens would participate most commonly by communicating with their fellow citizens over great distances by means of the printed word. The Founders placed particular emphasis on ensuring that the public could be well informed, and took great care to protect the openness of the marketplace of ideas so that knowledge could flow freely. Thus they not only protected freedom of assembly as a basic right, they made a special point—in the First Amendment—of protecting the freedom of the printing press.

Their world was dominated by the printed word. Just as the proverbial fish doesn't know it lives in water, the United States in its first half century knew nothing but the world of print: the Bible, the hymnal, the Declaration of Independence, our Constitution, our laws, the Congressional Record, newspapers, books, and pamphlets. Though they feared that the government might try to censor the printing press—as King George had done—the Founders could not imagine that America's public discourse would ever consist mainly of something other than printed words.

And yet, today, almost forty-five years have passed since the majority of Americans received their news and information from the printed word. Newspapers are hemorrhaging readers. Reading itself is in decline, not only in our country but in most of the world. The Republic of Letters has been invaded and occupied by the empire of television.

Radio, the Internet, movies, cell phones, iPods, computers, instant messaging, video games, and personal digital assistants all now vie for our attention—but it is television that still dominates the flow of information in modern America. In fact, according to an authoritative global study, Americans now watch television an average of *four hours and thirty-five minutes every day*—ninety minutes more than the world average. When you assume eight hours of work a day, six to eight hours of sleep, and a couple of hours to bathe, dress, eat, and commute, that is almost three-quarters of all the discretionary time that the average American has. And younger Americans, on average, spend even more time watching television.

The Internet is a formidable new medium of communication and a source of great hope for the future vitality of democracy. Eventually—maybe sooner rather than later—television as we now know it may be looked back on as a transition between the age of print and the age of the Internet. (I have sought to hasten the arrival of truly interactive television with a new kind of network—which I cofounded with my partner, Joel Hyatt—Current TV, which bridges television and the Internet.)

But today, television still reaches far more people than does the Internet. Moreover, the majority of Internet users report that they watch television—at least some of the time—*while* they use the Internet. Sixty percent of those who use both media simultaneously report that they *regularly* have the television on while they are using the Internet. Studies show not only a continued increase in the average time Americans spend watching television each day but also an increase in the average time spent by Internet users watching television while they use the Internet.

Television first overtook newsprint to become the dominant source of information in America in 1963. But for the next two decades, the television networks mimicked the nation's leading newspapers by faithfully following the standards of the journalism profession. Indeed, men like Edward R. Murrow led the profession in raising the bar.

In all the years since then, television's share of the total audience for news and information has continued to grow—and its lead over newsprint has continued to expand. Millions of Americans have simply stopped reading newspapers. Afternoon newspapers were the first to go broke. Now, virtually all newspapers are shrinking in profits, advertising, and circulation—and more than a few are even shrinking in their physical size. One day many years ago, a smart young political consultant turned to an older elected official and succinctly described a new reality in America's public discourse: "If it's not on television, it doesn't exist."

This "tipping point," when television replaced the printing press as America's dominant medium, involved far more than the simple substitution of one medium for another. The ability of television to instantly convey moving images as well as words and music to hundreds of millions of Americans simultaneously increased the impact and inherent power of the television medium over the printed word by several orders of magnitude. The suddenness of this dramatic change was like moving in a single decade from the sandal to the space shuttle, from splicing rope to splicing genes.

All of a sudden, in a single generation, Americans made a dramatic change in their daily routine, and started sitting motionless, staring at flickering images on a screen for more than thirty hours each week. Not only did television take over a larger share of the time and attention Americans devoted to news and information, it began to dominate a larger share of the public sphere as a whole. Moreover, as advertisers quickly discovered, television's power to motivate changes in behavior was also unprecedented.

The advertising of products, of course, is the principal business of television. And it is difficult to overstate the extent to which the pervasiveness of modern electronic advertising has reshaped our society. In the 1950s, John Kenneth Galbraith first described the way in which advertising altered the classical relationship by which supply and demand are balanced over time by the invisible hand of the marketplace. Modern advertising campaigns, he pointed out, were beginning to create high levels of demand for products that consumers never knew they wanted, much less needed.

The same phenomenon Galbraith noticed in the commercial marketplace is now the dominant fact of life in what used to be America's marketplace for ideas. The inherent value or validity of political propositions put forward by candidates for office is now largely irrelevant compared with the image-based advertising campaigns they use to shape the perceptions of voters. And the high cost of these commercials has radically increased the role of money in American politics—and the influence of those who contribute it.

That is why campaign finance reform, however well drafted, often misses the main point: so long as the dominant means of engaging in political dialogue is through purchasing expensive television advertising, money will continue in one way or another to dominate American politics. And as a result, ideas will continue to play a diminished role.

That is also why the House and Senate campaign committees in both parties now search for candidates who are multimillionaires and can buy the ads with their own personal resources. Little wonder that the halls of Congress now have a higher proportion of wealthy members.

When I first ran for Congress in 1976, I never took a poll during the entire campaign. Eight years later, however, when I ran statewide for the U.S. Senate, I did take polls and like most statewide candidates relied more heavily on electronic advertising to deliver my message to the voters. I vividly remember a turning point in that Senate campaign when my opponent, a fine public servant named Victor Ashe who has since become a close friend, was narrowing the lead I had in the polls. After a long and detailed review of all the polling information and careful testing of potential TV commercials, the anticipated response from my opponent's campaign and the planned response to the response, my campaign advisers made a recommendation and prediction that surprised me with its specificity: "If you run this ad at this many 'points' [a measure of the size of the advertising buy], and if Ashe responds as we anticipate, and then we purchase this many points to air our response to his response, the net result after three weeks will be an increase of 8.5 percent in your lead in the polls."

I authorized the plan and was astonished when three weeks later my lead had increased by exactly 8.5 percent. Though pleased, of course, for my own campaign, I had a sense of foreboding for what this revealed about our democracy. Clearly, at least to some degree, the "consent of the governed" was becoming a commodity to be purchased by the highest bidder. To the extent that money and the clever use of electronic mass media could be used to manipulate the outcome of elections, the role of reason began to diminish.

As a college student, I wrote my senior thesis on the impact of television on the balance of power among the three branches of government. In the course of that study, I pointed out the growing importance of visual rhetoric and body language over logic and reason. There are countless examples of this, but perhaps, understandably, the first one that comes to mind is from the 2000 campaign, long before the Supreme Court decision and the hanging chads, when the controversy over my sighs in the first debate with George W. Bush created an impression on television that for many viewers outweighed whatever positive benefits I might have otherwise gained in the verbal combat of ideas and substance. A lot of good that senior thesis did me.

The potential for manipulating mass opinions and feelings initially discovered by commercial advertisers is now being even more aggressively exploited by a new generation of media Machiavellis. The combination of ever more sophisticated public opinion sampling techniques and the increasing use of powerful computers to parse and subdivide the American people according to "psychographic" categories that identify their selective susceptibility to individually tailored appeals has further magnified the power of propagandistic electronic messaging that has created a harsh new reality for the functioning of our democracy.

As a result, our democracy is in danger of being hollowed out. The opinions of the voters are sometimes, in effect, being purchased—just as demand for new products is artificially created. Decades ago American journalist and political commentator Walter Lippmann wrote, "The manufacture of consent . . . was supposed to have died out with the appearance of democracy . . . but it has not died out. It has, in fact, improved enormously in technique . . . under the impact of propaganda, it is no longer plausible to believe in the original dogma of democracy."

I recoil at Lippmann's bleak dismissal of America's gift to human history. In order to reclaim our birthright, we Americans must resolve to repair the systemic decay of the public forum. We must create new ways to engage in a genuine and not manipulative conversation about our future. We must, for example, stop tolerating the rejection and distortion of science. We must insist on an end to the cynical use of pseudostudies known to be false for the purpose of intentionally clouding the public's ability to discern the truth. Americans in both parties should insist on the reestablishment of respect for the rule of reason. The climate crisis, in particular, should cause us to reject and transcend ideologically based distortions of the best available scientific evidence.

To be sure, we still share ideas about public matters. But the use of the printed word to work toward general agreement has declined. We rely more heavily now—for good or ill—on electronic images that can elicit emotional responses, often without requiring reflective thought. Like the boarded-up business district of a small town bypassed by an interstate highway, the marketplace of ideas in the form of printed words has emptied out. Video-rental stores and fast-food restaurants have replaced the hardware stores and groceries. It is the emptying out of the marketplace of ideas as we have known it in the past that accounts for the "strangeness" that now haunts our efforts to reason together about the choices we must make as a nation. The mental muscles of democracy have begun to atrophy.

As the dominance of television has grown, extremely important elements of American democracy have begun to be pushed to the sidelines. But the most serious loss by far has been the playing field itself. The "marketplace of ideas" so beloved and so carefully protected by our Founders was a space in which "truths," in John Stuart Mill's words, could be discovered and refined through "the fullest and freest comparison of opposite opinions." The print-based public sphere that had emerged from the books, pamphlets, and essays of the Enlightenment has, in the blinking eyes of a single generation, come to seem as remote as the horse and buggy.

Again, we need to be clear about the original relationship between the printed word, reason, and democracy. While a conversation about such a broad, abstract subject over such a big spread of time can seem awfully slippery, there are some simple truths to hold on to. The new possibilities that led our Founders to recognize that the rule of reason could be our new sovereign emerged as a result of broad social changes that can be traced straight back to Johannes Gutenberg's invention of the printing press. With time, the print revolution broke up the stagnant medieval information monopoly and led to an explosion of knowledge that was disseminated to masses of people who had previously received no knowledge whatsoever that wasn't transmitted from above by some hierarchy of power, either religious or secular.

Initially tantalized by the sudden appearance of the Bible and then other classic works in their own native tongues, people became literate by the millions. Their voracious hunger for wisdom from every source, religious and secular, stimulated the rapid proliferation of print technology and the emergence of a print-based culture that elevated the power and possibility of individuals to seize more control over their own destinies.

More and more people gained an appetite for current information about contemporary events and confidence in their own ability to use their reasoning capacity to sort through the available evidence relevant to decisions that affected their lives.

The American experiment was based on the emergence in the second half of the eighteenth century of a fresh new possibility in human affairs: that the rule of reason could be sovereign. You could say that the age of print begat the Age of Reason which begat the age of democracy. The eighteenth century witnessed more and more ordinary citizens able to use knowledge as a source of power to mediate between wealth and privilege. The democratic logic inherent in these new trends was blunted and forestalled by the legacy structures of power in Europe. But the intrepid migrants who ventured across the Atlantic—many of them motivated by a desire to escape the constraints of class and creed—carried the potent seeds of the Enlightenment and planted them in the fertile soil of the New World.

Our Founders understood this better than any others; they realized that a "well-informed citizenry" could govern itself and secure liberty for individuals by substituting reason for brute force. They decisively rejected the three-thousand-year-old superstitious belief in the divine right of kings to rule absolutely and arbitrarily. They reawakened the ancient Greek and Roman traditions of debating the wisest courses of action by exchanging information and opinions in new ways.

Whether it is called a public forum or a public sphere or a marketplace of ideas, the reality of open and free public discussion and debate was considered central to the operation of our democracy in America's earliest decades. Our first self-expression as a nation—"We the People"—made it clear where the ultimate source of authority lay.

It was universally understood that the ultimate check and balance for American government was its accountability to the people. And the public forum was the *place* where the people held the government accountable. That is why it was so important that the marketplace of ideas operated independent from and beyond the authority of government. The three most important characteristics of this marketplace of ideas were the following:

1. It was open to every individual, with no barriers to entry save the necessity of literacy. This access, it is crucial to add, applied not only to the *receipt* of information but also to the ability to *contribute* information directly into the flow of ideas that was available to all.
2. The fate of ideas contributed by individuals depended, for the most part, on an emergent meritocracy of ideas. Those judged by the market to be good rose to the top, regardless of the wealth or class of the individual responsible for them.
3. The accepted rules of discourse presumed that the participants were all governed by an unspoken duty to search for general agreement. That is what a "conversation of democracy" is all about.

What resulted from this shared democratic enterprise was a startling new development in human history. The liberating force of this new American reality was thrilling to all humankind. It ennobled the individual and unleashed the creativity of the human spirit. Thomas Jefferson declared, "I have sworn upon the altar of God eternal hostility against every form of tyranny over the mind of man."

The Age of Reason also had a dark side, of course. Claims to reason have justified appalling atrocities, including the so-called scientific racism that justified Nazi anti-Semitism and so much else. Moreover, the abstract nature of reason made some of its most zealous practitioners dangerously numb to human realities rooted in emotional attachments and shared feelings of responsibility for community, family, and nature. Critics of this tendency toward cold detachment and extremism first emerged as early as the 1700s.

For all its problems, however, the Enlightenment brought impressive advances in civilization. It set the stage for modern democracy and empowered individuals to use knowledge as a source of influence and power. America's democratic revolution succeeded where the others initially failed because our Founders understood that a well-designed self-government, protected by checks and balances, could be the instrument with which the people embodied their reasoned judgments into law. The rule of reason undergirded and strengthened the rule of law. But to an extent seldom appreciated, all of this—including especially the ability of the American people to exercise the reasoned collective judgments presumed in our Founders' design—depended on the particular characteristics of the marketplace of ideas as it operated during the age of print.

For example, the underlying premise of representative democracy was that the voters in each constituency would be able to communicate freely within the public forum with the candidates vying to be their representative in Congress and assumed further that they could rely on the free flow of information about that representative's subsequent performance in Congress in order to hold him accountable.

We celebrate the vision, wisdom, and courage of our Founders—and sometimes bemoan the apparent lack of these qualities in modern leaders. Yet the human nature of our Founders—a nature that they understood so well—is the same as our own. We have the same vulnerabilities and the same potential, the same weaknesses and the same strengths. The temptation to pursue special interests at the expense of the general welfare is hardly new to American politics. The suspicions by partisans of hidden agendas on the part of their adversaries were common in the era of our founding. Bitter partisanship and the "politics of personal destruction" often reached extremes far worse than those in the present era. Indeed, most of our current complaints are as timeless as the concern by middle-aged parents that the latest generation has lost all respect for values and is well on the road to decadence.

There is, however, something fundamentally new and different about our current crisis of democracy. Among those who share the feeling that something has gone terribly wrong there is wide disagreement about the causes of the problem. Some point to the increased role of special interests and the growing influence of money in American politics. Others point to the enhanced importance of image over substance and the superficial quality of public argument.

Still others bemoan public apathy and the declining participation in the electoral process and civic affairs, which many believe is related to increased cynicism toward and distrust of the integrity of our national institutions and processes. Many are also concerned about the increasingly sophisticated efforts to manipulate public opinion and to selectively control information relevant to collective decision making in a democracy.

Excessive partisanship is identified as a source of the problem by Americans of both political parties, and—especially—by the growing number of independents. Those on the Right lament the intrusion of government via taxes and regulation, while those on the Left decry the wholesale abandonment of the government's prior commitments to public education, health care, science, medical research, assistance to the poor, the young, and the elderly, and the withdrawal from regulating corporate behavior to protect the public interest. Paradoxically, more and more Americans also say they perceive few substantive differences between the two political parties.

There are grains of truth in all of these concerns. I have come to believe, however, that these perceived *causes* are actually *symptoms* of a much deeper crisis.

The present threat is not based on conflicting ideas about America's basic principles. It is based on several serious problems that stem from the dramatic and fundamental change in the way we communicate among ourselves. Our challenge now is to understand that change and see those problems for what they are.

Consider the rules by which our present public forum now operates and how different they are from the norms our Founders knew during the age of print. Today's massive flows of information are largely in only one direction. The world of television makes it virtually impossible for individuals to take part in what passes for a national conversation.

Individuals receive, but they cannot send. They absorb, but they cannot share. They hear, but they do not speak. They see constant motion, but they do not move themselves. The "well-informed citizenry" is in danger of becoming the "well-amused audience."

Ironically, television *programming* is actually more accessible to more people than any source of information has ever been in all of history. But here is the crucial distinction: It is accessible in only one direction. There is no true interactivity, and certainly no conversation. Television stations and networks are almost completely inaccessible to individual citizens and almost always uninterested in ideas contributed by individual citizens.

So, unlike the marketplace of ideas that emerged in the wake of the printing press, there is much less of an exchange of ideas in television's domain because of the imposing barriers to entry that exclude contributions from most citizens.

Along with the one-way nature of the public conversation on television and the distortion of journalism by entertainment values, there is another troubling characteristic of the television medium that is different from the print medium and less friendly to the traditions of democracy. The high capital investment required for the ownership and operation of a television station and the centralized nature of broadcast, cable, and satellite television networks have led to the increasing concentration of ownership by an ever smaller number of larger corporations that now effectively control the majority of television programming in America.

These conglomerates are apparently sometimes tempted to bend their news-programming choices to support the achievement of commercial objectives. The news divisions—which used to be seen as serving a public interest and were subsidized by the rest of the network—are now seen as profit centers designed to generate revenue and, sometimes, to advance the larger agenda of the corporation that owns them. They have fewer reporters, fewer stories, smaller budgets, less travel, fewer bureaus, less-independent judgment, more vulnerability to influence by management, and more dependence on government sources and canned public relations handouts. The coverage of political campaigns, for example, focuses on the "horse race" and little else. And the well-known axiom that guides most local television news is "If it bleeds, it leads." (To which some disheartened journalists add, "If it thinks, it stinks.") For these and other reasons, the U.S. press was recently found in a comprehensive international study to be only the fifty-third-freest press in the world. NBC, to take only one prominent example, is slashing its news division in order to boost profits: It is cutting $750 million from its budget, a considerable amount from the news division. This tragedy is compounded by the irony that this generation of journalists is the best-trained and most highly skilled in the history of their profession. But they are often not allowed to do the job they have been trained to do.

As Dan Rather put it, television news has been "dumbed down and tarted up." The purpose of television news now seems primarily to be to "glue eyeballs to the screen" in order to build ratings and sell advertising.

This was the point made by Jon Stewart, the brilliant host of *The Daily Show with Jon Stewart,* when he visited CNN's *Crossfire:* There should be a distinction between news and entertainment. It really matters. The subjugation of news by entertainment seriously harms our democracy: It leads to dysfunctional journalism that fails to inform the people. And when the people are not informed, they cannot hold government accountable when it is incompetent, corrupt, or both.

The natural tendency toward concentrated ownership of electronic broadcasting firms caused concern in the United States when the technology was first introduced. As early as the 1920s, when radio, the forerunner of television, first debuted in the United States, there was immediate apprehension about its potential impact on democracy. Later, in the 1930s, Joy Elmer Morgan, director of the National Committee on Education by Radio, wrote that if control of radio were concentrated in the hands of a few, "no nation can be free."

Since then, of course, the control of radio in the United States has, in fact, become much more concentrated. And radio is not the only place where big changes have taken place. Television news has undergone a series of dramatic changes. The movie *Network,* winner of the Best Screenplay Oscar in 1976, was presented as a farce but was actually a prophetic warning of the dangers of transforming news—which plays such an important role in our democracy—into profit-driven entertainment programming. The journalism profession morphed into the news business, which became the media industry and is now owned almost completely by conglomerates.

The German philosopher Jürgen Habermas describes what has happened as "the refeudalization of the public sphere." That may sound overly complex or obscure, but the phrase packs a lot of meaning. Feudalism, which thrived before the printing press democratized knowledge and made the idea of America thinkable, was a system in which wealth and power were intimately intertwined, and where knowledge played almost no mediating role. The great masses of the people were denied access to knowledge and, as a result, felt powerless.

And what if an individual citizen or group of citizens wants to enter the public debate by expressing their views on television? Since they cannot simply join the conversation, some of them have resorted to raising money in order to buy thirty seconds in which to express their opinion. But too often they are not allowed to do even that. MoveOn.org tried to buy an ad for the 2004 Super Bowl broadcast to express opposition to Bush's economic policy, which was then being debated by Congress. CBS told MoveOn that "issue advocacy" was not permissible. Then, CBS, having refused the MoveOn ad, began running advertisements by the White House in favor of one of the president's controversial policies. So MoveOn complained, and the White House ad was temporarily removed. By temporarily, I mean it was removed until the White House complained, and CBS immediately put the ad back on, yet still refused to present the MoveOn ad.

To understand the final reason why the news marketplace of ideas dominated by television is so different from the one that emerged in the world dominated by the printing press, it is important to distinguish the quality of vividness experienced by television viewers from the "vividness" experienced by readers. I believe that the vividness experienced in the reading of words is automatically modulated by the constant activation of the reasoning centers of the brain that are used in the process of cocreating the representation of reality the author has intended. By contrast, the visceral vividness portrayed on television has the capacity to trigger instinctual responses similar to those triggered by reality itself   and without being modulated by logic, reason, and reflective thought.

The simulation of reality accomplished in the television medium is so astonishingly vivid and compelling compared with the representations of reality conveyed by printed words that it signifies much more than an incremental change in the way people consume information. Books also convey compelling and vivid representations of reality, of course. But the reader actively participates in the conjuring of the reality the book's author is attempting to depict. Moreover, the parts of the human brain that are central to the reasoning process are continually activated by the very act of reading printed words: Words are composed of abstract symbols—letters—that have no intrinsic meaning themselves until they are strung together into recognizable sequences.

Television, by contrast, presents to its viewers a much more fully formed representation of reality—without requiring the creative collaboration that words have always demanded.

Marshall McLuhan's description of television as a "cool" medium—as opposed to the "hot" medium of print—was hard for me to understand when I read it forty years ago, because the source of "heat" in his metaphor is the mental work required in the alchemy of reading. McLuhan was almost alone in recognizing the new thermodynamic relationship between television viewers and the medium itself.

Years later, one of McLuhan's disciples, Neil Postman, said, "Every technology has a philosophy which is given expression in how the technology makes people use their minds, in what it makes us do with our bodies, in how it codifies the world, in which of our senses it amplifies, in which of our emotional and intellectual tendencies it disregards. This idea is the sum and substance of what the great Catholic prophet Marshall McLuhan meant when he coined the famous sentence 'The medium is the message.'"

While I understand McLuhan's words now, I think they still invite some confusion. Although it is true that television does not elicit the same cerebral response, it definitely does stimulate the flow of much more energy in different areas of the brain. And the passivity associated with watching television is at the expense of activity in parts of the brain associated with abstract thought, logic, and the reasoning process.

Any new dominant communications medium leads to a new information ecology in society that inevitably changes the way ideas, feelings, wealth, power, and influence are distributed—and the way collective decisions are made.

When a new technology emerges as the primary medium for the sharing of information—like the printing press in the fifteenth century or television in the twentieth century—those who adapt to the new technology have to literally change the way they process information. As a result, their brains may actually undergo subtle change.

When millions of people experience these same changes simultaneously in the course of a few decades, their interactions with one another begin to take new forms.

An individual who spends four and a half hours a day watching television is likely to have a very different pattern of brain activity from an individual who spends four and a half hours a day reading. Different parts of the brain are stimulated repetitively.

As I will describe in chapter 1, the human brain—like the brains of all vertebrates—is hardwired to immediately notice sudden movement in our field of vision. We not only notice, we are compelled to look. When our evolutionary predecessors gathered on the African savanna three million years ago and the leaves next to them moved, the ones who didn't look are not our ancestors.

Noticing sudden movement helped to alert the survivors to the presence of a predator, or to the nearness of prey, or to a potential mate. The ones who did notice passed on to us the genetic trait that neuroscientists call "the orienting response." And that is the brain syndrome continuously activated by television—sometimes as frequently as once per second. That is the reason the industry phrase *glue eyeballs to the screen* is actually more than a glib and idle boast. It is also a major part of the reason Americans watch the TV screen an average of four and a half hours a day.

In chapters 1 through 5, I identify and describe the enemies of reason. This section draws the connection between the withdrawal of reason from the public sphere and the resulting vacuum that is filled by fear, superstition, ideology, deception, intolerance, and obsessive secrecy as a means of tightening control over the information that a free society needs to govern itself according to reason-based democracy.

Chapters 6 through 8 assess the damage that has already occurred as a result of the progressive substitution of raw power and institutionalized corruption for reason and logic in policies important to our survival: national security, environmental security, energy security, the protection of our liberty, and the promotion of the general welfare. In each case, the most effective ways to heal this damage can be found in a deeper understanding of how the damage has been caused, and why.

In chapter 9, I offer a road map for restoring the health and vitality of American democracy and propose a strategy for the reintroduction of reason to its proper role at the heart of the deliberative process of self-government. As exciting as the Internet is, it still—for the time being—lacks the single most powerful characteristic of the television medium; because of its architecture and design it does not support the real-time mass distribution of full-motion video. This temporary limitation of the Internet—and, more important, the many strengths that make it a source of hope for the future of democracy—will also be explored in chapter 9.

CHAPTER ONE

The Politics of Fear

Fear is the most powerful enemy of reason. Both fear and reason are essential to human survival, but the relationship between them is unbalanced. Reason may sometimes dissipate fear, but fear frequently shuts down reason. As Edmund Burke wrote in England twenty years before the American Revolution, "No passion so effectually robs the mind of all its powers of acting and reasoning as fear."

Our Founders had a healthy respect for the threat fear poses to reason. They knew that, under the right circumstances, fear can trigger the temptation to surrender freedom to a demagogue promising strength and security in return. They worried that when fear displaces reason, the result is often irrational hatred and division. As Justice Louis D. Brandeis later wrote: "Men feared witches and burnt women."

Understanding this unequal relationship between fear and reason was crucial to the design of American self-government.

Our Founders rejected direct democracy because of concerns that fear might overwhelm reflective thought. But they counted heavily on the ability of a "well-informed citizenry" to reason together in ways that would minimize the destructive impact of illusory, exaggerated, or excessive fears. "When a man seriously reflects on the precariousness of human affairs, he will become convinced that it is infinitely wiser and safer to form a constitution of our own in a cool deliberate manner, while we have it in our power," wrote Thomas Paine in his legendary pamphlet *Common Sense*, specifically warning that the Founders should not take the risk of waiting until some fear seized the public imagination, in which event their reasoning processes would be hampered.

Nations succeed or fail and define their essential character by the way they challenge the unknown and cope with fear. And much depends on the quality of their leadership. If leaders exploit public fears to herd people in directions they might not otherwise choose, then fear itself can quickly become a self-perpetuating and freewheeling force that drains national will and weakens national character, diverting attention from real threats deserving of healthy and appropriate fear and sowing confusion about the essential choices that every nation must constantly make about its future.

Leadership means inspiring us to manage through our fears. Demagoguery means exploiting our fears for political gain. There is a crucial difference.

Fear and anxiety have always been a part of life and always will be. Fear is ubiquitous and universal in every human society. It is a normal part of the human condition. And it has always been an enemy of reason. The Roman philosopher and rhetoric teacher Lactantius wrote, "Where fear is present, wisdom cannot be."

We have always defined progress by our success in managing through our fears. Christopher Columbus, Meriwether Lewis and William Clark, Susan B. Anthony, and Neil Armstrong all found success by challenging the unknown and overcoming fear with courage and a sense of proportion that helped them overcome legitimate fears without being distracted by distorted and illusory fears.

The Founders of our country faced dire threats. If they failed in their endeavors, they would have been hanged as traitors. The very existence of our country was at risk. Yet in the teeth of those dangers, they insisted on establishing the freedoms that became the Bill of

Rights. Are members of Congress today in more danger than were their predecessors when the British army marched on the Capitol?

Are the dangers we now face so much greater than those that led Franklin Delano Roosevelt to famously remind us that the only thing we have to fear is fear itself? Is America in more danger now than when we faced worldwide fascism on the march—when our fathers fought and won a world war on two fronts simultaneously?

Is the world more dangerous than when we faced an ideological enemy with thousands of missiles poised to annihilate our country at a moment's notice? Fifty years ago, when the nuclear arms race with the Soviet Union was raising tensions in the world and McCarthyism was threatening our liberties at home, President Dwight Eisenhower belatedly said, "Any who act as if freedom's defenses are to be found in suppression and suspicion and fear confess a doctrine that is alien to America." Edward R. Murrow, whose courageous journalism was assaulted by Senator Joseph McCarthy, declared, "We will not be driven by fear into an age of unreason."

It is simply an insult to those who came before us and sacrificed so much on our behalf to imply that we have more to be fearful of than they did. In spite of the dangers they confronted, they faithfully protected our freedoms. It is up to us to do the same.

Yet something is palpably different today. Why in the early years of the twenty-first century are we so much more vulnerable to the politics of fear? There have always been leaders willing to fan public anxieties in order to present themselves as the protectors of the fearful. Demagogues have always promised security in return for the surrender of freedom. Why do we seem to be responding differently today?

The single most surprising new element in America's national conversation is the prominence and intensity of constant fear. Moreover, there is an uncharacteristic and persistent confusion about the sources of that fear; we seem to be having unusual difficulty in distinguishing between illusory threats and legitimate ones.

It is a serious indictment of the present quality of our political discourse that almost three-quarters of all Americans were so easily led to believe that Saddam Hussein was personally responsible for the attacks of September 11, 2001, and that so many Americans *still* believe that most of the hijackers on September 11 were Iraqis. And it is an indictment of the way our democracy is currently operating that more than 40 percent were so easily convinced that Iraq did in fact have nuclear weapons, even after the most important evidence presented— classified documents that depicted an attempt by Saddam Hussein's regime to purchase yellowcake uranium from the country of Niger— was revealed to have been forged.

Clearly, the current administration has misused fear to manipulate the political process, and I will return to this issue later in this chapter. But I think a far more important question is: How could our nation have become so uncharacteristically vulnerable to such an effective use of fear to manipulate our politics?

A free press is supposed to function as our democracy's immune system against such gross errors of fact and understanding. As Thomas Jefferson once said, "Error of opinion may be tolerated where reason is left free to combat it." So what happened? Why does our immune system no longer operate as it once did? For one thing, there's been a dramatic change in the nature of what philosopher Jürgen Habermas has described as "the structure of the public forum." As I described in the introduction, the public sphere is simply no longer as open to the vigorous and free exchange of ideas from individuals as it was when America was founded.

When errors of fact and judgment are no longer caught and neutralized by the nation's immune system, it is time to examine the problem and to work toward good health in our political discourse. In order to do this, we need to start paying more attention to new discoveries about the way fear affects the thinking process. And, in fact, recent advances in neuroscience offer new and interesting insights into the nature of fear.

For most of the last century, the human brain was studied almost exclusively in the context of accidents and unusual head injuries. Doctors would note the part of the brain taken out by the injury and then, after careful observation of strange behaviors, would slowly determine what functions had been controlled by the injured part. But now scientists are able to observe healthy brains in normal operation, measuring current, blood flow, and chemical activity that indicate which part of the brain is most active at a particular time.

New technologies in any field can have a revolutionizing impact. When Galileo used new and more powerful telescopes to study the heavens in greater detail, he was able to see the movements of the planets around the sun and the movements of Jupiter's moons around Jupiter in order to describe in compelling detail the comprehensive new model of the solar system first proposed by Copernicus. It was the new technology itself that empowered Galileo to describe a reality that was impossible to perceive so clearly until the new technology of the telescope made it possible.

In almost exactly the same way, the new technology called "functional magnetic resonance imaging," or FMRI, has revolutionized the ability of neuroscientists to look inside the operations of a living human brain and observe which regions of the brain are being used at which times and in response to which stimuli. Just as Galileo could suddenly see the moons of Jupiter, neuroscientists are now able for the first time to see the proper relationships among areas of the brain such as the amygdala and the hippocampus and the neocortex, to name only a few.

An entirely new understanding of the brain is coming forth, and one of the areas that has been richest in discoveries has to do with how we as human beings function in relation to fear. The implications for democracy are profound.

In a democracy, the common (if usually unstated) assumption is that citizens operate as rational human beings, reasoning their way through the problems presented to them as if every question could be analyzed rationally and debated fairly until there is a well-reasoned collective conclusion. But the new research demonstrates that, of course, this is not the way it works at all.

One of the world's leading neuroscientists, Dr. Vilayanur S. Ramachandran, has written, "Our mental life is governed mainly by a cauldron of emotions, motives and desires which we are barely conscious of, and what we call our conscious life is usually an elaborate post hoc rationalization of things we really do for other reasons."

There are other mental structures that govern feelings and emotions, and these structures have a greater impact on decision making than logic and reason. Moreover, emotions have much more power to affect reason than reason does to affect emotions—particularly the emotion of fear.

A scientist at Stony Brook University, Charles Taber, went so far as to say, "The Enlightenment model of dispassionate reason as the duty of citizenship is empirically bankrupt."

In the words of New York University neuroscientist Joseph LeDoux, author of *The Emotional Brain*, "Connections from the emotional systems to the cognitive systems are stronger than connections from the cognitive systems to the emotional systems." Our capacity for fear is "hardwired" in the brain as an ancient strategy that gives us the ability to respond instantly when survival may be at stake. But fear is not the only arousing emotion that is "hardwired" to quickly activate responses. The amygdala, for example, is almost certainly involved in speeding other responses important to our species's survival, such as the urge to reproduce. (It may be partly for that reason that sexual titillation along with fear is also a staple ingredient of modern television programming.) By contrast, reason is centered in parts of the brain that have most recently evolved and depends upon more subtle processes that give us the ability to discern the emergence of threats before they become immediate and to distinguish between legitimate threats and illusory ones.

Neurologists and brain researchers describe how disturbing images go straight to a part of the brain that is not mediated by language or reasoned analysis. There are actually two parallel pathways from the visual centers to the rest of the brain, and one of them serves as a crude but instantaneous warning system. (Evolution often forces a tradeoff between speed and accuracy.) Moreover, whatever the cause of the fear, the phenomenon itself is difficult to turn off once it's turned on.

Psychologists have studied the way we make decisions in the presence of great uncertainty and have found that we develop shortcuts—called "heuristics"—to help us make important choices. And one of the most important shortcuts that we use is called "the affect heuristic." We often make snap judgments based principally on our emotional reactions rather than considering all options rationally and making choices carefully.

This shortcut is actually a useful trait. It allows us to make quicker decisions, and it helps us avoid dangerous situations. However, our use of emotions to make decisions can also cloud judgment. When an emotional reaction like fear is especially strong, it can completely overwhelm our reasoning process.

Moreover, just as fear can interfere with reason in the presence of an imminent threat, it can also exercise the same power over reason in the realms of memory. We mistakenly assume that memory is the exclusive province of reason, but in fact those regions of the brain that give us our capacity for fear have their own memory circuits. Over the course of our lives, we emotionally tag traumatic experiences as memories that are especially accessible to recall—either consciously or unconsciously—and they are constantly being retrieved to guide us in new situations, especially when a rapid response is required.

Most of us are familiar with the phenomenon of post-traumatic stress disorder (PTSD), which is common to rape victims, child abuse victims, and combat veterans, among others. Normally, when an experience is translated into memory, it's given a sort of "time tag," a mechanism that gives us the ability when we recall those experiences to sense how long ago the events we recall occurred and a rough understanding of their temporal sequence. You can sense that the remembered experience was before this and after that. Or that it was ten weeks ago or eleven weeks ago.

However, when traumatic events—those involving anxiety or pain—are stored in memory, the process is different. All bets are off. The amygdala is activated, and that memory is coded and stored differently. In effect, the "time tag" is removed—so that when the traumatic experiences are later recalled, they feel "present." And the memory has the ability to activate the fear response in the present moment—even though the trauma being remembered was a long time ago—because the intensity of the memory causes part of the brain to react as if the trauma were happening again right now. PTSD is the constant intrusion into the mind of traumatic memories and a reexperiencing of the events as if the event had just happened. As Dr. Ramachandran has pointed out, it is this preoccupation with the trauma that can be so disabling.

Even if we know intellectually that the events were long ago, the specialized and robust memory circuits in the fear centers of the brain reexperience the traumatic events when they are remembered and drive the same kinds of responses—such as a faster heartbeat and increased feelings of fear—that would be driven if the experiences were actually occurring at the time.

Structural similarities between previous experiences and subsequent ones can cause the fear centers of the brain to pull memories forward and force them into the present moment. If a subsequent experience is even superficially similar to a traumatic memory, it can wield incredible power over emotions and can trigger the same fear responses evoked by the original trauma.

Moreover, reasoned analysis of the superficial nature of these structural similarities has very little influence over the fear center of the brain and seldom dissipates the power of the fearful memory. Yet the fear center has incredible influence over the reasoning process and also over the way memories are shaped. As UCLA research psychologist Dr. Michael Fanselow describes, "The available evidence suggests the amygdala learns and stores information about fear-arousing events *but also modulates* storage of other types of information *in different brain regions*" (emphasis added).

When human beings developed a higher order of thinking, we gained an advantage in being able to anticipate emerging threats. We gained the ability to conceptualize threats instead of just perceiving them. But we also gained the ability to conceptualize *imaginary* threats. And when groups of people are persuaded to conceptualize these imaginary threats, they can activate the fear response as powerfully as would *real* threats.

This ability to conceive of something that activates the amygdala and starts the fear response is particularly significant because of another important and closely related phenomenon, called "vicarious traumatization." If someone, such as a family member or an individual with whom we identify has experienced trauma, that person's feelings can be communicated to us even though we didn't directly experience the traumatic event.

Recent research proves that the telling of traumatic stories to those who feel linked by identity to the victims of trauma—whether the shared identity is ethnic, religious, historical, cultural, linguistic, tribal, or nationalistic—can actually produce emotional and physical responses in the listener similar to those experienced by the victims.

Indeed, physiologists have recently discovered a new class of neurons, called "mirror neurons," that create a powerful physical capacity for empathy. Dr. Ramachandran described the startling significance of this new finding to me:

It has long been known that neurons in this region (a part of the brain called the anterior cingulate that receives a major input from the amygdala) fire when you poke the patient to cause pain—so they were called "pain sensing neurons" on the assumption that they alert the organism to potential danger—leading to avoidance. But researchers in Toronto found that in human patients some of these cells responded not only when the patient himself was poked with a needle—as expected—but also fired equally when the patient watched *another* patient being poked. These neurons (mirror neurons) were dissolving the barrier between the "self" and others—showing that our brains are actually "wired up" for empathy and compassion. Notice that one isn't being metaphorical in saying this; the neurons in question simply can't tell if you or the other person is being poked. It's as if the mirror neurons were doing a virtual reality simulation of what's going on in the other person's brain—thereby almost "feeling" the other's pain. (I call them Dalai Lama cells.)

Therapists first discovered the powerful phenomenon of vicarious traumatization well before the discovery of the mirror neurons that explain how it works. Dr. I. Lisa McCann and Dr. Laurie Ann Pearlman offer the original definition of vicarious traumatization as "the enduring psychological consequences for therapists of exposure to the traumatic experience of victim clients. Persons who work with victims may experience profound psychological effects, effects that can be disruptive and painful for the helper and persist for months or years after work with traumatized persons."

Throughout the world, stories about past traumas and tragedies are passed down from one generation to the next. Long before television added new punch and power to the ability of storytellers to elicit emotional responses, vivid verbal descriptions of traumas physically suffered by others evoked extremely powerful reactions—even centuries after the original traumas occurred.

In the early summer of 2001, Tipper and I went to Greece. While we were there, the pope made a historic visit to Greece, and was met with thousands of angry demonstrators holding signs, yelling epithets. I looked into what was going on. They were angry about something that had happened eight hundred years ago: The Fourth Crusade had stopped off in Constantinople, sacked the city, and weakened it for the later overthrow by the Turks. And they're angry today, eight hundred years later.

To take a second example, Slobodan Milošević, in the early summer of 1989, went to the plains of Kosovo on the six-hundredth anniversary of the battle that defeated the Serbian Empire in its heyday. Government spokesmen said a million and a half people came. Western estimates said a million people came, covering the hillsides to listen to him speak. In his speech, Milošević revivified the battle of six hundred years earlier. And in the immediate aftermath of that collective retraumatization, a brutal campaign of violent expulsion began against the Croats and the Bosnians and the Kosovars at least in part because there was a vicarious experience of a trauma six centuries earlier that activated in the physical bodies of the individuals present, in this generation a response as if they were reliving that fear of so long ago.

If you look at the conflicts on the Indian subcontinent, in Sri Lanka, in Africa, in Northern Ireland, in the Middle East—indeed, in almost every conflict zone in the entire world—you will find an element of amygdala politics based on vicarious traumatization, feeding off memories of past tragedies. In each case, there is a political process that attempts to solve these conflicts through reasoned discourse. But such a response is insufficient to dissipate the continuing power of the reawakened and revivified traumatic memories. We need new mechanisms, like the Truth and Reconciliation Commission in South Africa—or mechanisms not yet invented—to deal with the role of collective vicarious traumatic memory in driving long-running conflicts.

The principal way we now tell stories in our culture is over television. As I noted, forty years have passed since the majority of Americans adopted television as their primary source of information. As we've seen, its dominance has become so extensive that the average American spends two-thirds of his or her "discretionary time" (time other than working, sleeping, and commuting) watching television. And virtually all significant political communication now takes place within the confines of flickering thirty-second television advertisements.

Research shows that television can produce "vicarious traumatization" for millions. Survey findings after the attacks of September 11 showed that people who had frequently watched television exhibited more symptoms of traumatization than less frequent TV viewers. One analyst of this study said of respondents describing their reactions to 9/11, "Those who watched the most television reported the most stress."

The physical effects of watching trauma on television—the rise in blood pressure and heart rate—are the same as if an individual has actually experienced the traumatic event directly. Moreover, it has been documented that television can create false memories that are just as powerful as normal memories. When recalled, television-created memories have the same control over the emotional system as do real memories.

And the consequences are predictable. People who watch television news routinely have the impression that the cities where they live are far more dangerous than they really are. Researchers have also found that even when statistics measuring specific crimes actually show steady decreases, the measured fear of those same crimes goes up as television portrayal of those crimes goes up. And the portrayal of crime often increases because consultants for television station owners have advised their clients that viewership increases when violent crime leads newscasts. This phenomenon has reshaped local television news.

Many of the national morning programs now lead with crime and murders, and we'll watch them for hours because they are so compelling. The visual imagery on television can activate parts of the brain involved in emotions in a way that reading about the same event cannot.

Television's ability to evoke the fear response is especially significant because Americans spend so much of their lives watching TV. An important explanation for why we spend so much time motionless in front of the screen is that television constantly triggers the "orienting response" in our brains.

As I noted in the introduction, the purpose of the orienting response is to immediately establish in the present moment whether or not fear is appropriate by determining whether or not the sudden movement that has attracted attention is evidence of a legitimate threat. (The orienting response also serves to immediately focus attention on potential prey or on individuals of the opposite sex.) When there is a sudden movement in our field of vision, somewhere deep below the conscious brain a message is sent: *LOOK!* So we do. When our ancestors saw the leaves move, their emotional response was different from and more subtle than fear. The response might be described as "Red Alert! Pay attention!"

Now, television commercials and many action sequences on television routinely activate that orienting reflex once per second. And since we in this country, on average, watch television more than four and a half hours per day, those circuits of the brain are constantly being activated.

The constant and repetitive triggering of the orienting response induces a quasi-hypnotic state. It partially immobilizes viewers and creates an addiction to the constant stimulation of two areas of the brain: the amygdala and the hippocampus (part of the brain's memory and contextualizing system). It's almost as though we have a "receptor" for television in our brains.

When I was a boy growing up on our family farm in the summers, I learned how to hypnotize chickens. You hold the chicken down and then circle your finger around its head, making sure that its eyes trace your hand movement. After a sufficient number of circles, the chicken will become entranced and completely immobile. There's a lot you can do with a hypnotized chicken. You can use it as a paperweight, or you can use it as a doorstop, and either way, the chicken will sit there motionless, staring blankly. (What you can't do is use it as a football.

Something about being thrown through the air seemed to wake that chicken right up.)

It turns out that the immobility response in animals is an area that has received some scholarly attention, and here is one thing the scientists have found: The immobility response is *strongly* influenced by fear. A fear stimulus causes the chicken's amygdala to signal the release of neurochemicals, and controlled experiments show that they make immobility much more likely.

No, I'm not saying that television viewers are like hypnotized chickens. But there may be some lessons for us larger-brained humans in the experiences of barnyard hens. I remember times in my youth when I spent hours in front of a TV without noticing how much time had passed. My own experience tells me that extended television watching can be mind numbing.

That is one of the reasons why I feel so passionately about connecting the television medium to the Internet and opening it up to the creativity and talent of individuals. I believe it is extremely important to pay considerably more attention to the quality and integrity of television programming made by citizens. That is also one of the reasons I am concerned about the potential for exploitation of the television medium by those who seek to use it to manipulate public opinion in ways that bypass reason and logic.

Television's quasi-hypnotic effect is one reason that the political economy supported by the television industry is as different from the vibrant politics of America's first century as those politics were different from the feudalism that thrived on the ignorance of the masses of people in the Dark Ages.

Our systematic exposure to fear and other arousal stimuli on television can be exploited by the clever public relations specialist, advertiser, or politician. Barry Glassner, a professor of sociology at the University of Southern California, argues that there are three techniques that together make up "fearmongering": repetition, making the irregular seem regular, and misdirection. By using these narrative tools, anyone with a loud platform can ratchet up public anxieties and fears, distorting public discourse and reason.

There are, of course, many historical examples of vivid imagery producing vicarious traumatization that has been used for positive purposes. For example, the images of civil rights protesters being threatened with snarling dogs and being brutalized with fire hoses helped mobilize ordinary Americans to become part of a broader movement for social justice. In my own experience, I have learned that visual images—pictures, graphs, cartoons, and computer models—communicate information about the climate crisis at a level deeper than words alone could convey. Similarly, the horrifying pictures that came back to us from both Vietnam and the Iraq war helped facilitate shifts in public sentiment against failing wars that needed to end.

Even though logic and reason have played more prominent roles in the medium of print, they can also be used along with images to powerful and positive effect in the television medium. In fact, visual images of suffering are significant precisely because they can help generate empathy and goodwill. The horrifying pictures from inside Abu Ghraib prison communicated the essence of the wrongdoing there far more powerfully than any words could have. Even so, when such strong feelings are manipulated, the possibility for abuse becomes considerable.

It is well documented that humans are especially fearful of threats that can be easily pictured or imagined. For example, one study found that people are willing to spend significantly more for flight insurance that covers "death from 'terrorist acts'" than for flight insurance that covers "death from 'all possible causes.'" Now, logically, flight insurance for death by any cause would cover terrorism in addition to a number of other potential problems. But something about the buzzword *terrorism* creates a vivid impression that generates excessive fear.

The flight insurance example highlights another psychological phenomenon that is important to understanding how fear influences our thinking: "probability neglect." Social scientists have found that when confronted with either an enormous threat or a huge reward, people tend to focus on the magnitude of the consequence and ignore the probability.

Consider how the Bush administration has used some of the techniques identified by Professor Glassner. Repeating the same threat over and over again, misdirecting attention (from al-Qaeda to Saddam Hussein), and using vivid imagery (a "mushroom cloud over an American city").

September 11 had a profound impact on all of us. But after initially responding in an entirely appropriate way, the administration began to heighten and distort public fear of terrorism to create a political case for attacking Iraq. Despite the absence of proof, Iraq was said to be working hand in hand with al-Qaeda and to be on the verge of a nuclear weapons capability. Defeating Saddam was conflated with bringing war to the terrorists, even though it really meant diverting attention and resources from those who actually attacked us.

When the president of the United States stood before the people of this nation and invited us to "imagine" a terrorist attack with a nuclear weapon, he was referring to terrorists who actually had no connection to Iraq. But because our nation had been subjected to the horrors of 9/11, when our president said "imagine with me this new fear," it was easy enough to bypass the reasoning process that might otherwise have led people to ask, "Wait a minute, Mr. President, where's your evidence?"

Even if you believe that Iraq might have posed a threat to us, I hope you will agree that our nation would have benefited from a full and thorough debate about the wisdom of invading that country. Had we weighed the potential benefits of an invasion against the potential risks, perhaps we could have prevented some of the tragic events now unfolding there.

Terrorism relies on the stimulation of fear for political ends. Indeed, its specific goal is to distort the political reality of a nation by creating fear in the general population that is hugely disproportionate to the actual danger that the terrorists are capable of posing. Ironically, President Bush's response to the terrorist attack of September 11 was, in effect, to further distort America's political reality by creating a new fear of Iraq that was hugely disproportionate to the actual danger Iraq was capable of posing. That is one of the reasons it was so troubling to so many when in 2004 the widely respected arms expert David Kay concluded a lengthy, extensive investigation into the administration's claim that Iraq posed an enormous threat because it had weapons of mass destruction with the words *We were all wrong.*

As we now know, of course, there was absolutely no connection between Osama bin Laden and Saddam Hussein. In spite of that fact, President Bush actually said to the nation at a time of greatly enhanced vulnerability to the fear of attack, "You can't distinguish between al-Qaeda and Saddam."

History will surely judge America's decision to invade and occupy a fragile and unstable nation that did not attack us and posed no threat to us as a decision that was not only tragic but absurd. Saddam Hussein was a brutal dictator, to be sure, but not one who posed an imminent danger to us. It is a decision that could have been made only at a moment in time when reason was playing a sharply diminished role in our national deliberations.

Thomas Jefferson would have recognized the linkage between absurd tragedy and the absence of reason. As he wrote to James Smith in 1822, "Man, once surrendering his reason, has no remaining guard against absurdities the most monstrous, and like a ship without rudder, is the sport of every wind."

I spoke at the Iowa Democratic Convention in the fall of 2001. Earlier in August, I had prepared a very different kind of speech. But in the aftermath of this tragedy, I proudly, with complete and total sincerity, stood before the Democrats of Iowa and said, "George W. Bush is my president, and I will follow him, as will we all, in this time of crisis." I was one of millions who felt that same sentiment and gave the president my total trust, asking him to lead us wisely and well. But he redirected the focus of America's revenge onto Iraq, a nation that had nothing whatsoever to do with September 11.

The fear campaign aimed at selling the Iraq war was timed precisely for the kickoff of the 2002 midterm election. The president's chief of staff explained the timing as a marketing decision. It was timed, Andrew Card said, for the post–Labor Day advertising period because that's when advertising campaigns for "new products," as he referred to it, are normally launched. The implication of his metaphor was that the old product—the war against Osama bin Laden—had lost some of its pizzazz. And in the immediate run-up to the election campaign of 2002, a new product—the war against Iraq—was being launched. For everything there is a season, particularly for the politics of fear.

The president went to war verbally against terrorists in virtually every campaign speech and fund-raising dinner for his political party. It was his main political theme. Democratic candidates like Senator Max Cleland in Georgia, a triple-amputee Vietnam vet, were labeled unpatriotic for voting counter to the White House's wishes on obscure amendments to the homeland security bill.

And when Tom DeLay, the former Republican leader in the House of Representatives, was embroiled in an effort to pick up more congressional seats in Texas by forcing a highly unusual redistricting vote in the state senate, he was able to track down Democratic legislators who fled the state to prevent a quorum—and thus prevent the vote—by enlisting the help of President Bush's new Department of Homeland Security. As many as thirteen employees of the Federal Aviation Administration conducted an eight-hour search, joined by at least one FBI agent (though several other agents who were asked to help refused to do so). DeLay was admonished by the House Ethics Committee but refused to acknowledge any wrongdoing.

By locating the Democrats quickly with the technology put in place for tracking terrorists, the Republicans were able to succeed in focusing public pressure on the weakest of the senators and forced passage of their new political redistricting plan. Thanks in part to the efforts

of three different federal agencies, Bush and DeLay were able to celebrate the gain of up to seven new Republican congressional seats.

This persistent effort to politicize the war in Iraq and the war
against terrorism for partisan advantage is obviously harmful to the
prospects for bipartisan support of the nation's security policies. By
sharp contrast, consider the different approach that was taken by Prime
Minister Winston Churchill during the terrible days of October 1943
when, in the midst of World War II, he faced a controversy with the
potential to divide his bipartisan coalition. He said,

> What holds us together is the prosecution of the war. No . . .
> man has been asked to give up his convictions. That would be
> indecent and improper. We are held together by something out-
> side, which rivets our attention. The principle that we work on
> is, "Everything for the war, whether controversial or not, and
> nothing controversial that is not bona fide for the war." That is
> our position. We must also be careful that a pretext is not made
> of war needs to introduce far-reaching social or political changes
> by a side wind.

What Churchill warned against is exactly what the Bush administration has attempted to do, using the war against terrorism for partisan advantage and introducing far-reaching changes in social policy
in order to consolidate its political power.

On many other issues as well, it is now clear that the Bush administration has resorted to the language and politics of fear in order to
short-circuit debate and drive the public agenda without regard to the
evidence, the facts, or the public interest. As I will discuss later in
chapter 5, the administration has not hesitated to use fear of terrorism to attack measures in place for a generation to prevent a repetition of Cold War abuses of authority by the FBI and the intelligence
community. Fear of terrorism has also conveniently distracted the
American people from pesky domestic issues such as the economy,

which was beginning to seriously worry the White House in the summer of 2002.

Rather than leading with a call to courage, this administration has chosen to lead by inciting fear. In the 2006 election campaign, Bush was even more explicit, saying that "if Democrats win, the terrorists win."

There is legitimate fear, of course, and a legitimate and responsible way to address it. But fear of death rouses us like no other. It is unconscionable to use forged documents and false arguments to generate such panic by convincing Americans that terrorists are going to detonate nuclear weapons in cities where they live.

When physical survival is connected to a conjured fear, that fear has a qualitatively different aspect. All fears should be talked about and can be talked about in a responsible way if they're real and if they're dealt with in a way that has integrity. But the intentional creation of false fears for political purposes is harmful to our democracy.

Of course, the use of fear as a political tool is not new. American history is rife with examples, "Remember the *Maine*" and the Gulf of Tonkin Resolution to mention only two. I personally recall the way President Richard Nixon used the fear of violent crime in the midterm elections of 1970.

It was a campaign I saw firsthand. My father, who was the bravest politician I have ever known, was slandered as unpatriotic because he opposed the Vietnam War; he was accused of being an atheist because he opposed a constitutional amendment to foster government-sponsored prayer in the public schools.

I was in the military at the time, on my way to Vietnam as an army journalist in an engineering battalion. I was on leave the week of the election. Law and order, court-ordered busing, a campaign of fear emphasizing crime—these were the other big issues that year. It was a sleazy campaign by Nixon, one that is now regarded by political historians as a watershed, marking a sharp decline in the tone of our national discourse.

In many ways, George W. Bush reminds me more of Nixon than of any other president. Like Bush, Nixon subordinated virtually every principle to his hunger for reelection. He instituted wage and price controls with as little regard for his conservative principles as President Bush has shown in piling up trillions of dollars of debt.

After the oil embargo of 1973, Nixon secretly threatened a military invasion of the Middle Eastern oil fields. Now Bush has actually done it, keeping his true intentions secret, as Nixon did. After he was driven from office in disgrace, Nixon confided to one of his regular interlocutors: "People react to fear, not love. They don't teach that in Sunday school, but it's true."

Speaking on national television the night before that 1970 election, Senator Ed Muskie of Maine addressed the real choice confronting the voters: "There are only two kinds of politics. They're not radical and reactionary or conservative and liberal or even Democratic and Republican. There are only the politics of fear and the politics of trust. One says you are encircled by monstrous dangers. Give us power over your freedom so we may protect you. The other says the world is a baffling and hazardous place, but it can be shaped to the will of men.

"Cast your vote," he concluded, "for trust in the ancient traditions of this home for freedom."

The next day, my father was defeated—defeated by the politics of fear. But his courage in standing for principle made me so proud and inspired me. I really felt that he had won something more important than an election. In his speech that night, he stood the old segregationist slogan on its head and defiantly promised, "The truth shall rise again." I wasn't the only person who heard that promise, nor was I the only one for whom that hope still rings loud and true.

But before such a hope can be realized, we need to understand the implications of fear's new prominence in our democracy. In the following chapter, I will explore why, in an atmosphere of constant fear, the public is more likely to discard reason and turn to leaders who demonstrate dogmatic faith in ideological viewpoints. These new demagogues don't actually offer greater security from danger, but their simplistic and frequently vitriolic beliefs and statements can provide comfort to a fearful society.

Unfortunately, the rise of these leaders serves only to exacerbate the decline of reason and further jeopardize our democracy.

CHAPTER TWO

Blinding the Faithful

The relationship between faith, reason, and fear sometimes resembles the children's game of rock, paper, scissors. Fear displaces reason, reason challenges faith, faith overcomes fear. In a book banned by the church during the decade of Galileo's trial in the seventeenth century, *Religio Medici*, Thomas Browne wrote, "As reason is a rebel to faith, so passion is a rebel to reason." Browne was one of many who struggled during the early Enlightenment with the conflicting claims of ultimate authority made by the church, the rule of reason, and human nature. He concluded that faith, reason, and passion "may be all Kings, and yet make but one monarchy: every one exercising his sovereignty and prerogative in a due time and place, according to the restraint and limit of circumstance."

During the century and a half that followed—from Galileo's imprisonment to America's independence—many Enlightenment thinkers began to insist that reason alone must occupy the throne as the new sovereign source of authority. "Fix reason firmly in her seat, and call to her tribunal every fact, every opinion," wrote Thomas Jefferson. "Question with boldness even the existence of a God; because if there be one, He must more approve of the homage of reason, than that of blind-folded fear."

Jefferson and our other Founders believed that the progressive unfolding of the Enlightenment would allow reason to assume important duties that had been performed by blind faith. They had confidence that the twin daughters of reason—science and law—would enlighten us and empower us to restrain our passions and build our courage. They believed that in the process, the American people would find a new source of security from existential fear in a self-government based on the rule of reason.

Though most of the American Revolutionaries never adopted the extreme anticlerical views of their French counterparts, they nevertheless felt keenly that organized religion in the old world had been a cynical ally of the political despotism they aspired to overthrow. After all, many of them were descended from immigrants fleeing oppression and religious persecution. Jefferson wrote that throughout history, the state-sanctioned religious authority "has been hostile to liberty. He is always in alliance with the despot, abetting his abuses in return for protection to his own. It is easier to acquire wealth and power by this combination than by deserving them."

In his very last letter, written ten days before his death (a few hours before that of John Adams) on the fiftieth anniversary of the Declaration of Independence, Jefferson expressed his hope that the Declaration would arouse people throughout the world

to burst the chains under which monkish ignorance and superstition had persuaded them to bind themselves, and to assume the blessings & security of self-government. That form, which we have substituted, restores the free right to the unbounded exercise of reason and freedom of opinion. All eyes are opened, or opening, to the rights of man. The general spread of the light of science has already laid open to every view the palpable truth, that the mass of mankind has not been born with saddles on their backs, nor a favored few booted and spurred, ready to ride them legitimately by the grace of God.

It is important to note that what Jefferson warned against was not faith itself—nor even organized religion itself. He was warning us against the combination of religious dogma and governmental power. He and our other Founders fought just as hard *for* the free exercise of religion by individuals as they fought *against* the establishment of religion by government.

It is also one of America's most painful ironies that Jefferson and many of our other Founders often seemed so blind to the immorality of their own participation in slavery. How could Jefferson write with such force and clarity about the contemptuous idea that some people were "born with saddles on their backs" and not immediately free the slaves he owned? Another point: Many of those who began the abolitionist movement were more motivated by their religious beliefs than by reason; and the fact that faith led them more quickly to the truth about slavery calls into question Jefferson's easy conclusion that reason is superior to faith. Still, for most people, a balance between reason and faith is a better guide than either alone.

With a few exceptions, our Founders were not irreligious. They knew then—as most of us feel now—that despite the many clashes between reason and faith, these cohabit much more easily in the mind than do reason and fear. As John Donne wrote at the beginning of the seventeenth century, "Reason is our soul's left hand, Faith her right."

Fear, however, can disrupt the easy balance between reason and faith—especially irrational fear of a kind less readily dispelled by reason. When fear crowds out reason, many people feel a greater need for the comforting certainty of absolute faith. And they become more vulnerable to the appeals of secular leaders who profess absolute certainty in simplistic explanations portraying all problems as manifestations of the struggle between good and evil.

It may well be that the global epidemic of fundamentalism—Muslim, Christian, Hindu, and Jewish, among others—has been partly caused by the dizzying pace of technologically driven change.

This unprecedented globalizing tsunami has disrupted many age-old traditional patterns in families, communities, markets, environments, and cultures all around the world.

To brace themselves and their families against disturbing and disorienting change, people instinctively reach for the strongest tree they can find—which is often the one that seems to have the deepest roots. As people cling ever more firmly to their religious traditions, they can become more vulnerable to ideas and influences that reason might filter out in less fearful times.

If dogma and blind faith rush in to fill the vacuum left by reason's departure, they allow for the exercise of new forms of power more arbitrary and less derived from the consent of the governed. In simple terms, when fear and anxiety play a larger role in our society, logic and reason play a diminished role in our collective decision making.

Unfortunately, the new expressions of power that surface in such circumstances often spring from the deep, poisoned wells of racism, ultranationalism, religious strife, tribalism, anti-Semitism, sexism, and homophobia, among others. And the passions thus mobilized are exploited most of all by those who claim divine authority to restore security and order.

Throughout history, our innate fear of others-who-are-different-from-us has combined all too frequently with some malignant dogma, masquerading as a message from God, to unleash the most horrific violence and oppression in the repertoire of hell. Moreover, this deadly form of exclusivist group passion can be virtually invulnerable to reason. So it is especially useful to demagogues who learn how to fan it and exploit it to gain and consolidate power.

One of the most important contributions of America to the world was the precision of our Founders in separating the relationship between God and government. God's role in establishing the basis for government, they believed, was to endow every individual with "certain unalienable rights"—not to endow any particular leader with a divine right to exercise power over others.

Having replaced the divine right of kings with the divine rights of individuals, our Founders overthrew the monarchy and designed a self-government according to the strictures of reason. And they took special care to insulate the ongoing deliberations of democracy against the recombination of fear and dogma, by guarding against any effort by government to establish in law any trace of divine justification for the exercise of power.

They were also keenly aware of the thin and permeable boundary between religious fervor and power-seeking political agendas. "A religious sect may degenerate into a political faction," wrote James Madison, but the new American nation would nevertheless be protected against the ungovernable combination of religious fervor and political power as long as the Constitution prohibited the federal government from establishing any particular creed as preeminent.

This principle was so well established that in 1797 the U.S. Senate unanimously approved, and President John Adams signed, a treaty that contained the following declaration: "The United States is not a Christian nation any more than it is a Jewish or Mohammedan Nation."

In the absence of a national religion, the guarantee of freedom for individuals to believe what they wish would inevitably produce a panoply of different doctrines. The Founders understood that the way to protect and defend people of faith—and I am one—is by preventing any one sect from dominating.

Thus, Madison continued, even if a passionate religious sect became a political faction in one part of the nation, "the variety of sects dispersed over the entire face of it must secure the national councils against any danger from that source." In other words, the separation of these sects would guarantee that their respective efforts to exercise power would cancel out one another.

Our Founders relied time and again on this same Newtonian system of checks and counterweights in order to protect the Republic against the abusive combination of religion and political power. They trusted in the mechanics of balance because they knew that human beings would always seek power. Therefore, the only way to create a safe forum for reason was to disperse power into separate sources that would constantly push against one another in a self-balancing system. And they followed one guiding principle above all others in their effort to establish an equipoise that allowed rational discourse to maintain its equilibrium: Prevent the concentration of too much power in the hands of a single person or small group.

Over sixty years ago, in the middle of World War II, Justice Robert Jackson wrote, "If there is any big star in our constitutional constellation, it is that no official, high or petty, can prescribe what shall be orthodox in politics, nationalism, religion, or other matters of opinion." His words are no less true today.

Any effort by any government official in America to claim any divine right is therefore blasphemy. Government, in the American design, has absolutely *no* God-given rights. Its moral authority comes from the integrity of its deliberative processes and our own participation in those processes. Its derivation of just power from the consent of the governed must flow according to the rule of law. As John Adams first wrote in Massachusetts, we are "a government of laws and not of men."

The separation of church and state was thus based not only on the Founders' insights into fear, faith, and reason, but also on their new awareness of the nature of power. They understood that the love of power can become so intoxicating that it overwhelms reason. It was actually this distrust of concentrated power that led them not only to separate organized religion from the exercise of governmental authority, but also to separate the powers of the national government into three coequal branches and embed each in a complex web of checks and balances designed to further prevent the aggregation of too much power in any one branch.

Laws were to be deliberated carefully and crafted within a legislative branch that was itself insulated against the danger of concentrated power with its own separation into two coequal chambers, each endowed with a different set of perspectives and incentives—and with special provisions designed to protect passionately held minority views from being overrun by majority opinions.

Each of these laws was to be administered by an executive whose power was also constrained and circumscribed by the Constitution. Then, as a further protection against the abusive use of governmental power, every law was also subjected to review by a Supreme Court, whose members—once appointed and confirmed—served for life and whose duty was to ensure that the principles embodied in the Constitution were not violated by any law, either in its wording or in its execution.

But this intricate clockwork mechanism of American government has always depended on a "ghost in the machine." The ghost animating the Constitution's machinery is not holy; it is us, all of us, the proverbial "well-informed citizenry." We may be endowed with individual rights by our Creator, but we act to protect those rights and govern our nation with the instruments of reason.

The immune system of American democracy has operated more effectively when citizens of the nation had a greater opportunity to examine "every fact, every opinion" before reason's tribunal. Even though there has never been a time when the system worked perfectly, we have had greater success as a nation when there has been more open discussion of the options before us. But our continued willingness and competence as citizens to play that essential role has now been called into question. Our facility with rational analysis is not what it used to be. The truth is, reading and writing simply don't play as important a role in how we interact with the world as they used to.

Our ability to operate the intricate machinery of self-government has always depended, to an underappreciated degree, on a widespread familiarity and competence with printed words. The Constitution, all of our Founders' explanations of their intent, all of the laws passed by Congress, and all of the Supreme Court decisions of the last 218 years are in printed words. As citizens, if we are not well practiced in and thoroughly familiar with the use of words as handles with which to grasp our power as citizens, we have a diminished ability to "fix reason firmly in her seat."

The metaphor of our "immune system" protecting our democratic system has recently been enriched by new understandings about how our biological immune system operates. The brain and the immune system have something important in common: Neither is fully formed at birth; both continue to develop rapidly during infancy. We humans have the longest extended period of infancy of any creatures in nature. This characteristic of our species—called "neoteny"—has profound implications for our tendency to absorb vast amounts of culture, tradition, and beliefs into the "operating system" of our brains. Psychological and relationship patterns—including dysfunctions— and all manner of other habits and behaviors are passed down from one generation to the next.

The immune system calibrates itself during infancy and childhood as it produces antibodies in response to threats to health. When the antibodies are no longer needed, the genetic codes necessary for reproducing them are stored by the immune system so that they are readily accessible in case there must be an immediate surge in the production of these antibodies to repel subsequent threats. (In much the same way, traumatic memories remain preferentially accessible, stored in the fear center of the brain.)

Scientists have recently discovered that the modern practice of quickly treating infants with massive doses of antibiotics at the first sign of a threatening pathogen has had a disturbing side effect: It deprives the immune system of its ability to "learn" how it should respond quickly and appropriately to pathogens. As a result, the normal "close order drill" of a healthy immune system can become freewheeling, loose, and inexact in its responses to threats and can become confused into responding inappropriately to benign insults as if they were deadly threats. The increased incidence of asthma and other immune system disorders may be more attributable to this disabling of the immune system than to the new prevalence of pathogens in the environment.

It may well be that the disuse of democracy's calisthenics—the sharp decline in reading and writing—and the bombardment of every new fear with television commercials and simplistic nostrums disguised as solutions for the indicated fear has given American democracy an immune system disorder that prevents the citizenry from responding precisely, appropriately, and effectively to serious threats to the health of our democracy. So all of a sudden we overreact to illusory threats and underreact to real threats.

The disclosure that our government had been cruelly and routinely torturing captured prisoners—and was continuing to do so as official policy—provoked surprisingly little public outcry, even though it threatened America's values and moral authority in the world. Similarly, the disclosure that the executive branch had been conducting mass eavesdropping on American citizens without respecting the constitutional requirement that it obtain judicial warrants—and was continuing to do so—caused so little controversy that the Congress actually adopted legislation approving and affirming the practice. Yet this action threatened the integrity of the Bill of Rights, which is at the heart of America's gift to human history.

At the same time, the majority of citizens were led to wholeheartedly approve and endorse the invasion of a country that did not attack us and posed no threat to us. And there was little opposition expressed to the redeployment of U.S. troops and other war-fighting resources from the hot pursuit of the terrorists who actually *did* attack us and who actually *do* pose an ongoing threat.

So how could we have become so confused about the difference between real threats and illusory threats? Are we now exhibiting the kind of freewheeling and loose response to dangers facing the Republic that makes us less capable of maintaining the healthy operation of

American constitutional government? And even if you disagree with my conclusions about the choices the administration made, wouldn't we be better off if we had had a full and open debate about them?

By portraying the invasion of Iraq as the central front in an epic struggle between good and evil, President Bush sought to cloak his policy of unprovoked war in the garb of religious faith. America had been momentarily stunned, of course, by the ferocity and magnitude of the terrorist attacks on September 11, 2001. The fear of further attacks and the intense anger we all felt at those who killed our fellow citizens made our country unusually willing to follow the leadership of our president and strike back at targets of his choosing.

Initially, he wisely sent troops into Afghanistan to attack the terrorists and disrupt their bases. But soon thereafter, Bush began to redirect the nation's desire for revenge away from Osama bin Laden and toward Saddam Hussein. He offered Americans a way to cut through the complexities of foreign policy by sorting every nation in the world into two simple categories: "You're either with us or you are against us." He described Iraq as part of "the axis of evil" and offered forged evidence that Hussein was seeking to develop atomic bombs. Ironically, the other two members of that "axis"—Iran and North Korea—have used the last six years to actually pursue nuclear weapons programs.

Well before he began beating the drums for war against Iraq, Bush had already announced that his chosen enemy was evil itself. The day after 9/11, Bush announced, "This will be a monumental struggle of good versus evil, but good will prevail." Two days later, I was sitting in the audience at the National Cathedral when Bush proclaimed that his "responsibility to history" was to "rid the world of evil." I actually thought that most of the president's speech that day was excellent, and I told him so. But I remember being astonished at the grandiosity and hubris of his odd and disturbing claim that he could and would "rid the world of evil."

Really?

The following week, in addressing a joint session of Congress, Bush said God had foreordained the outcome of the conflict in which we were engaged because "freedom and fear, justice and cruelty, have always been at war, and we know that God is not neutral between them."

As others have noted, Bush's view of his policies in the context of a fateful spiritual conflict between good and evil does not really represent Christian doctrine. It actually more closely resembles an ancient Christian heresy called Manichaeism—rejected by Christianity more than a thousand years ago—that sought to divide all of reality into two simple categories, absolute good and absolute evil.

Simplicity is always more appealing than complexity, and faith is always more comforting than doubt. Both religious faith and uncomplicated explanations of the world are even more highly valued at a time of great fear. Moreover, during times of great uncertainty and public anxiety, any leader who combines simplistic policies with claims of divine guidance is more likely to escape difficult questions based on glaring logical flaws in his arguments.

There are many people in both political parties who worry that there is something deeply troubling about President Bush's relationship to reason, his disdain for facts, and his lack of curiosity about any new information that might produce a deeper understanding of the problems and policies that he is supposed to wrestle with on behalf of the country.

Yet Bush's incuriosity and seeming immunity to doubt is sometimes interpreted by people who see and hear him on television as evidence of the strength of his conviction, even though it is this very inflexibility—this willful refusal even to entertain alternative opinions or conflicting evidence—that poses the most serious danger to our country.

By the same token, the simplicity of many of Bush's pronouncements is often misinterpreted as evidence that he has penetrated to the core of a complex issue, when in fact exactly the opposite is true:

They often mark his refusal even to *consider* complexity. And that's particularly troubling in a world where the challenges America faces are often quite complex and require rigorous, sustained, disciplined analysis.

Yet I don't remember a single newspaper, commentator, or political leader ever questioning the president's claim that our nation's objective should be to "rid the world of evil." Further, I heard precious little questioning of the preposterous logic by which the president and vice president had conflated Osama bin Laden and Saddam Hussein. It was as if the nation had decided to suspend the normal rigors of logical analysis while we pursued war against a noun (terror) and a nation (Iraq) that had absolutely nothing to do with the attack we were seeking to avenge.

After invoking the language and symbols of religion to bypass reason and convince the country to go to war, Bush found it increasingly necessary to disdain and dispute inconvenient facts that began to surface in public discussions. He sometimes seemed to wage war against reason itself in his effort to deny obvious truths that were totally inconsistent with the false impressions the nation had been given prior to making the decision to invade. He and his team seemed to approach every question of fact as a partisan fight to the finish.

Those who questioned the faulty assumptions on which the war was based were attacked as unpatriotic. Those who pointed to the forged evidence and glaring inconsistencies were accused of supporting terrorism. One of Bush's congressional allies, John Boehner, then House majority leader, said, "If you want to let the terrorists win in Iraq, just vote for the Democrats."

This same pattern has characterized the effort to silence dissenting views *within* the executive branch, to censor information that may be inconsistent with its stated ideological goals, and to demand conformity from all executive branch employees.

Those inside the administration who sounded alarms about the increasingly troubling signs that our nation was marching with blind faith into a strategic quagmire were intimidated, threatened, and censored. For example, the administration undercut the four-star general who was chief of staff of the U.S. Army, General Eric Shinseki, by naming his successor fourteen months before his retirement. And Major General John Batiste testified last year that anyone in the Pentagon who asked about postwar planning was threatened with being fired.

Astonishingly, the bipartisan Iraq Study Group felt it was necessary to include in its report last year a recommendation that the White House restore the tradition of candor in the relationship between civilian leaders and the uniformed military and allow generals and admirals to tell the truth and give honest recommendations without fear of retribution. I use the word *astonishing* because I remember when American citizens—in their role as voters—would have so severely punished such outrageous abuses, especially in time of war, that it would have been inconceivable that a bipartisan panel of "experts" would need to advise the president to allow his generals to tell the truth.

The framers of the Constitution understood the threat posed to rational debate by the use of intimidation to silence truth tellers. As Alexander Hamilton put it in Federalist No. 73, "A power over a man's support is a power over his will." As another example of this phenomenon, before the Iraq war began, CIA analysts who strongly disagreed with the White House assertion that Osama bin Laden was linked to Saddam Hussein found themselves under pressure at work and became fearful of losing promotions and salary increases. And tragically, the CIA failed to correct a manifestly false view that there was a linkage between al-Qaeda and the government of Iraq.

That is similar to what happened in the 1960s to FBI officials who disagreed with J. Edgar Hoover's view that Dr. Martin Luther King was closely connected to Communists. The head of the FBI's domestic intelligence division said that as a result of his efforts to tell the truth about King's innocence, he and his colleagues became isolated and pressured. "It was evident that we had to change our ways or we would all be out on the street. . . . The men and I discussed how to get out of trouble. To be in trouble with Mr. Hoover was a serious matter. These men were trying to buy homes, had mortgages on homes, children in school. They lived in fear of getting transferred, losing money on their homes, as they usually did. . . . So they wanted another memorandum written to get us out of the trouble that we were in." Soon, there was no more difference of opinion within the FBI, and the false accusation became the unanimous view.

The very idea of self-government depends on open and honest debate as the preferred method for pursuing the truth—and a shared respect for the rule of reason as the best way to establish the truth. The Bush administration routinely shows disrespect for that whole basic process. It claims divine guidance. It feels it already knows the truth and isn't very curious to learn about any facts that might contradict it.

For example, Bush described the war in Iraq as a "crusade," disregarding the obvious fact that the sectarian implications of that description might make the task for our troops more difficult in a Muslim nation that had repeatedly fought off invasions by Christian crusaders in the Middle Ages.

One of the generals in charge of war policy, William G. Boykin, went on a speaking tour of conservative evangelical groups in his spare time to declare—from the pulpit, in uniform—that our nation was in a holy war as a "Christian nation battling Satan." Boykin may have felt safe in using the language of the Crusades—even though the United States was desperately seeking Muslim allies at the time—because his commander in chief had repeatedly used religious language and symbols in his presentation of his policy. And Bush was far from the only fundamentalist politician taking this approach. As recently as Christmas 2006, Congressman Robin Hayes (R-NC) proposed that the only enduring solution for the multisided sectarian civil war in Iraq was "spreading the message of Jesus Christ. . . . Everything depends on everyone learning about the birth of the Savior." Well, Congressman, I consider Jesus to be my Savior also, but Iraq is a Muslim country.

General Boykin was never removed from his job. This was the same General Boykin, by the way, who helped organize the use of abusive treatment of prisoners in Iraq. And given the origins of the new policy approving torture, it is not surprising that the abuse was directed not only at the prisoners' bodies, but also at their religious beliefs. Many prisoners testified that guards forced them, under pain of torture, to curse their religion, eat pork, and drink alcohol in violation of the rules of their faith. One of them told a newspaper reporter that he was first ordered to denounce Islam, and then, after his leg was broken, one of his torturers started hitting it and "ordered me to thank Jesus that I'm alive."

These examples are so horrifying, in part, because they are so contrary to what America is all about. What makes the United States special in the history of nations is our commitment to the rule of law and our devotion to democracy and the rights of individuals. Because the Founders were insightful students of human nature, they knew that there is good and evil in every person. They feared the abuse of power precisely because they understood that each of us lives every day with an internal system of checks and balances, and none of us can be relied on to be virtuous if we are allowed to attain an unhealthy degree of power over our fellow citizens.

Consider the balancing of internal impulses described by one of the soldiers at Abu Ghraib convicted of abusing prisoners, Specialist Charles A. Graner, Jr. Graner was confronted by his colleague, specialist Joseph M. Darby, who would become a courageous whistleblower. When Darby asked Graner to explain the actions captured in the photographs Darby discovered on the photo disk, Graner replied, "The Christian in me says it's wrong. But the corrections officer says, 'I love to make a grown man piss on himself.' "

What happened at that prison, it is now clear, was not the result of random acts by a "few bad apples." It was the natural consequence of the Bush administration policy that dismantled the constraints of law and the Geneva Conventions, made war on America's system of checks and balances, and evaded accountability and responsibility for the actions it ordered.

The abuse of the prisoners at Abu Ghraib flowed directly from the abuse of the truth that characterized the administration's march to war and the abuse of the trust that was placed in President Bush by the American people in the aftermath of September 11.

When you boil down precisely what went wrong with the Bush Iraq policy, it's fairly simple. He waged the politics of blind faith. He used a counterfeit combination of misdirected vengeance and misguided dogma to dominate the national discussion, bypass reason, silence dissent, and intimidate those who questioned his logic both inside and outside the administration.

He adopted an ideologically driven view of Iraq that was tragically at odds with reality. Everything that has gone wrong since has been in one way or another the result of the spectacular clash between the bundle of misconceptions that were gullibly consumed before the war and the all too painful reality that our troops and contractors and diplomats and taxpayers have encountered since it began.

When that painful reality began to displace illusion in the public's mind, the president made increasingly strenuous efforts to silence the messengers of truth and create his own version of reality. His seeming contempt for the rule of reason and his early successes in persuading people to believe in his dogma-driven view of the world apparently tempted him to the hubristic and deeply dangerous illusion that reality itself has become a commodity that can be created and sold with clever propaganda and public relations skills.

Did he himself believe what he was telling the country? It is hard to know. In the words of British author and journalist George Orwell: "We are all capable of believing things which we know to be untrue, and then, when we are finally proved wrong, impudently twisting the facts so as to show that we were right. Intellectually, it is possible to carry on this process for an indefinite time: the only check on it is that sooner or later a false belief bumps up against solid reality, usually on a battlefield."

There have been other collisions between President Bush's "created reality" and America's actual reality. The president's distortion and rejection of the best available evidence on climate change mirrors his modus operandi in misrepresenting and suppressing the best evidence available on the threat posed by Iraq. And his budget policy—which transformed a $5 trillion surplus into a $4 trillion deficit—has been, in its own way, just as spectacular a collision between illusion and reality as the Iraq war. Again, it was the result of completely rejecting the best available evidence on the threat posed to America's economy by his tax and spending proposals.

Some mistakenly malign the president as not being smart enough to have normal curiosity about separating fact from myth. Others seem convinced that his personal religious conversion experience was so profound that he relies on religious faith in place of logical analysis.

But I reject both of those cartoon images.

I know President Bush is plenty smart, and I have no doubt that his religious belief is both genuine and an important motivation for many things that he does in life, as my faith is for me and as it is for most people. I'm convinced, however, that most of the president's frequent departures from fact-based analysis have much more to do with his right-wing political and economic ideology than with the Bible. I've alluded to James Madison's warning, over two centuries old, that "a religious sect may degenerate into a political faction." Now, with the radical Right, we have a political faction disguised as a religious sect, and the president of the United States is *heading* it. The obvious irony is that Bush uses a religious blind faith to hide what is actually an extremist political philosophy with a disdain for social justice that is anything but pious by the standards of any respected faith tradition I know.

The truth about this particular brand of faith-based politics is that President Bush has stolen the symbolism and body language of religion and used it to disguise the most radical effort in American history to take what belongs to the American people and give as much of it as possible to the already wealthy and privileged. And these wealthy and privileged individuals look at his agenda and they say, as Vice President Dick Cheney said to former secretary of the Treasury Paul O'Neill about massive tax cuts that they both knew would create an enormous budget deficit, "This is our due."

Make no mistake: It is the president's reactionary ideology, not his religious faith, that is the source of his troubling inflexibility. Whatever his religious views, President Bush has such an absolute certainty in the validity of his rigid right-wing ideology that he does not feel the same desire that many of us would in gathering facts relevant to the questions at hand. As a result, he ignores the warnings of his own experts, forbids dissent, and often refuses to test his assumptions against the best available evidence. He is, in fact, out of touch with reality, and his recklessness risks the safety and security of the American people.

The Bush administration has demonstrated contempt for the basic tenets of a rational decision-making process, defined as one in which an honest emphasis is placed on getting good facts and then letting good facts drive decisions: Instead, the hallmark of the current administration is a systematic effort to manipulate facts in service to a totalistic ideology that is felt to be more important than the mandates of basic honesty.

More than three hundred years ago, John Locke, one of the architects of the English Enlightenment that was so influential in shaping the philosophy of our Founders, wrote, "Every sect, as far as reason will help them, make use of it gladly; and where it fails them, they cry out, 'It is a matter of faith, and above reason.'" Thus, it is crucially important to be precise in describing exactly what belief system it is that Bush accepts so uncritically and insulates from any logical challenge or even debate.

The surprising recent dominance of American politics by right-wing politicians whose core beliefs are usually wildly at odds with the opinions of the majority of Americans is one that resulted from the careful building of a coalition of interest groups that have little in common with one another besides a desire for power that can be devoted to the achievement of a narrow agenda. This coalition of supporters includes both right-wing religious extremists and exceptionally greedy economic special interests, both groups seeking more and more power for their own separate purposes. All have agreed to support one another's agendas even when it is ideologically inconsistent to do so. The only consistent loser in these exchanges is the American citizen. As a whole, this coalition reveals exactly what our Founders warned against: that a faction might come to dominate politics and pursue power for its own sake.

In case after case, the president has pursued policies chosen in advance of the facts—policies designed to benefit friends and supporters. These supporters have, in turn, benefited the president with enormous contributions and political muscle. This self-reinforcing cycle of mutual back-scratching has pushed government policy further and further away from the public interest. So it should not be surprising when the president uses tactics that deprive the American people of any opportunity to effectively subject his arguments to the kind of informed scrutiny that is essential to our system of checks and balances.

The first important group in this coalition is what I would call the economic royalists, who are primarily interested in eliminating as much of their own taxation as possible and removing all inconvenient regulatory obstacles. Their ideology—which they and Bush believe with almost religious fervor—is based on several key elements:

First, there is no such thing as "the public interest"; that phrase represents a dangerous fiction created as an excuse to impose unfair burdens on the wealthy and powerful.

Second, laws and regulations are also bad—except when they can be used on behalf of this group, which turns out to be often. It follows, therefore, that whenever laws must be enforced and regulations administered, it is important to assign those responsibilities to individuals who can be depended upon not to fall prey to the hated illusion that there is such a thing as the public interest, but who will instead reliably serve the narrow and specific interests of this small group. Some of these activities will be discussed further in chapter 3.

What members of this coalition seem to spend much of their time and energy worrying about is the impact of government policy on the behavior of poor people. They are deeply concerned, for example, that government programs to provide health care, housing, social insurance, and other financial support will adversely affect work incentives. They are also opposed to the minimum wage, the forty-hour workweek, job safety laws, consumer protection, the right to sue an HMO (even as they seek the authority to intervene in American families' medical decisions), the right to privacy, and the right to clean air and water. In short, if they were to achieve their ambition, they would eliminate an economic blueprint that created most of the safeguards and protections established for middle-class families throughout the twentieth century.

This group has provided the bulk of the resources that have financed the now extensive network of foundations, think tanks, political action committees, media companies, and front groups capable of simulating grassroots activism and mounting a sustained assault on any reasoning process that threatens their economic goals. Many of the problems President Bush has caused for this country stem from the marriage of these resources to his belief in the infallibility of this right-wing Republican ideology that often puts the highest priority on the interests of the wealthy and of large corporations.

The second branch of this coalition is made up of the foreign policy hawks whose policy preferences range from unprovoked invasions to economic imperialism. Their overarching goal is to maximize U.S. influence around the world. Treaties and agreements are considered antithetical to orthodoxy, because they can interfere with the exercise of power the same way domestic laws can. The Geneva Conventions and the U.S. law prohibiting torture were both described by President Bush's former White House counsel as "quaint" and then effectively discarded as a constraint, so that Bush and former secretary of defense Donald Rumsfeld could institute policies that resulted in the widespread torture of detainees in Iraq, Afghanistan, Guantánamo, and numerous secret locations elsewhere. And even though Pentagon officials confirmed that Rumsfeld was personally involved in reviewing the specific extreme measures authorized to be used by interrogators at Guantánamo (procedures that served as the basis for those used in Iraq), he was not held accountable for the most shameful and humiliating violation of American principles in recent memory.

The way in which President Bush tries to create his own reality reminds me of when Richard Nixon once told the interviewer David Frost: "If the president, for example, approves something, approves an action because of national security or, in this case, because of a threat to internal peace and order of significant order, then the president's decision in this instance is one that enables those who carry it out to carry it out without violating the law."

This is exactly the rationale offered by the White House to support its position that Bush's inherent power as commander in chief makes everything he does "legal" by definition. Torture, according to this twisted logic, is just fine as long as the president orders it. Or as Nixon famously put it, "When the president does it, that means it's not illegal."

This may be more than a facile comparison between two failed presidents. Bush's two most influential advisers—Dick Cheney and Donald Rumsfeld—both worked very closely with President Nixon when he was in the Oval Office. From all reports, Cheney and Rumsfeld were the most enthusiastic advocates of the Iraq invasion and the decision to suspend the prohibitions against torture in the Geneva Conventions. It is no secret that both men looked at the rollback of unexamined presidential authority after Watergate with abhorrence.

The progressive abandonment of concern for reason or evidence has required the administration to develop a highly effective propaganda machine with which it attempts to embed in the public mind mythologies that grow out of one central doctrine upon which all the special interests agree: Government is very bad and should be done away with as much as possible—except the parts of it that redirect money through big contracts to industries that have won their way into the inner circle.

This coalition gains access to the public through a cabal of pundits, commentators, and "reporters"—call it the Limbaugh-Hannity-Drudge axis. This fifth column in the fourth estate is made up of propagandists pretending to be journalists. Through multiple overlapping outlets covering radio, television, and the Internet, they relentlessly force-feed the American people right-wing talking points and ultra-conservative dogma disguised as news and infotainment—24 hours a day, 7 days a week, 365 days a year. It is quite a spectacle.

What is most troubling to me is the promotion of hatred as entertainment. Moreover, they have actively conspired to fan the flames of a vicious hatred aimed at one group in particular: Americans with progressive political views. They speak of "liberals" with the kind of dripping contempt and virulent hostility that used to be associated with racism and sectarian religious strife. One of the best-known right-wing commentators, Ann Coulter, advised her audience that she was in favor of executing an American citizen who had joined the Taliban "in order to physically intimidate liberals by making them realize that they could be killed, too."

One of the coalition's "constitutional scholars," Edwin Vieira, echoed Coulter's hateful rant at a conference on the so-called Judicial War on Faith by explaining how he would recommend handling the Supreme Court. He actually quoted Joseph Stalin, saying that Stalin "had a slogan and it worked pretty well for him whenever he ran into difficulty: 'No man no problem.' " The only way to explain an American constitutional scholar endorsing ad hominem attacks on

Supreme Court justices is to assume that he has abandoned reason and surrendered to dogma. Moreover, by quoting Stalin—a homicidal dictator whose only peers are Mao and Hitler—he had to realize that people might interpret this as a vague threat of physical violence against justices whose opinions violated right-wing orthodoxy.

Former House Republican leader Tom DeLay also used language apparently suggesting that violence against judges may even have been appropriate. "Judges need to be intimidated," he said. "We're going to go after them in a big way." The tragic episode involving Terri Schiavo, the brain-dead woman who captured the nation's attention in 2005, provoked his most ominous threat to the bench. After judges ruled in favor of her husband's decision to remove her feeding tube, DeLay said, "The time will come for the men responsible for this to pay for their behavior."

Of course, the Schiavo affair revealed something larger about the Bush coalition's zeal. It proved that they are willing to shoot themselves in the foot to defend the purity of their sect's dogma. That's what happened when religious conservatives pressured the president and Senate majority leader to call a special session of Congress to pass a bill that would force reinsertion of a feeding tube to artificially keep a woman in a vegetative state alive. Bush and former Senate majority leader Bill Frist agreed, playing politics with the Schiavo family's private tragedy. The overwhelming majority of Americans in both political parties told the president and the majority in Congress that they strongly disagreed with this extremist approach. The episode's blowback demonstrated the limits of the coalition's radical strategy. In extreme cases, it turns out, the public finds the dangerous mixture of religion and politics repugnant.

Most people of faith I know in both parties have been getting a bellyful of this push by extremists to cloak their political agenda in religiosity, mix it up in their unholy blend of religion and politics, and then force it on everyone else.

The emergence of an ultraconservative, antigovernment dogma

that increasingly relies on the encouragement of mass hostility toward nonbelievers is an extremely troubling new development in America's public forum. As we've seen, it turns James Madison's prophecy on its head: A political faction has degenerated into a quasi-religious sect. It is a sect that sounds as if it believes America is in the early stages of an ideological civil war. It promotes its core beliefs as if they are impervious to reason. And it is unleashing and encouraging ugly and violent impulses.

This right-wing sect often manifests a complete lack of empathy toward other Americans whom it identifies as its ideological enemies. This curious trait can make the mouthpieces of the radical Right appear to be coldly insensitive. For example, when several widows of victims killed in the 9/11 attacks expressed impatience with the Bush administration's unwillingness to cooperate with investigators trying to find out why the warnings were ignored, the widows were immediately attacked and vilified by a chorus of right-wing commentators, who all seemed to be reading from the same tone-deaf script.

To take another example, one of the radio hosts in this group, Neal Boortz, was whipping up public anger at the victims of Hurricane Katrina when they expressed impatience with the Bush administration's incompetent rescue and relief efforts. In the course of his diatribe, he commented on a news story about one Katrina victim who had received no support after losing everything. Boortz criticized her for not having a job and then recommended that she turn to prostitution. "If that's the only way she can take care of herself," he said, "it sure beats the hell out of sucking off the taxpayers."

Comprising the final pillar of this coalition are extreme religious conservatives and fundamentalists, many of whom want to roll back most of the progressive social changes of the twentieth century, including many women's rights, social integration, the social safety net, and the government social programs of the Progressive Era, the New Deal, and the Great Society.

While the economic royalists provide the financial support for this new coalition, a group of ultraconservative religious leaders (who actually are primarily politicians) provide manpower and voter turnout. They serve a special purpose with their constant efforts to cloak the right-wing faction's political agenda in religious camouflage. Many of them also have their own media outlets and are part of the propagandist wing of the coalition. Of course, many of these ministers are genuinely and deeply concerned about the wave of disorienting change that has contributed to the rise of fundamentalism all over the world. And some of them, to their credit, are now emerging as thoughtful critics of distinctly un-Christian elements of the right-wing agenda. But others are just cynical, garden-variety political hacks dressed in clerical collars. Jerry Falwell, for example, seized upon the nation's tragedy only two days after 9/11 as an opportunity to inspire more hatred of Americans with progressive views—identifying them, as usual, as enemies of Christianity.

"I really believe that the pagans and the abortionists, and the feminists, and the gays and the lesbians . . . ," he began, "the ACLU, People for the American Way—all of them who have tried to secularize America—I point the finger in their face and say, 'You helped this [terrorist attack] happen.'"

In the same way, James Dobson, the leader of Focus on the Family, demonstrated just how quickly a religious minister could morph into a political attack dog. During the 2004 election, at a political rally in support of a Republican candidate for Senate, he argued that only Republicans would stand up for Christian values. He said of a prominent Democratic senator, Patrick Leahy, "I don't know if he hates God, but he hates God's people."

I think it's important to expose the fundamental flaw in the basic arguments of these zealots. The unifying theme now being pushed by this coalition is actually an American heresy, a highly developed political philosophy that is fundamentally at odds with the founding principles of the United States of America. Once again, here is what they have backward: In America, we believe that God endowed individuals with unalienable rights; we do *not* believe that God has endowed George Bush—or any political leader—with a divine right to exercise power. In fact, here in America we believe it is blasphemy to assert that the Creator of the universe has chosen to endorse a particular political party.

The historic temptation for religious zealots to subordinate the rule of law to their ideological fervor is perhaps captured best in words given by the author of the play *A Man for All Seasons* to its hero, Sir Thomas More. When More's zealous son-in-law proposes that he will cut down any law in England that serves as an obstacle to his hot pursuit of the Devil, More replies, "And when the last law was down, and the Devil turned round on you—where would you hide, Roper, the laws all being flat? This country's planted thick with laws from coast to coast—man's laws, not God's—and if you cut them down—and you're just the man to do it—d'you really think you could stand upright in the winds that would blow then?"

A great many laws and constitutional principles have been cut down in recent years. To take another example, those desiring to weaken the separation of church and state have tried to undermine the independence of the judiciary and stack the courts with politically responsive judges who do not share the traditional American wariness of establishing religious dogma in law. Toward this end, these zealots have sought to deprive the U.S. Senate of its rule requiring a supramajority to end debate on the confirmation of judges. The zeal with which they have attacked the rule of law reminds me of Sir Thomas More's son-in-law. The Senate's rule has stood for more than two centuries as a protection for unlimited debate. I will discuss the importance of the filibuster as a democratic tool in chapter 8, but worth considering here is how it prevents those in power from governing by faith alone.

The filibuster has been used for devilish purposes on occasion in American history, but far more frequently it has been used to protect the rights of a minority. Indeed, it has often been cited as a model for other nations struggling to reconcile the majoritarian features of democracy with a respectful constitutional role for minority rights.

Ironically, Georgia senator Johnny Isakson reported in a Senate floor speech that he had asked a Kurdish leader in Iraq if he was worried that the majority Shiites would overrun the minority. Isakson proudly said that the Kurdish leader responded, "Oh, no, we have a secret weapon: Filibuster."

In order to cut down this occasional refuge of a scoundrel, the right-wing sect proposed to cut down the dignity and independence of the Senate itself, reduce its power, and accelerate a decline in its stature that was already far advanced.

What makes their zeal so dangerous for our country is their willingness to do serious damage to our American democracy in order to satisfy their lust for a one-party domination of all three branches of government and the enactment of dogma as policy.

They seek nothing less than absolute power. Their grand design is an all-powerful executive using a weakened legislature to fashion a compliant judiciary in its own image. They endeavor to break down the separation of powers. And in place of the current system, they seek to establish a system in which power is unified in the service of a narrow ideology serving a narrow set of interests.

It is truly *power* that is key to understanding the cynical manipulation of faith and the assault on reason. Over time, this administration has focused more and more of its attention on the operations of this vicious cycle, and slowly but surely, its need for more and more power has become an all-consuming goal. It is love of power for its own sake that is the original sin of this presidency.

As Aristotle once said of virtue, respect for the rule of law is one thing; it is indivisible. And as long as it remains indivisible, so will our country. But if either major political party is ever so beguiled by a lust for power that it abandons this unifying principle, then the fabric of our democracy will tear.

CHAPTER THREE

The Politics of Wealth

Adam Smith's *The Wealth of Nations* and America's Declaration of Independence were published in the same year. In both, men were understood to be units of independent judgment, capable of making decisions upon the basis of freely available information, the collective result being the wisest possible allocations of wealth (in the case of the former, work) and political power (in the case of the latter).

Capitalism and democracy shared the same internal logic: Free markets and representative democracy were both assumed to operate best when individuals made rational decisions—whether they were buying and selling property or accepting and rejecting propositions. Both works took for granted the existence of a public sphere defined by the printed word to which all literate individuals had equal access. And both shared a common enemy: despotic rulers capable of using arbitrary power to confiscate property and restrict liberty.

The inner structure of liberty is a double helix: One strand— political freedom—spirals upward in tandem with the other strand— economic freedom. But the two strands, though intertwined, must remain separate in order for the structure of freedom to maintain its integrity. If political and economic freedoms have been siblings in the history of liberty, it is the incestuous coupling of wealth and power that poses the deadliest threat to democracy. If wealth can be easily exchanged for power, then the concentration of either can double the corrupting potential of both. Freedom's helix then spirals downward toward unhealthy combinations of concentrated political and economic power.

That is what has happened throughout human history. Over and over again, wealth and power have become concentrated in the hands of a few who consolidate and perpetuate their control at the expense of the many. This default pattern has appeared in many variations and has been interrupted by rare and memorable exceptions, including ancient Athens and the brief Roman Republic.

The establishment of the United States represented the most hopeful departure from that pattern. For the first time in history, large numbers of individuals were empowered to use knowledge on a regular basis to mediate between wealth and power. And because the only legitimate source of power in America was to be the consent of the governed, wealth was not to be bartered for political power.

The derivation of just power from the consent of the governed depends upon the integrity of the reasoning process through which that consent is given. If the reasoning process is corrupted by money and deception, then the consent of the governed is based on false premises, and any power thus derived is inherently counterfeit and unjust. If the consent of the governed is extorted through the manipulation of mass fears, or embezzled with claims of divine guidance, democracy is impoverished. If the suspension of reason causes a significant portion of the citizenry to lose confidence in the integrity of the process, democracy can be bankrupted.

If citizens no longer participate, those among them who notice signs of corruption or illogic have no way to voice their concerns and summon the attention of others who, upon examining the same evidence, might share their dismay. No critical mass of opposition can form among individuals who are isolated from one another, looking through one-way mirrors in soundproof rooms, shouting if they wish but still unheard. If enough citizens cease to participate in its process, democracy dies.

Our Founders worried about the dangers of concentrated wealth. Even Alexander Hamilton, the great conservative, wrote just before the Constitutional Convention about "the real disposition of human nature" that could lead to misfortune in the new nation: "As riches increase and accumulate in few hands; as luxury prevails in society; virtue will be in a greater degree considered as only a graceful appendage of wealth, and the tendency of things will be to depart from the republican standard."

The Roman historian Plutarch, whose histories were well known to many of our Founders, had warned that an "imbalance between rich and poor is the oldest and most fatal ailment of all Republics."

The founder of capitalism, Adam Smith, wrote in *The Wealth of Nations* about the wealthy and powerful corrupt elites throughout the history of the world prior to the dawn of the new age: "All for ourselves and nothing for other people seems, in every age of the world, to have been the vile maxim of the masters of mankind."

And of course, the apostle Paul wrote in his letter to Timothy: "The love of money is the root of all evil."

Dr. Samuel Johnson, who was also widely read by our Founders, wrote in the 1750s that in a republic, reason has "power to warn us against evil." It is that quality of alertness that our Founders understood to be particularly vulnerable to the seductive appeal of power. In the words of Johnson's contemporary Immanuel Kant, the most influential European philosopher of the Enlightenment: "The enjoyment of power inevitably corrupts the judgment of reason, and perverts its liberty."

As noted in the introduction, the idea of self-government became feasible after the printing press—and, in its wake, the Enlightenment—distributed knowledge widely to individuals and created a marketplace of ideas based on the rule of reason. As soon as decisions could be freely discussed and debated, reason began to displace wealth as the principal source of power.

When the operations of a government are open to full examination by its citizens and subjected to vigorous discussion and debate, then the corrupt misuse of public power for private gain becomes more difficult to conceal. If the rule of reason is the standard by which every use of official power is evaluated, then even the most complex schemes to violate the public's trust can be uncovered and policed by a well-informed citizenry. Moreover, when ideas rise or fall according to merit, reason tends to drive us toward decisions that reflect the best available wisdom of the group as a whole.

But reason alone is not enough. There must be a public forum accessible to all within which individuals can communicate freely to illuminate unwise as well as illegitimate uses of power. Hannah Arendt, who wrote about totalitarianism in the twentieth century, emphasized the importance of the public realm to this process: "The only remedies against the misuse of public power by private individuals lie in the public realm itself, in the light which exhibits each deed enacted within its boundaries, in the very visibility to which it exposes all those who enter it."

If the forum is not fully open, then those who control access become gatekeepers. If they charge money in return for access, then those with more money have a greater ability to participate. Good ideas in the minds of men and women who cannot afford the price of admission to the public forum are then no longer available for consideration. When their opinions are blocked, the meritocracy of ideas that has always been the beating heart of democratic theory begins to suffer damage. The conversation of democracy then comes untethered from the rule of reason and can be manipulated.

That is exactly what has been happening in America. The replacement of an easily accessible, print-based marketplace of ideas with a restricted-access, television-based realm has led to a radical transformation of the nature and operation of the marketplace of ideas in the United States.

When only those who have wealth can afford to enter the principal forum in which the majority of people receive their information, then those who can pay the price of admission automatically become more influential. Their opinions become more important than the opinions of others. The nation's priorities then change.

To take just one of many examples, for the past several years, the felt need to eliminate inheritance taxes on the wealthiest 1/100 of 1 percent of the families in America (the only taxpayers who are still subject to it) has been treated as a *much* more important priority than the need to provide at least minimal access to health care for tens of millions of families who currently have no access to health care coverage at all.

When wealth determines access to the public forum, it causes similar distortions during election campaigns. In modern America, the candidate who amasses the largest amount of money is guaranteed to dominate the semblance of political discourse that is used by the voters as the basis for making their choices.

The communication between candidates for national office and American voters is currently based almost entirely on one-way thirty-second television commercials purchased by the candidates at great expense with money donated to them largely by elites, many of whom are interested in purchasing specific policy outcomes with their contributions. Cash must be collected from those who have it. Those who have cash are typically motivated to give it to the candidates who promise postelection behavior that will be pleasing to the contributors—upon whom everything depends in this system. This behavior would not necessarily be pleasing at all to the voters if they knew what was going on. But both candidates and contributors are capable of ignoring the true interests of the voters, because the voters' opinions can now be shaped by mass advertising campaigns, which can be purchased.

Moreover, in the Congress as a whole—both House and Senate—the enhanced role of money in the reelection process, coupled with the sharply diminished role for reasoned deliberation and debate, has produced an atmosphere conducive to pervasive institutionalized corruption. The scandal involving disgraced lobbyist Jack Abramoff was only the tip of a giant iceberg that threatens the integrity of the entire legislative branch of government. Steps are now being taken in the new Congress to limit this threat, but the underlying problem is still present.

The frequent response of reformers has been to propose new laws and regulations purporting to govern the amounts of money individuals and groups can give to candidates, to require more disclosure of these transfers of cash, and to prohibit certain particularly offensive forms of this institutionalized corruption.

Predictably, however, since the underlying problem is the lack of effective participation by the people in reviewing and analyzing the decisions and policies of their elected officials, these new laws and regulations also escape effective scrutiny and thus are routinely violated—in spirit if not in letter. New forms of old abuses outrace the legislative and regulatory process so completely that it would be humorous were they not the signs of a dangerous downward spiral for our democracy.

As long as individual citizens are not able to use logic and reason as the instruments with which they can dissect and meticulously examine ideas, opinions, policies, and laws, corrupt forces will shape those policies and laws instead. It is the public's lack of participation that empowers its abusers. It is the public's enforced muteness that prevents people from joining with others in a collective effort to once again wield reason to mediate between wealth and power.

When the public merely watches and listens and does not have a speaking part, the entire exercise is fraudulent. It might be called

American Democracy: The Movie. It looks and sounds almost real, but its true purpose is the presentation of a semblance of participatory democracy in order to produce a counterfeit version of the consent of the governed. With no ability to test the propositions presented or explore the facets of policies not revealed, the public is often persuaded to endorse and applaud policies that are actually harmful to its interests.

Since voters still have the real power to elect their leaders, those who wish to exchange wealth for power must do so, in part, by paying for elaborate public relations campaigns to try to shape the opinions of the millions who spend so much time watching television. At times it seems as if a genuine democratic conversation is taking place, but it flows mainly in one direction—from those who have raised enough money to buy the television advertising to those who watch the ads and have little effective means for communicating in the opposite direction.

The word *corruption* comes from the Latin *corruptus,* which means "to break or to destroy." Corruption destroys and breaks that trust which is absolutely essential for the delicate alchemy at the heart of representative democracy. In its contemporary form, corruption almost always involves an incestuous coupling of power and money and describes the exchange of money for the misuse of public power. It matters not whether the exchange is initiated by the person with the money or the person with the power; it is the exchange itself that is the essence of the corruption. It matters not if the private enrichment is with cash or with its equivalent in influence, prestige, status, or power; the harm is done by the fraudulent substitution of wealth for reason in the determination of how the power is used. It matters not if the purchased use of power is seen as beneficial by some or even by many; it is the dishonesty of the transaction that carries the poison.

When the decision-making process is no longer dominated by reason, it quickly becomes far more vulnerable to outcomes determined by the use of raw power, and the temptation to corruption grows accordingly. And sure enough, in recent years there has been a series of gross examples of corruption and the fraudulent abuse of public power for private ends. The activities that now do the most harm to the health and integrity of American democracy are for the most part legal. And all of the abuses have one thing in common: The perpetrators have clearly assumed that they have little to fear from public outrage and that very few people will learn about their misdeeds.

All of them *assume* an ignorant public. Bush would not be able credibly to label a bill that increases air pollution "the clear skies initiative"—or call a bill that increases clear-cutting of national forests "the healthy forests initiative"—unless he was *confident* that the public was never going to know what these bills actually did.

Nor could he appoint Ken Lay from Enron to play such a prominent role in handpicking members to the Federal Energy Regulatory Commission (Lay's choices were conveyed directly to the White House personnel officer, and there is every indication that Lay participated in interviewing prospects) unless the president felt totally comfortable that no one would pay attention to an obscure policy apparatus like the FERC. After members of the FERC were appointed with Mr. Lay's personal review and approval, Enron went on to bilk the electric ratepayers of California and other states without the inconvenience of federal regulators trying to protect citizens from the company's criminal behavior.

Likewise, this explains why many of the most important Environmental Protection Agency (EPA) positions have been carefully filled with lawyers and lobbyists representing the worst polluters in their respective industries, ensuring that those polluters are not inconvenienced by the actual enforcement of the laws against excessive pollution.

The private foxes have been placed in charge of the public henhouses. And shockingly, the same pattern has been followed in many other agencies and departments. But there is precious little outrage because there is so little two-way conversation left in our democracy.

Trees are falling in the forest right and left, but they don't seem to be making a sound. This behavior could never take place if there were the slightest chance that such institutionalized corruption would be exposed in a public forum that had relevance to the outcome of elections.

Thomas Jefferson warned that the concentration of power in the executive branch would lead to corruption unless there was full and vigorous scrutiny of its appointments by the public. Appointed positions in the federal government would, in effect, be auctioned off to the business interests most affected by the decisions made by those appointed. "Withdrawn from the eyes of the people," he wrote, "they [federal offices] may more secretly be bought and sold, as at market."

In Bush's ideology, there is an interweaving of the agendas of large corporations that support him and his own ostensibly public agenda for the government that he leads. Their preferences become his policies, and his politics becomes their business. The White House is evidently so beholden to the coalition of interests that has supported it financially that it feels it has to give them whatever they want and do whatever they say. While President Bush likes to project an image of strength and courage, the truth is that in the presence of his large financial contributors and powerful political supporters, he is morally timid—so much so that he seldom if ever says "no" to them on anything—no matter what the public interest might mandate.

Machiavelli illuminated this phenomenon five centuries ago in Florence: "A Prince who would maintain his authority is often compelled to be other than good. For when the class, be it the people, the soldiers, or the nobles, on whom you judge it necessary to rely for your support, is corrupt, you must needs adapt yourself to its humours, and satisfy these, in which case virtuous conduct will only prejudice you."

Just as the appointment of industry lobbyists to key positions in agencies that oversee their former employers results in a kind of institutionalized corruption and the abandonment of law enforcement and regulations at home, the outrageous decision to brazenly grant sole-source no-bid contracts worth $10 billion to Vice President Cheney's former company Halliburton—which paid him $150,000 annually until 2005—has convinced many observers that incompetence, cronyism, and corruption have played a significant role in undermining U.S. policy in Iraq.

Not coincidentally, the first audits of the massive sums flowing through the U.S. authorities in Iraq now show that billions of dollars in money appropriated by Congress and Iraqi oil revenue have disappeared with absolutely no record of where they went, to whom, for what, or when. And charges of massive corruption are now widespread.

The president has rejected recommendations of antiterrorism experts to increase domestic security because large contributors in the chemical industry, the hazardous materials industry, and the nuclear industry oppose these measures. Even though his own Coast Guard recommends increased port security, he has chosen instead to reject the recommendation, relying on information provided to him by the commercial interests managing the ports, who don't want the expense and inconvenience of implementing new security measures.

He has also undermined the Medicare program with a radical new proposal prepared by the major pharmaceutical companies, also large campaign contributors. The Bush appointee in charge of Medicare was secretly ordered, we learned after the fact, to withhold from the Congress the truth about the president's proposal and its real cost until the Congress had finished voting on it. When a number of congressmen balked at supporting the proposal, the president's henchmen made a mockery of the rules of Congress by holding the fifteen-minute vote open for more than two hours while they brazenly attempted to bribe and intimidate members of Congress who had initially voted against the president and forced them to change their votes in sufficient numbers to cause the proposal to pass narrowly. I will return to the deception involved in selling this program to the Congress in chapter 4.

These and other activities make it abundantly clear that the Bush White House represents a new departure in the history of the presidency. He appears at times to be so eager to accommodate his supporters and contributors that there often seems to be little he is not willing to do for them—even if it comes at the expense of the public interest.

When he assumed office, President George W. Bush said, "I didn't—I swear I didn't—get into politics to feather my nest or feather my friends' nests."

The essential cruelty of Bush's game is that he takes an astonishingly selfish and greedy collection of economic and political proposals and then cloaks them with a phony moral authority, thus misleading many Americans who have a deep and genuine desire to do good in the world. And in the process he convinces these Americans to lend unquestioning support for proposals that actually hurt their families and their communities.

An increasing number of Republicans, including veterans of the Reagan White House and even the father of the modern conservative movement, William F. Buckley Jr., are now openly expressing dismay over the epic failures of the Bush presidency.

The United States has survived many assaults on its integrity and has endured lengthy periods during which high levels of corruption twisted the nation's goals and distorted the operations of democracy. But in every prior instance, the people, the press, the courts, and the Congress restored the integrity of the system through the use of reason. This is different; the absolute dominance of the politics of wealth today is something new.

During the Enlightenment, when reason often was given primacy over the church and the monarchy, the two traditional sources of valuation in the public sphere—the political system and the market system—were seen as natural philosophical allies.

Our Founders put their faith in the ability of a free people to use the power of reason to protect the Republic against the evil they feared most: a concentration of political power that might develop into tyranny. Capitalism was seen as operating in a separate sphere altogether.

Money itself was not considered the problem, because ultimately, money has significance only to the extent that others agree to accept it in exchange for goods or services or behaviors. And in the new American Republic, it was inconceivable that power could be purchased with money. Power was to be allocated in a different sphere altogether—the democratic sphere—where the rule of reason was sovereign.

The boundary between these two spheres has shifted back and forth over time and has often been a source of tension. Indeed, this fault line can be seen in the contrast between Adam Smith's phrase "life, liberty, and the pursuit of property" and Jefferson's famous words in the Declaration of Independence, "Life, liberty and the pursuit of happiness."

Almost two years before the Declaration of Independence, the First Continental Congress had adopted a precursor to the declaration known as the Declaration of Colonial Rights, in which they used the phrase "life, liberty, and property." (The phrase "pursuit of happiness" was first coined in 1759 by Dr. Samuel Johnson.) In commenting upon James Madison's first draft of the Constitution, Thomas Jefferson wrote in 1787 that he intended to "insist" on attaching a Bill of Rights that would declare, "1. Religion shall be free; 2. Printing presses free; 3. Trials by jury preserved in all cases; 4. No monopolies in commerce; 5. No standing army."

This concern over "monopolies in commerce" would resurface repeatedly and demonstrated that even though democracy and capitalism were seen as complementary and mutually reinforcing, the internal contradictions of "democratic capitalism" were there from the beginning. Democracy begins with the premise that all are created equal. Capitalism begins with the premise that competition will inevitably produce inequality, depending on differences in talent, industriousness, and fortune. The two value systems have been the reigning philosophies in two different spheres of life.

The "fault line" that marked the boundary between capitalism and democracy generated tremors during the first years of the Republic. Deep beneath the surface, much more powerful tectonic pressures were building. Slavery—America's original sin—forced a collision be-tween the rock-hard edges of two ideas—"property" and "freedom"—that were pushing against each other with almost equal force. But in the last decades of the eighteenth century, these two tectonic plates seemed to make up a solid sheet of bedrock on which the American Republic could be based.

One of the first tensions was in the requirement of property own-ership for voting. John Adams wrote in a letter in 1776 that "the same reasoning" that led to a demand to drop the requirement of property ownership would lead to other demands: "New claims will arise; women will demand the vote; lads [under twenty-one] will think their rights not enough attended to; and every man who has not a farthing, will demand an equal voice with any other, in all acts of state. It tends to confound and destroy all distinctions, and prostrate all ranks to one common level."

He was right in predicting that other demands would follow, even if he was wrong in his attempt to preemptively oppose them. Moreover, the logic with which Adams and others made property ownership a requirement for voter eligibility was weak. As a result, it was inevitable that the strong desires for freedom stoked by America's independence would break these two concepts apart.

Initially, our Founders valued and highlighted the role that prop-erty and wealth could play in promoting free self-government by guar-anteeing a basis for independence of judgment on the part of citizens. They did not see wealth in and of itself as a bad thing.

On the contrary, affluence—up to a point—was recognized as a positive force for securing political freedom. Moreover, one strand of the Protestant Reformation influential in America implied that pros-perity might well be a sign that God had marked its possessor as one of the chosen few destined for heaven.

When the American Revolutionaries rebelled against the English king, they recognized in one another's property both a badge of inde-pendent thought and an incentive to band together. They were almost as concerned about the king's imposition of unjust taxes and his threat to their property as they were about his threat to their liberty. As Jefferson wrote in the Declaration of Independence: "And for the support of this Declaration, with a firm reliance on the protection of divine Providence, we mutually pledge to each other our Lives, our Fortunes and our sacred Honor."

The "landed gentry" of colonial America were, after all, the heirs of the noblemen and merchants who had drafted the Magna Carta half a millennium earlier. Even then, economic independence from the king had fueled a desire for more political freedom.

The requirement of property ownership as a condition for the right to vote was, in a way, yet another manifestation of the Founders' mistrust of concentrated power. An individual who did not own property was likely to be dependent on others and therefore under the sway of others and thus not capable of basing his vote on reason that was unpolluted by the exercise of economic power over his judgment. This reflected their contemporary understanding of how political freedom had emerged from the Dark Ages; individuals who had amassed enough property to feel a degree of independence from the monarchy were able to see clearly enough to steer by the light of reason.

The Founders recognized the ownership of property as an indicator, however imprecise, of competence in the world and rationality in thought—precisely the qualities one would want in a confederation of independent thinkers whose collective judgment would form the basis for self-government.

Inevitably, however, the logic of democracy pushed aside the requirement of property ownership for voting. The most famous and most devastating argument was from Benjamin Franklin, who put the case for expanding the franchise beyond property owners very simply:

Today a man owns a jackass worth fifty dollars and he is entitled to a vote; but before the next election the jackass dies. The man in the meantime has become more experienced, his knowledge of the principles of government, and his acquaintance with mankind, are more extensive, and he is therefore better qualified to make a proper selection of rulers—but the jackass is dead and the man cannot vote. Now, gentlemen, pray inform me, in whom is the right of suffrage? In the man or in the jackass?

Unfortunately, neither logic nor morality was sufficient to dispel the corrupt understanding of "property" that was at the heart of slavery. Slavery was a living, breathing mockery of the guiding principle of democracy. The inclusion of the odious "three-fifths" clause in the original U.S. Constitution marked the prevailing moral blindness of America's Founders where slavery was concerned. Even though sanctioned by the Constitution of 1789, it was an example of the corruption of democracy by the enforcement of an immoral property "right."

Abraham Lincoln's later decision to emancipate the slaves—in the midst of the Civil War that slavery caused—came after a long history of a widespread abolitionist movement. Almost a century later, the American civil rights movement of the mid-twentieth century, like the abolitionist movement a century earlier, fought for the full political freedom of African Americans by using the language and symbols of the struggle by Moses three thousand years earlier to free Jews from slavery.

The natural resonance of its message came not only because of the predominance in America of the Judeo-Christian tradition that Jews and African Americans shared, and not only because the movement was a continuation of the same struggle that ended slavery one hundred years earlier in the United States; it came also because we simply take it for granted that political freedom and economic freedom are intertwined.

During the cataclysm of the Civil War, the United States was violently split apart, primarily on the issue of slavery. The line of division was not only between North and South, but between those who sought to perfect the logic of democracy and those who insisted on a perversion of capitalism by fighting to retain the right to own other human beings. "Democratic capitalism"—as it had been understood previously in America—was no longer the bedrock on which the nation had been founded, but two massive separate monoliths that split apart and then came crashing violently toward each other. As freedom triumphed, the market for buying and selling human beings was destroyed.

Lincoln's transcendent victory for the freedom of the human spirit saved the Republic. But in order to win the war, Lincoln was forced to rely on corporations that produced munitions, transported troops by rail, and focused the industrial strength of the North against the largely agrarian economy of the South. In the process, Lincoln removed many constraints that had kept the power of corporations in check during the first seven decades of the Republic.

Thomas Jefferson had expressed concern about what he saw as the encroaching danger *in 1821*—more than a decade after he left the presidency: "Our country is now taking so steady a course as to show by what road it will pass to destruction, to wit: by consolidation of power first, and then corruption, its necessary consequence. The engine of consolidation will be the Federal judiciary; the two other branches the corrupting and corrupted instruments."

Echoing Jefferson, President Andrew Jackson warned against the dangers of too much corporate power, saying that it raised the question of "whether the people of the United States are to govern through representatives chosen by their unbiased suffrages, or whether the money and power of a great corporation are to be secretly exerted to influence their judgment and control their decisions."

In spite of such concerns articulated in different ways by several of our early presidents, the role of corporations was still limited until the Civil War. Lincoln may have perceived the dangers he was enhancing and some historians attribute the following statement to him:

We may congratulate ourselves that this cruel war is nearing its end. . . . But I see in the near future a crisis approaching that unnerves me and causes me to tremble for the safety of my country. As a result of the war, corporations have been enthroned and an era of corruption in high places will follow, and the money power of the country will endeavor to prolong its reign by working upon the prejudices of the people until all wealth is aggregated in a few hands and the Republic is destroyed. I feel at this moment more anxiety for the safety of my country than ever before, even in the midst of war. God grant that my suspicions may prove groundless.

Lincoln's fears, of course, were not groundless. Only twenty-two years later, the "money powers" against which he warned secured in the Supreme Court a decision that has been interpreted ever since in ways that pervert the purpose of the Fourteenth Amendment, which was intended to confer upon former slaves all the individual rights granted by the Constitution to "persons."

The 1886 Supreme Court decision *Santa Clara County v. Southern Pacific Railroad* has been cited for decades—especially since the conservative takeover in 1980—to uphold the proposition that corporations are, legally speaking, "persons" and thus protected under the Fourteenth Amendment. It was one of many developments that marked the ascendancy of corporate power in both the economic and political spheres of American life. By the end of the nineteenth century, the "monopolies in commerce" that Jefferson had wanted to prohibit in the Bill of Rights were full-blown monsters, crushing competition from smaller businesses, bleeding farmers with extortionate shipping costs, and buying politicians at every level of government.

In the half century between the American Civil War and the beginning of World War I, the transformation of work and the economy contributed with these many other factors to set the stage for several social movements aimed at using political power to remedy abuses and problems experienced by working people in the industrial age. The growing importance of mass production in manufacturing and railroads in transportation triggered the mass migration from the farms to the factories. The new concentration of wealth in the hands of industrialists contributed with many other factors to a perceived worsening of the cyclical depressions that had a harsher effect on families that were more dependent on paychecks than they had been when living on the farm. These hardships combined with abuses—such as lax safety standards for those working with powerful and deadly machinery; child labor in industrial work settings, mines, factories, and other unhealthy environments; new threats to health and safety from the mass production and handling of foods and medicines; abusive treatment of employees; and unhealthful food—to form a list of grievances shared by large numbers in proximity to one another.

In spite of the abuses associated with monopolies, concentrated wealth, and the corruption of politicians, America's public forum was still open and accessible to individuals, many of whom argued eloquently and powerfully for new laws to constrain these abuses. Upton Sinclair, Ida Tarbell, and the other reforming journalists who received the label "muckrakers" were able to awaken the conscience of America with their printed words—because printed words still represented the principal medium of communication in every part of American life.

The Progressive movement in the first decade of the twentieth century gave voice and force of law to a growing desire to ameliorate these harms. Because reformers were still able to use reason to mediate between wealth and power, the boundary line between democracy and capitalism began to move back in favor of democracy. Theodore Roosevelt, two weeks before becoming president in the fall of 1901, after the assassination of President William McKinley, said, "The vast individual and corporate fortunes, the vast combinations of capital which have marked the development of our industrial system, create new conditions, and necessitate a change from the old attitude of the state and the nation toward property."

Halfway through his second term, after winning many battles against monopolies on behalf of the public interest, Roosevelt said, in April 1906, "Behind the ostensible government sits enthroned an invisible government owing no allegiance and acknowledging no responsibility to the people. To destroy this invisible government, to befoul the unholy alliance between corrupt business and corrupt politics, is the first task of the statesmanship of the day."

All of the reform movements that began in the first decades of the twentieth century were based on appeals to reason. In the tradition of Thomas Paine, reformers laid out with clear logic a description of the abuses they saw, the suffering that resulted, and the need for governmental action to impose remedies that were not forthcoming in the market of its own accord. The reading public, upon absorbing these compelling narratives, gave them political force by repeating them to their elected representatives in the form of a demand that new laws be passed.

In the late nineteenth century, the industrial revolution, urbanization, and the new connections linking East to West and North to South, including the railroads and the telegraph lines, were among the forces that led to the emergence of a mass market and fueled the consolidation of newspaper ownership into national chains such as the Hearst newspapers. "Yellow journalism" brought some of the worst abuses in the history of newsprint, appealing to the basest instincts of Americans, often with gross fabrications. Even though competition among newspapers in most cities was far more robust than it is today, the role of the pamphleteers and independent printing presses had long since begun to diminish, compared with the growing power of newspaper chains.

Soon, however, the nature of America's public forum would change even more dramatically with the introduction of the first electronic mass medium, radio.

Whereas the printing press allowed the public to participate in the national conversation—through letters, pamphlets, and newspapers—radio was something new: a one-way mass medium that instantly delivered the same information, or "content," to every home with a receiver over a vast area. As professor of sociology Paul Starr noted in his book *The Creation of the Media,* the national radio networks that established dominance in most markets by the 1930s, NBC and CBS, effectively reached every home in the nation.

Radio was distinct not only in that it was a one-way medium, but also because it allowed political leaders and those who could afford to broadcast to enter the homes of listeners from thousands of miles away. It was this second characteristic that enabled radio to create the "mass audience." Radio allowed the broadcaster to bypass traditional institutions such as political parties, labor unions, and associations to communicate directly with the listener. Anyone capable of broadcasting could join millions of families every night.

The societal impacts of this revolutionary technology were very different in the United States from those in the rest of the world. In the United States, the defenders of democracy insisted that constraints be placed on the new medium. The "equal time rule" ensured that political parties and candidates for office received equal amounts of airtime; the Fairness Doctrine ensured that differing points of view were included in programming; and the "public interest standard" required all of those in the small group granted licenses to keep the public interest always in mind—upon penalty of losing the license to someone else if they did not.

Elsewhere in the world, particularly in nations without a long democratic tradition, radio was introduced without the safeguards that were put in place in the United States. Moreover, the political atmosphere in much of the world was highly volatile during this interwar period.

The U.S. victory in World War I had contributed to economic prosperity for the decade between the end of the war and the beginning of the Great Depression. But Germany had lost the war and was suffering the punitive economic impact of the Versailles Treaty. The resulting malaise set the stage for a radical transformation and combination of both the economic and the political spheres.

World War I saw the end of the rule of the royal houses in Russia, Germany, and the Austro-Hungarian Empire. The echoes of ancient Rome could be heard in the transfer of power from the kaiser and the czar (both titles derived from Caesar) and the fall of the last multistate empire in Europe, which was a lineal descendant of the Holy Roman Empire, itself a pale imitation of the power that was Rome. And of course, in the rubble of the desperate and defeated Austria walked a seething, twisted, frustrated artist who would come to see himself as heir to the Holy Roman Empire, which he styled the First Reich, and the German Empire of the kaiser, which he called the Second Reich.

In 1922, less than five years after the armistice that ended World War I, Joseph Stalin was named general secretary of the Communist Party in the newly formed Union of Soviet Socialist Republics, and the leader of the new Fascist Party in Italy, Benito Mussolini, was named prime minister of a coalition government. A half year earlier, Adolf Hitler had been named chairman of the new National Socialist Party in Germany.

All three would require several years to consolidate their power. Each one mobilized support for his malignant, totalitarian ideology by using the powerful new medium for mass communication that also debuted on the world stage in 1922: radio.

Totalitarianism appeared in three distinctive designs: Nazism and fascism were fraternal twins and cousins to communism. Even though the first two saw the third as their mortal enemy, all three relied materially on propaganda delivered over the radio to engineer total state control over all political and economic power. Whatever their doctrinal differences, the result was the same in all totalitarian regimes: The freedom and rights of the individual were effectively eliminated.

Without the introduction of radio, it is doubtful that these totalitarian regimes would have commanded the obedience of the people in the manner they did. As Joseph Goebbels, Hitler's minister of propaganda, would say later, "It would not have been possible for us to take power or to use it in the ways we have without the radio. . . . The radio is the most influential and important intermediary between a spiritual movement and the nation, between the idea and the people."

Similarly, Italian historian Gianni Isola, studying Mussolini's consolidation of power, wrote, "Broadcasting was born in Italy under Fascism, and Fascism used it, right from the beginning, for propaganda." Marco Palla, another Italian scholar writing about Mussolini, adds, "The effect of the State's ubiquitous presence, made possible by the means of radio, was probably more influential than any other instrument of propaganda."

Propaganda became a science, but the word actually dates back to the Counter-Reformation—a period when the Catholic Church paid new attention to improving the effectiveness of its efforts at persuasion designed to win the hearts and minds of Europeans who were converting to Protestantism in large numbers. Perhaps for that reason, the word *propaganda* still does not have the same pejorative meaning in Europe that it does in the United States.

But we understand the word—and the phenomenon it represents—as something new in the twentieth century. And watching Goebbels's mastery of propaganda allowed us to understand how sinister it can be. *ARBEIT MACHT FREI (WORK IS FREEDOM)*—the sign above the entrance of the Nazi extermination camps—symbolizes the evil uses to which psychology-based persuasion was put by the Nazis.

Psychology-based communication was first developed by another Austrian of Hitler's generation, Edward Bernays, Sigmund Freud's nephew. Bernays adapted the revolutionary insights of his uncle to create the modern science of mass persuasion—based not on reason, but on the manipulation of subconscious feelings and impulses. Bernays, considered the father of public relations, left Austria long before the Nazi rise to power and immigrated to the United States, where he transformed commercial advertising and began a similar transformation of political persuasion.

The combination of psychologically driven public relations and electronic mass media broadcasting led to modern propaganda. Reason was displaced not only by the substitution of broadcasting for print, but also by the science of PR as the principal language by which communication occurs in the public forum—for both commercial and political purposes.

One of Bernays's first breakthroughs involved his work for the American Tobacco Company, when he interviewed psychoanalysts to discover the reason women in the 1920s would not smoke cigarettes. Upon learning their view that women of the era saw cigarettes as phallic symbols of male power and thus inappropriate for women, Bernays hired a group of women to dress and act as suffragists. They marched down New York's Fifth Avenue in a parade for women's rights and upon passing news photographers pulled out and lit cigarettes, proclaiming them "torches of freedom." The strategy worked to break women's resistance to cigarettes.

A second victory involved another corporate client, Betty Crocker. Bernays discovered that women were not buying cake mixes because they felt ashamed to present their husbands with a cake that required so little work. Bernays advised changing the formula to require the addition of a fresh egg, and once again, the strategy worked. Women felt they had done enough to deserve praise for their baking and the cake mix started selling robustly.

Bernays's business partner, Paul Mazur, understood the larger significance of the new techniques of mass persuasion. "We must shift America from a needs to desires culture," Mazur said. "People must be trained to desire, to want new things, even before the old have been entirely consumed. We must shape a new mentality. Man's desires must overshadow his needs."

"Advertising," George Orwell is often quoted as saying, "is the rattling of a stick inside a swill bucket." Amid all these lofty terms, it is worth remembering what we're talking about.

What should have been most disturbing about the introduction of these new techniques is the threat they posed to the internal logic of capitalism. The invisible hand of Adam Smith was giving way to invisible puppet strings manipulated by marketers who were now able to manufacture demand.

As noted in the introduction, John Kenneth Galbraith demonstrated more than fifty years ago the raw power of electronic mass advertising, which—when fueled by enough money—was capable of artificially creating demand for products that consumers had had no idea they needed or wanted. Advertising's distortion of the pull of demand complicates Adam Smith's metaphor of the invisible hand, to say the least; this distortion amplifies the internal contradictions between capitalism and democracy. (These contradictions are far less glaring than were those between communism and democracy, by any measure. Galbraith is said to have quipped, "Under capitalism man exploits man. Under communism it's just the opposite.")

Another consequence of the new importance of mass electronic advertising in the marketplace is that there are now many industries in the United States where competition is effectively limited to companies that have the concentrated wealth necessary to mount huge marketing campaigns. The inherent quality of the product in question and its price still matter a lot, of course—but the ability of new competitors, including small entrepreneurs, to suddenly have an impact on competition with a genuinely better mousetrap is sharply reduced. The resulting concentration of corporate wealth in the hands of a smaller number of larger conglomerates has occurred at the same time that political power has come to be more concentrated in the hands of a smaller number of people.

There is, as a result, a powerful motive for those who seek large gains from corrupt schemes to find ways of suspending or interrupting the rule of reason as the standard by which their behavior will be measured. But not even the most ambitious swindler could have imagined that the rule of reason could have been weakened as a dominant force in the public forum in the manner that it has following the transition from a print-based forum to an electronic media–based forum.

Inevitably, Bernays also began to apply his psychological and mass-marketing insights to the sale of political ideas. "If we understand the mechanism and motives of the group mind," he said, "is it not possible to control and regiment the masses according to our will without their knowing about it? The recent practice of propaganda has proved that it is possible, at least up to a certain point and within certain limits."

In 1922—as the world was first taking notice of radio, Mussolini, Hitler, and Stalin—Walter Lippmann first proposed that friends of democracy should also adopt the techniques of propaganda, though he did not use the word. He used instead a phrase that to me is even more chilling: "the manufacture of consent." This catchphrase was later seized upon by opponents of his philosophy, including MIT professor of linguistics Noam Chomsky, who later chose as the title of one of his books "Manufacturing Consent."

Though well-meaning, Lippmann was cynical in his analysis, elitist in his prescription, and completely unrealistic about the damage that would be done to democracy if the ultimate decisions were made by a "specialized governing class" and then sold to the people with propaganda. That is precisely what happened with the invasion of Iraq.

"The knowledge of how to create consent will alter every political calculation and modify every political premise," Lippmann said. "As a result of psychological research, coupled with the modern means of communication, the practice of democracy has turned a corner. A revolution is taking place, infinitely more significant than any shift of economic power."

In the following decade, President Franklin Delano Roosevelt used radio to communicate over the heads of newspaper editors and other intermediaries to bring about a dramatic shift in the boundary between democracy and capitalism when he built public support for the New Deal agenda.

But the legal constraints placed on the radio medium in the United States prevented its use for the type of cynical political manipulation that occurred in many other countries—in Europe, Asia, Latin America, and Africa.

These constraints were removed during the Reagan administration, in the name of "free speech," and the results have been horrendous. Our Founders could never have imagined that the marketplace of ideas would change so profoundly that the "consent of the governed"—the very source of legitimate political power in a democracy—could become a commodity.

And radio, of course, was the precursor of an infinitely more powerful broadcasting medium, television.

As noted in the introduction, television is also a one-way medium. Individuals receive but do not send, they listen but do not speak, they are given information but do not share it in return, they do not comment on it in ways that others can hear. Therefore, automatically, their ability to use the tools of reason as participants in the national conversation is suspended.

There is an entirely separate set of consequences related to this change in the nature of the public forum, and it is not rooted this time in the impact on perceptions or the impact on the operations of the brain or the internal balance between reason, fear, and faith. It is rooted this time in the sheer economic realities of the physics of the medium itself. Because it has, until recently, been a centralized system, it requires large capital investments to simultaneously control or purchase the production of programming and to distribute it from a single point to hundreds of millions of people. This has led to the control of television programming and distribution by those with large amounts of wealth.

In addition, the number of voices in the media is shrinking while the influence is growing for those whose voices are heard. This process of ownership change is already so far advanced that it has alarmed even conservative Republican members of Congress, causing them to join with members of the Democratic Party to oppose the efforts of the Federal Communications Commission (FCC) to make the world of information even safer for monopoly.

For the first generation of television broadcasting, the physics of the medium included reliance on the electromagnetic spectrum for distribution and the separation of one channel from others by enough wavelengths that the net result was severe scarcity of available frequencies suitable for distribution. Two consequences flowed from those physics. One, the scarcity meant that only a few frequencies or channels could be used in each individual geographic area. Two, government was thrust into the role of deciding who would be given the privilege of using these scarce resources and according to what criteria.

The economics of broadcasting influenced the next three generations of television distribution: cable, satellite, and Internet. In each case, the specific design and physics of the distribution system influenced the economic structure of the system. With respect to cable distribution, cable was a natural monopoly in the sense that an electric utility or terrestrial telephone network is a natural monopoly. Because it is in the interest of the community to limit the number of cables and lines attached to wooden poles around the community or buried underneath the streets, the economics of a utility push it toward a natural monopoly.

Therefore, the same two vulnerabilities to corruption appear. One, you need massive amounts of wealth to construct and maintain and operate such a system. Two, you need political influence to receive the necessary government blessing to be the sole natural monopolist, and you need government indulgences for all the policy choices that flow out of the criteria used to make that choice. Similarly, in the case of satellite distribution, the cost of launching satellites into orbit sharply limits the number of companies capable of affording it.

Some expect that the Internet, the third system for distributing television, might eventually bring dramatic changes to the way in which television is created and distributed. This will be explored further in chapter 9, "A Well-Connected Citizenry."

Thus, one of the most obvious and dangerous consolidations of power has formed in the media, where powerful conglomerates have used their wealth to gain more power and consequently more wealth. Physical and economic constraints on access to television in particular made this outcome largely inevitable. It's hard to understate how much media ownership has changed in the space of a generation. Today, it's rare to see a family-run media business with deep pride in its independence and a journalistic tradition that has survived over half a dozen generations. Such businesses are now part of conglomerates whose obligations involve meeting Wall Street's expectations rather than the Founders' expectations of the requisite for a well-informed citizenry.

Now that the conglomerates can dominate the expressions of opinion that flood the minds of the citizenry and selectively choose the ideas that are amplified so loudly as to drown out others that, whatever their validity, do not have wealthy patrons, the result is a de facto coup d'état overthrowing the rule of reason. Greed and wealth now allocate power in our society, and that power is used in turn to further increase and concentrate wealth and power in the hands of the few. If this sounds overly strident, please read on, as I get down to cases.

CHAPTER FOUR

Convenient Untruths

The last two centuries have demonstrated the superiority of free market economies over centralized economies and the superiority of democracy over forms of government that concentrate power in the hands of a few. In both cases, the root of that superiority lies in the open flow of information.

Thomas Jefferson saw open communication as the key to the success of the American experiment: "Which we trust will end in establishing the fact, that man may be governed by reason and truth. Our first object should therefore be, to leave open to him all the avenues to truth." Adam Smith, who described the collective wisdom of free markets as the "invisible hand," also considered the free flow of information essential to the efficiency of capitalism. When information is freely available to individuals and flows unimpeded throughout the political or economic system, the important decisions are not always made by the same small group of people. Instead, the ability to make judgments is widely distributed throughout the entire system, so each individual can contribute to the collective wisdom.

Decisions that are made in this manner usually turn out to be better decisions than those made by any small group, which is inherently more vulnerable to the dangers of limited information and special pleading. Participatory democracy, because of its openness and accountability, helps to minimize mistakes in national policy decisions.

The new science of information theory offers a way to understand why democracy—like capitalism—is simply more efficient at making good decisions over time. A few years ago, a friend of mine who is a computer scientist, Danny Hillis, patiently tried to explain to me the workings of a massively parallel supercomputer by pointing out that the first computers relied on a central processing unit surrounded by a field of memory. To find the answer to a particular problem, the CPU would send out a query to the field of memory to retrieve data, then bring it back to the center for processing. The result would then be placed back in the memory. All this necessitated three trips, back and forth, consuming precious time and generating unwanted heat.

The architectural breakthrough associated with massive parallelism was to break up the power of the CPU and distribute it throughout the memory field to lots of smaller separate "microprocessors"—each one co-located with the portion of the memory field it was responsible for processing. When a task has to be performed, all of the processors work simultaneously, and each processes a small quantity of information, then all of the separate parts of the answer are brought simultaneously to the center, where they are assembled. The result: one trip, less time, less energy, less heat.

The metaphor of massive parallelism, or "distributed intelligence," offers an explanation for why our representative democracy is superior to a governmental system run by a dictator or a king. Where totalitarian regimes rely on a "central processor" to dictate all commands, representative democracies depend on the power and insight of people spread throughout the society, each located adjacent to the part of society in which he or she is most interested.

In the case of free market capitalism, decision making is even more widely dispersed. The Soviet Union's economy collapsed because it relied on a central processor to make all economic decisions, and it didn't work very well. Innovation withered, and corruption took root. The North Korean economy continues to rely on a central processor, and today its people are starving. But capitalist economies distribute the power to those located outside the center—entrepreneurs and consumers, who make their own decisions independent of one another—and the accumulated wisdom marries supply to demand and allocates both efficiently.

To take a third example, many of the latest techniques from the world of management rely on the same principles of distributed intelligence, even if they don't call it that. By distributing intelligence and information and responsibility to workers on the front lines, organizations are transforming themselves, serving customers better, and producing greater value.

Each of these examples relies for its success on the same basic architecture. Instead of insisting that all decisions be made in a single place, the power is widely distributed throughout the organization. Each individual's portion of the answer is then assembled as part of a collective conclusion. In capitalism, it's called supply and demand; in representative democracy, it's called self-determination. In each case, it is essential that all the individuals involved share some basic characteristics: for example, the freedom to obtain information that flows unimpeded throughout the system.

The challenge for any organization is not simply to establish these conditions, but to nurture and sustain them. There's no better example of how to do that than the U.S. Constitution, with its checks and balances and careful design intended to sustain the creativity of self-government, even after more than two hundred years. Our Constitution is, in a sense, the software guiding the operations of a massively parallel system for processing political decisions.

However, the role information plays in our democracy has been profoundly transformed with the new dominance of television over the printing press. The one-way nature of the television medium—at least as it has been structured up until now—coupled with the relatively small number of television networks and the increased concentration of ownership, has increased the temptation for those in political power to seek a greater degree of control over the information concerning their activities that is conveyed to the American people by the news media.

All recent occupants of the White House—including the administration in which I served—have paid more attention to the information that is released by the government and have been tempted to try to manage the impressions formed in the minds of Americans. Unfortunately, during the present administration, this temptation has led to a sharp increase in the use of secrecy, a determined assault on the integrity of scientific research findings that might undercut the administration's effort to intimidate and silence the bearers of any information that might be used to challenge the decisions this White House has made.

Worse still, the current White House has engaged in an unprecedented and sustained campaign of mass deception—especially where its policies in Iraq are concerned. Active deception by those in power makes true deliberation and meaningful debate by the people virtually impossible. When any administration lies to the people, it weakens America's ability to make wise collective decisions about our Republic.

Now that the full extent of this historic fiasco is becoming clear, it is important to understand how such a horrible set of mistakes could have been made in a great democracy. And it is already obvious that the administration's abnormal and un-American approach to secrecy, censorship, and massive systematic deception is the principal explanation for how America embraced this catastrophe.

Five years after President Bush first made his case for an invasion of Iraq, it is now clear that virtually all the arguments he made were based on falsehoods. If we as the public knew then what we know now about Iraq, the list of tragic mistakes might not be so long. The president has chosen to ignore—and indeed often to suppress—studies, reports, and facts that were contrary to the false impressions he was in the process of fostering in the minds of the American people.

The administration has chosen instead to focus on convenient untruths presented with superficial, emotional, and manipulative appeals that are not worthy of American democracy. This group has exploited fears for partisan political gain and its members have postured themselves as bold defenders of our country while actually weakening, not strengthening, America.

We were told by the president that war was his last choice. But it is now clear that it was always his first preference. His former secretary of the Treasury, Paul O'Neill, confirmed that Iraq was "topic A" at the very first meeting of the Bush National Security Council just ten days after the inauguration: "It was all about finding *a way to do it.*"

We were told that the president would give the international system every opportunity to function, but we now know that he allowed that system to operate only briefly as a sop to his secretary of state and for cosmetic reasons.

The first rationale presented for the war was to destroy Iraq's weapons of mass destruction, which of course turned out not to exist. We now know from the statements of Paul Wolfowitz, former deputy secretary of defense, that this rationale was cynically chosen after a careful analysis of American public opinion showed that this was the one argument likely to be most effective in persuading the voters to support an invasion.

It was as if the Bush White House had adopted Walter Lippmann's recommendation to decide in advance what policies it wanted to follow and then to construct a propagandistic mass persuasion campaign to "manufacture" the consent of the people to do what the "specialized governing class" had already made up its mind to do.

As if on cue—and there is no doubt that there *was* a cue; the PR campaign was highly orchestrated—numerous administration spokespersons fanned out to give statements to the national media that a "mushroom cloud" might threaten American cities unless we invaded

Iraq to prevent Saddam Hussein from giving a nuclear weapon to the same terrorist group that had already attacked us with deadly consequences.

The nation was told that Saddam had purchased enrichment technology and that he was seeking supplies of uranium ore in Africa. And the administration was seemingly immune to any feeling of embarrassment or contrition when the evidence they offered to support both assertions turned out to be completely false.

Imagine for a moment that you are president of the United States. And imagine that you are standing before a joint session of Congress on live national television, speaking on the one occasion of the year when the Constitution commands the president to speak directly to the Congress and the American people about the state of the Union, and you deliver an important point on the issue of war and peace. And after your speech, the United Nations' experts on nuclear proliferation publicly announce that the document you have been given is a forgery.

This actually happened, of course. President Bush told the American people that he had documentary proof that Saddam Hussein was seeking yellowcake uranium in the African nation of Niger and implied that this was clearly for the purpose of enriching uranium for nuclear bombs. Then he asked the country to imagine how horrible it would be if one of the bombs made from this yellowcake exploded in a mushroom cloud and destroyed an American city. But two weeks later, the head of the United Nations agency monitoring nuclear weapons proliferation, Nobel Peace Prize winner Mohamed ElBaradei, issued a statement revealing to the world that the document upon which President Bush had based this pungent narrative was actually forged.

If you had been president and had stood before a joint session of Congress and delivered a speech watched by one billion people on live worldwide television, and you had presented to this vast audience crucial evidence for your case to go to war that you subsequently discovered was not only false but *forged,* would you feel embarrassed? Would you insist that someone be held accountable for giving you a forged document? Would you have any interest in figuring out who had forged the document and why? And in determining how it got into your hands? And why you were encouraged to rely so heavily on it in your State of the Union address? Would you feel remorse that you had presented such an important falsehood to the nation that relied on you for leadership?

Sir Arthur Conan Doyle wrote one of his famous Sherlock Holmes detective stories in which the key clue was "the dog that didn't bark." In this case, the White House hasn't even growled about who forged the document that got into the hands of the president of the United States and was used on national television. And amazingly, the White House still doesn't seem to care who forged that document. Four years later, there still hasn't been any responsibility assigned for this deceitfulness.

In the same State of the Union address, Bush also claimed that the UN weapons inspectors had found that Saddam Hussein had acquired specialized aluminum tubes designed to be used for enriching uranium for atomic bombs. But numerous experts at the Department of Energy and elsewhere in the intelligence community were certain that the information being presented to our country by the president was completely wrong. In the United States, the true experts on uranium enrichment are at Oak Ridge, in my home state of Tennessee, where most enrichment has taken place. They told me early on that in their opinion, there was zero possibility that the tubes in question were for the purpose of enrichment. Yet they said they felt intimidated at the Oak Ridge facility from making any public statement that disagreed with the assertions being made to the people by President Bush.

In almost every case, the intelligence used by the White House to make its case for war was stretched beyond recognition, distorted, and misrepresented. And in every case, when the evidence was questioned, there was a determined disinterest in learning the truth. On the contrary, there was an inflexible insistence on carrying out preconceived policies regardless of the evidence. First the verdict, then the trial.

As a result of the 9/11 Commission report, we now know that within hours after the attack of September 11, 2001, Secretary Rumsfeld was busy attempting to find a way to link Saddam Hussein with the attack. We have the sworn testimony of the president's White House head of counterterrorism, Richard Clarke, that on the day after the attack, September 12, the president wanted to connect the attacks to Saddam. Further, Clarke recounted on the news program *60 Minutes:*

> The president dragged me into a room with a couple of other people, shut the door, and said, "I want you to find whether Iraq did this." . . . I said, "Mr. President. We've done this before. We have been looking at this. We looked at it with an open mind. Mr. President, there's no connection." He came back at me and said, "Iraq. Saddam. Find out if there's a connection." . . . We got together all the FBI experts, all the CIA experts. They all cleared the report, and we sent it up to the president and it got bounced by the national security adviser or deputy. It got bounced and was sent back saying, "Wrong answer. Do it again.". . . And I don't think he, the president, sees memos that he wouldn't like the answer.

This was the day after the attack, and the president did not ask about Osama bin Laden. He did not ask Mr. Clarke, the veteran counterterrorism czar under both Democratic and Republican presidents, about al-Qaeda. He did not ask about Saudi Arabia or any other country other than Iraq.

When Clarke responded to that first question by saying that Iraq was not responsible for the attack and that al-Qaeda was, the president persisted in focusing on Iraq. So Clarke spent his time on this day after the worst attack in the history of the United States on our soil, as the man in charge of counterterrorism in the White House, trying to find a link between the attack and someone who had absolutely nothing to do with it. This is not criticism by hindsight. This is the way the president was thinking at the time he was planning America's response to the attack. This was not an unfortunate misreading of the available evidence, causing a mistaken link between al-Qaeda and Iraq. This was something else: a willful choice to make a specific linkage, whether evidence existed to support it or not.

When he was preparing to invade Iraq, President Bush repeatedly gave the clear impression that Iraq was an ally and partner to the terrorist group that attacked us, al-Qaeda. In fact, not long after the attacks of 9/11, President Bush made a decision to start mentioning Osama bin Laden and Saddam Hussein in the same breath, in a cynical mantra designed to fuse them together as one in the public's mind. He repeatedly used this device in a highly disciplined manner to create a false impression in the minds of the American people that Saddam Hussein was responsible for 9/11.

In a comment that some felt belongs in a file marked "Jokes That Reveal Deeper Meaning," President Bush said, "See, in my line of work, you got to keep repeating things over and over and over again for the truth to sink in, to kind of catapult the propaganda."

Usually, he was pretty tricky in his exact wording. Indeed, President Bush's consistent and careful artifice is itself evidence that he knew full well he was telling an artful and important lie, visibly circumnavigating the truth, over and over again, as if he had practiced how to avoid encountering it.

Almost 2,500 years ago, one of the first serious students of demagoguery, Socrates, said, "Whenever, therefore, people are deceived and form opinions wide of the truth, it is clear that the error has slid into their minds through the medium of certain resemblances to that truth." But President Bush and Vice President Cheney also sometimes slipped away from their usual tricky wording and in careless moments resorted to statements that bore no resemblance to the truth at all but were clearly outright falsehoods on their face.

In the fall of 2002, President Bush actually told the country, "You can't distinguish between al-Qaeda and Saddam." He also said, "The true threat facing our country is an al-Qaeda-type network trained and armed by Saddam." At the same time, Vice President Cheney was repeating his claim that "there is overwhelming evidence there was a connection between al-Qaeda and the Iraqi government." By the spring, Secretary of State Colin Powell was in front of the United Nations (an appearance he now says he regrets), claiming a "sinister nexus between Iraq and the al-Qaeda terrorist network."

But the president continued to dismiss all questions about his statements by saying, "The reason I keep insisting that there was a relationship between Iraq and Saddam and al-Qaeda was because there was a relationship between Iraq and al-Qaeda." And he continued to provide no evidence whatsoever.

By the time members of the administration were done, public opinion polls showed that fully 70 percent of the people had gotten the message that Bush wanted them to get; they were convinced that Saddam Hussein was responsible for the 9/11 attacks.

The myth that Iraq and al-Qaeda were working together was not the result of an innocent and ignorant mistake by the White House. The president and vice president ignored clear warnings, well before the war began—from the Pentagon's Defense Intelligence Agency and from the CIA, in classified reports given directly to the White House—that the claim was false. Well before the war, intelligence officials in Europe had also made clear there was no link. "We have found no evidence of any links between Iraq and al-Qaeda," one top European terrorism investigator said in 2002. "If there were such links, we would have found them, but we have found no serious connections whatsoever."

The propagation of this myth by the White House was not an example of negligence. When the administration is told specifically and repeatedly by the most authoritative sources that there is no linkage, but then in spite of the best evidence continues to make bold and confident assertions to the American people that leave the impression with 70 percent of the country that Saddam Hussein was linked to al-Qaeda and was primarily responsible for the 9/11 attack, this can only be labeled deception.

At least some within the president's own party admitted the same thing. Senator Chuck Hagel, who sits on the Foreign Relations Committee, said point-blank, "Saddam is not in league with al-Qaeda. I have not seen any intelligence that would lead me to connect Saddam Hussein with al-Qaeda." But these voices and others did not stop the deliberate campaign to mislead America. Over a period of several years, the president and vice president used their carefully crafted language to first create and then reinforce the fear that al-Qaeda was going to be armed by Iraq.

After the invasion, an exhaustive search for evidence of a linkage found none, and by August 2003, former Bush administration national security and intelligence officials had been forced to admit that the evidence used to make this Iraq–al-Qaeda claim contradicted the conclusions of key intelligence agencies. "Our conclusion was that Saddam would certainly not provide weapons of mass destruction or WMD knowledge to al-Qaeda because they were mortal enemies," said Greg Thielmann, a weapons analyst who worked at the State Department's Bureau of Intelligence and Research. "Saddam would have seen al-Qaeda as a threat, and al-Qaeda would have opposed Saddam as the kind of secular government they hated."

So when the bipartisan 9/11 Commission issued its report a year later finding no credible evidence of an Iraqi–al-Qaeda connection, it should not have caught the White House off guard. Yet instead of the candor that Americans needed and deserved from their leaders, the White House reasserted its view that there was linkage. Vice President Cheney, for example, claimed that he probably had more information than the commission had and said, "There clearly was a relationship" for which there was "overwhelming evidence." Cheney put forward this question: "Was Iraq involved with al-Qaeda in the attack on 9/11? We don't know."

As the author Thomas Pynchon once wrote, "If they can get you asking the wrong questions, they don't have to worry about the answers."

But the administration does now seem finally to be worried about the answers. Vice President Cheney lashed out at *The New York Times* for having the nerve to print a headline declaring PANEL FINDS NO QAEDA-IRAQ TIE—which was by then merely a clear statement of the obvious. Piling one falsehood on top of another, Cheney then said that there was no "fundamental split here and now between what the president said and what the commission said." He even tried to deny that he had ever personally been responsible for helping to create the false impression that there was linkage between al-Qaeda and Iraq.

Appropriately enough, his interview ended up as fodder for *The Daily Show with Jon Stewart*. Stewart played Cheney's outright denial that he had ever said that representatives of al-Qaeda and Iraqi intelligence met in Prague, and then Stewart froze Cheney's image and played the exact video clip when Cheney had indeed said exactly that in exactly the words he had denied. He caught him on videotape in a blatant lie. At that point, Stewart said, addressing himself to Cheney's frozen image on the television screen, "It's my duty to inform you that your pants are on fire."

Even Secretary Rumsfeld, who saw all of the intelligence available to President Bush that might bear on the alleged connection between al-Qaeda and Saddam Hussein, finally admitted under tough repeated questioning from reporters, "To my knowledge, I have not seen any strong, hard evidence that links the two."

We now know that Rumsfeld's assistant, Douglas Feith, established a separate and parallel "intelligence" operation inside the Pentagon that was used to present flawed information directly to the president without the knowledge of the CIA and the other professional centers of intelligence gathering and analysis in the U.S. government.

The White House had an overwhelming political interest in sustaining the belief in the minds of the American people that Hussein was in partnership with bin Laden. They dared not admit the truth out of fear that they would look like complete fools for launching our country into a reckless and unnecessary war against a nation that posed no immediate threat to us whatsoever. Among those Americans who still believe there is a linkage—and astonishingly, there are still many—there remains very strong support for the president's decision to invade Iraq. But among those who accept the truth that there was no connection, support for the war in Iraq and the decision to launch it has disappeared very quickly.

That's understandable, because if Iraq had nothing to do with the 9/11 attack, and had no connection to the organization that launched the attack, then that means the president took us to war when he didn't have to and that over three thousand American service members have been killed and thousands more have been wounded and many thousands of Iraqis have been killed and wounded—unnecessarily.

The lie about a connection between al-Qaeda and Iraq was also the key to justifying the constitutional power grab by the president. And in the end, for this administration, it is all about power. As long as their big, flamboyant lie remained an established fact in the public's mind, President Bush was seen by the majority as justified in taking for himself the power to make war on his whim. He was seen as justified in suspending many civil liberties at his personal discretion. And he could continue to distort the political reality experienced by the American people.

Is it possible that Bush and Cheney truly believed the false assertions they foisted on the American people and our allies? Leonardo da Vinci once wrote, "The greatest deception men suffer is from their own opinions." And investigative journalist I. F. Stone wrote in *In a*

Time of Torment: "All governments lie, but disaster lies in wait for countries whose officials smoke the same hashish they give out." If Bush and Cheney actually believed in the linkage that they asserted—in spite of all the evidence to the contrary presented to them contemporaneously—that would by itself, in light of the available evidence, make them genuinely unfit to lead our nation. On the other hand, if they knew the truth and lied, massively and repeatedly, isn't that worse? Are they too gullible or too dishonest?

In 2004, the late former Republican governor of Minnesota, Elmer Andersen, announced in Minneapolis that for the first time in his life, he had decided to oppose an incumbent president of his own party because Bush and Cheney, in his words, "believe their own spin. Both men spew outright untruths with evangelistic fervor." He attributed his switch to President Bush's "misguided and blatantly false misrepresentations of the threat of weapons of mass destruction. The terrorist seat," he said, "was Afghanistan. Iraq had no connection to this act of terror, was not a serious threat to the United States, as this president claimed, and there was no relation, it is now obvious, to any serious weaponry."

After the tragedy of Vietnam, the U.S. military made an impressive commitment to learning everything it could from the experience in Southeast Asia. By using logic and reason to dissect each and every mistake that had been made, our military leaders engineered a historic transformation of the uniformed services. The first Persian Gulf War and the intervention in Bosnia were among the successes that came from integrating the lessons of Vietnam into a new and much more effective approach to military strategy.

Unfortunately, the Pentagon was forced to discard many of these lessons during its preparations for invading Iraq. For example, the size of the U.S. invasion force, we now know, was far smaller than military experts had recommended. In February 2003, before the war began, Army Chief of Staff General Eric Shinseki told Congress that the occupation could require several hundred thousand troops, but the

White House had already decided that a much smaller force was adequate. Rather than engaging in a reasoned debate on the question, they undercut Shinseki for disagreeing with their preconceived notion—even though he was an expert and they were not.

The other generals and admirals got the message and stopped expressing disagreement with the White House. Shinseki had been right, of course, and most of the uniformed officers at the upper echelons of the Pentagon knew he was right. But the decision-making process was one that did not allow for principled differences. As a result, the policy selected was not informed by the collective wisdom.

During his effort to persuade Congress to endorse his decision to prepare for an invasion, President Bush promised that if he took the nation to war, it would only be on the basis of the most carefully worked out plans. Instead, we now know, in sharp contrast with what he told us at the time, that he went to war virtually without clear thought and certainly without preparation for the aftermath that has tragically now claimed more than three thousand American lives and many tens of thousands of Iraqi lives.

A small group of willful men in the administration—many of whom had avoided service in the military when they were younger—substituted their judgment for that of the nation's military leaders and led the nation to make a catastrophic error. Their conclusion that we needed only a small invasion force was based on the same mistaken assumption that led to their arrogant refusal to prepare a plan for the occupation of Iraq after the invasion. They assumed that American service members would be greeted by cheering Iraqis offering garlands of flowers—and that these same grateful Iraqis would quickly establish free markets and a healthy functioning democracy.

Unfortunately, of course, this assumption was also dead wrong. We now know from the CIA that a comprehensive and authoritative analysis of the likely consequences of the invasion—prepared long beforehand—accurately predicted the chaos, popular resentment, and growing likelihood of civil war and that this analysis was presented to the president.

This miscalculation, we now know, was also completely avoidable. But information that would have prevented this mistake was suppressed. Two months before the Iraq war began, President Bush received detailed and comprehensive secret reports warning him that the likely result of an American-led invasion of Iraq would be increased support for Islamic fundamentalism, deep divisions in Iraqi society, high levels of violent internal conflict, and guerrilla warfare aimed at U.S. forces.

Yet in spite of those analyses, President Bush chose to suppress those warnings and conceal that information, and instead he went right on conveying to the American people the absurdly Pollyannaish view of highly questionable and obviously biased sources like Ahmed Chalabi, a convicted felon.

The Bush administration began making payments to Chalabi's organization and gave him a seat adjacent to First Lady Laura Bush at the State of the Union address. They then flew him into Baghdad on a military jet with a private security force. However, the following year the administration claimed he was actually a spy for Iran who had been hoodwinking the president all along with phony facts and false predictions. Now Chalabi is a top official of the new government in Baghdad.

It has become common for President Bush to rely on special interests, like the one represented by Chalabi, for basic information about the policies important to these interests. ExxonMobil, for example, has apparently been his most trusted source of information about the climate crisis. Chemical companies are his most trusted sources on whether or not particular chemicals are hazardous to the environment. The major pharmaceutical companies are his most trusted advisers on the health risks of new drugs. Insurance companies are considered the most reliable source of data on any policy that affects them. And so forth.

And then, amazingly, the president seems to trust what these special interests tell him over and above objective information prepared for him by independent analysts who are charged with protecting the public interest. Since his ideology teaches him contempt for the very notion of "the public interest," he actually prefers to rely on biased information prepared by sources of questionable reliability—like Chalabi—who have a private interest in a particular policy outcome. The president has, in effect, outsourced the truth.

An extensive investigation published in the Knight Ridder newspapers uncovered the astonishing truth that even as the invasion began, there was literally *no plan at all* for the postwar period. Indeed, on the eve of war, when the formal presentation of America's plan to the military leaders and intelligence officers and others neared its conclusion, the slide describing President Bush's plan for the postwar phase was labeled "To Be Provided" because it simply did not exist.

Three weeks after the invasion, Lieutenant General William Wallace, commander of V Corps, the second most important U.S. military official in Iraq, was asked by a journalist about the plans for the postinvasion period. Astonishingly, Wallace's reply was, "Well, we're making this up here as we go along."

We now know from Paul Bremer, the person chosen by President Bush to be in charge of U.S. policy in Iraq immediately following the invasion, that he was repeatedly telling the White House that there were insufficient troops on the ground to make the policy a success. Yet at the very time Bremer was telling the White House these views, President Bush was simultaneously asserting to the American people that we had more than enough troops on the ground and that he was relying on the American leaders in Baghdad for his opinion that no more were needed.

Even as the growing chaos and violence in Iraq were becoming painfully obvious to anyone watching the television news, President Bush went out of his way to demean the significance of a formal national intelligence estimate warning that his policy in Iraq was falling apart and events were spinning out of control. Bush described this rigorous and formal analysis as, in his words, "just guessing."

We have also learned in *The Washington Post* that at the same time the president was falsely asserting to the American people that he was making sure he was providing all the equipment and supplies to the soldiers that their commanders said they needed, at that moment, the top military commander in Iraq, Lieutenant General Ricardo Sanchez, was pleading desperately and repeatedly for a response to his request for more equipment and more body armor, among other things, to protect the troops. And he wrote that under this situation, the army units he was commanding were "struggling just to maintain ... relatively low readiness rates."

We were told also that our allies would join in a massive coalition so that we would not bear the burden alone. And of course we are now bearing that burden almost entirely alone. More than 90 percent of the non-Iraqi soldiers are American, and the U.S. taxpayers have now paid more than $700 billion for a war that has already lasted longer than our involvement in World War II, from Pearl Harbor to V-E Day.

Bush also claimed that gaining dominance of Iraqi oil fields for American producers was never part of his calculation. Instead, he insisted, he was going to war in order to deal with an imminent threat to the United States. But again the evidence shows clearly that there was no such imminent threat and that Bush knew that at the time— or at least had been told that by those in the best position to know.

Further, there is now far more evidence than was available at the time of the invasion to suggest that Iraqi oil supplies may have played a much bigger role in the administration's overall decision than anyone realized. We now know, for example, from a document dated just two weeks to the day after Bush's inauguration, that his National Security Council was ordered to meld its review of operational policies toward "rogue states" (including Iraq) with the secretive Cheney Energy Task Force's "actions regarding the capture of new and existing oil and gas fields."

We know from documents obtained in discovery proceedings against that Cheney task force, by the odd combination of the conservative group Judicial Watch and the Sierra Club, that one of the documents that was receiving scrutiny by the task force during that same time period was a highly detailed map of Iraq—showing none of the cities, none of the places where people lived, but showing in great detail the location of every single oil deposit known to exist in the country, with dotted lines demarcating blocks for promising exploration—a map that, in the words of a Canadian journalist, resembled a butcher's drawing of a steer with the prime cuts delineated by dotted lines.

The administration has fought a pitched battle in the courts for more than six years to continue denying the American people the ability to know which special interests and which lobbyists advised Vice President Cheney on the design of the new energy policy. We know that Ken Lay was involved in vetting appointees to the Federal Energy Regulatory Commission, and we've seen some of the evidence of what Enron did to circumvent the regulators. But we do not yet know who was at the table with Cheney discussing how to get access to Iraq's oil reserves.

We know that Cheney himself, while heading Halliburton, did a considerable amount of business with Iraq—even though it was under UN sanctions at the time. And we know that Cheney stated in a public speech to the Institute of Petroleum in London in 1999, more than a year before becoming vice president, that over the coming decade the world would need, in his opinion, fifty million additional barrels of oil each day.

"Where is it going to come from?" Cheney asked, and then, answering his own question, he said: "The Middle East, with two-thirds of the world's oil and the lowest cost, is still where the prize ultimately lies."

Then, in the spring of 2001, when Vice President Cheney issued the administration's national energy plan, the one that had been devised in secret by corporations and lobbyists that he still refuses to name, the report included this declaration: "The Persian Gulf will be a primary focus of U.S. international energy policy."

That same year, Bush melded the national energy policy with his foreign policy toward rogue states like Iraq. Later that summer, in one of the more bizarre parts of Bush's policy process, Richard Perle, before he was forced to resign on conflict-of-interest charges as chairman of the Defense Policy Board, solicited a presentation to the board by a Rand Corporation analyst who recommended that the United States consider military seizure of Saudi Arabia's oil fields.

The board did not adopt that recommendation. But the cynical belief by some that oil played an outsize role in Bush's perception and policy toward Iraq was later enhanced when it became clear that one of the few facilities in the entire country that was secured by U.S. troops following the invasion was Iraq's oil ministry. The Iraqi National Museum with its priceless archaeological treasures dating from the birth of human civilization; the electric facilities so crucial to maintaining a standard of living for Iraqi citizens during the occupation that was soon to begin; schools, hospitals, and ministries of every kind—all of those were left to the looters.

Moreover, in early 2007, the government that the United States helped to establish in Baghdad enacted legislation that was written in Washington to give U.S. and British oil companies the dominant role in exploiting the massive oil reserves of Iraq. I will discuss this legislation at greater length later in chapter 7.

The historic misjudgments that led to the tragedy of America's invasion of Iraq were all easily avoidable. The administration's arrogant control of information and the massive deception perpetrated on the American people in order to gain approval for a dishonest policy led to the worst strategic mistake in the history of the United States. But the damage they have done to our country is not limited to the misallocation of military and economic and political resources. Nor is it limited even to the loss of blood and treasure. Whenever a chief executive spends prodigious amounts of energy in an effort to convince the American people of a falsehood, he damages the fabric of democracy and the belief in the fundamental integrity of our self-government.

Unfortunately, Iraq is far from the only area where the White House has relied on deception to gain approval for radically new policies and where subsequently available information shows that the president actually had analyses from reputable sources that directly contradicted what he was telling the American people. And in virtually every one of these cases, it is now evident, the information rejected by the president later turned out to be accurate. The president chose instead to rely on information provided to him from sources that often had a direct interest, financial or otherwise, in the radically new policy that the president adopted—information that subsequently turned out to be false. And in those cases where those policies have been implemented, the consequences have been to the detriment of the American people, often catastrophically so.

The kinds of unnatural, undemocratic activities in which this administration has engaged in order to aggrandize power have also included an unprecedented use of secrecy. Former White House counsel John Dean wrote recently, "Bush and Cheney are a throwback to the Nixon time. All government business is filtered through a political process at this White House, which is the most secretive ever to run the United States."

John F. Kennedy once said, "The very word *secrecy* is repugnant in a free and open society; and we as a people are inherently and historically opposed to secret societies, to secret oaths, and to secret proceedings." But in 2003, *U.S. News & World Report* had this to say about the current White House: "The Bush administration has quietly but efficiently dropped a shroud of secrecy across many critical operations of the federal government, cloaking its own affairs from scrutiny and removing from the public domain important information on health, safety and environmental matters."

The withdrawal of information from the public sphere appears to be driven mainly by political concerns. For example, they have imposed a veil of secrecy over Bush's gubernatorial papers from the years in which he was governor of Texas. There couldn't be many serious threats to national security in those papers. Similarly, they have withheld information about Vice President Cheney's continuing financial involvement with the company he used to run, Halliburton.

To head off complaints from our nation's governors over how much they would receive under federal programs, the Bush administration simply stopped printing the primary state budget report.

When mass layoffs became too embarrassing, this administration simply stopped publishing the regular layoff report that economists and others have been receiving for decades.

More than six thousand documents have been removed by the Bush administration from governmental Web sites, including, to cite only one example, a document on the Environmental Protection Agency (EPA) Web site giving citizens crucial information on how to identify chemical hazards near where their families live.

Moreover, this administration has established a new exemption that enables them to refuse the release to the press and the public of important health, safety, and environmental information submitted to the government by businesses—merely by calling it "critical infrastructure." There have been recent efforts, for example, to pull back huge numbers of declassified documents from the National Archives and reclassify them, even after they have long been in the public domain.

It is astonishing how little outrage is generated by each new effort to impose tighter controls over the information that is made available to the people in our democracy.

For example, during the height of the scandal involving the former lobbyist Jack Abramoff, convicted of crimes related to influence peddling and corruption, investigative reporters seeking to document the many contacts between Abramoff and the White House were told that any such contacts, if they existed at all, were minimal and that

President Bush did not even know Abramoff. All of the voluminous circumstantial evidence pointed in the opposite direction, and one of the obvious sources of information to resolve the controversy were the White House visitor logs, maintained by the Secret Service, which indicate who entered the White House and when. The response of the White House to requests for those logs was to work out a compromise by which some but not all of the information requested was released.

Then, without notice to the press or the public, the White House forced the Secret Service to change its long-standing policy and impose secrecy from that point forward on all of the visitor logs at the White House.

Ironically, one of the leading scientific experts on global warming in NASA, Dr. James E. Hansen, has been ordered to go in the opposite direction and start keeping a careful log of all his visitors for the administration so that it can monitor and control his discussions of global warming. Hansen has also been ordered not to talk to members of the press, although that order appears to have been ineffective.

In an effort to muddy the clear consensus of the scientific community on global warming, the White House also directed major changes and deletions to an EPA report—changes so egregious that the agency said it was too embarrassed to use the language insisted upon by the political employees at the White House. Scientific warnings about the catastrophic consequences of unchecked global warming were censored by a political appointee in the White House, Philip Cooney, who had no scientific training. Sometimes we seem very far indeed from an age when Jefferson could write of his "conviction that science is important to the preservation of our republican government, and that it is also essential to its protection against foreign power."

George Deutsch, a twenty-four-year-old Bush political appointee to NASA, not only had no scientific training, he ultimately resigned after it was revealed that he had never graduated from college at all.

But while he was there, he instructed all NASA scientists to always refer to the big bang as a *theory* rather than as science. Mr. Deutsch, who was an intern in the Bush-Cheney campaign, instructed the NASA scientists in a memo that the big bang is "not proven fact; it is opinion. This is more than a science issue, it is a religious issue."

In fact, there are a number of scientific issues that have been treated by the Bush administration as primarily religious issues. Among them are the life-and-death issues related to research into human stem cells. The subordination of the best scientific evidence to ideologically driven beliefs is yet another strategy for controlling policy by distorting and suppressing the best available information.

As the poet Thomas Moore wrote in the early nineteenth century, "But Faith, fanatic faith, once wedded fast to some dear falsehood, hugs it to the last."

The administration has also adopted a new policy on the Freedom of Information Act that actively encourages federal agencies to fully consider all potential reasons for nondisclosure, regardless of whether the disclosure would be harmful. In other words, the federal government will now actively resist complying with any request for information.

By closely guarding information about their own behavior, members of this administration are dismantling a fundamental element of accountability in American government, because as long as the government's actions are secret, it cannot be held accountable. A government for the people and by the people should be transparent *to* the people. However, the Bush administration has sought to deprive the public of necessary information for decision making by shrouding many policies with a veil of secrecy. In fact, I cannot remember any administration adopting this kind of persistent, systematic abuse of the truth and the institutionalization of dishonesty as a routine part of the policy process.

There are numerous cases in which the administration withdrew information from the public sphere when the facts in question did not support the administration's position. For example, during this administration's attempt to persuade Congress to enact the Medicare prescription drug benefit, many in the House and Senate raised concerns about the cost and design of the program. But rather than engaging in open debate on the basis of factual data, the administration withheld facts and prevented the Congress from hearing testimony that it sought from the principal administration expert who had compiled information showing in advance of the vote that, indeed, the true cost estimates were far higher than the numbers given to Congress by the president.

Deprived of that information, and believing the false numbers given to it instead, the Congress approved the program. Tragically, the entire initiative is now collapsing all over the country, with the administration making an appeal to major insurance companies to volunteer to bail it out.

Medicare head Thomas Scully resigned in December 2003 after charges that he actually threatened one of his actuaries in order to hide the true cost of the program that Congress was debating. After overseeing the single largest expansion of the federal program in thirty years and leaving in disgrace, Scully became a lobbyist for health care companies.

The intimidation of the Medicare actuary was unfortunately not an isolated case. The administration's efforts to control the flow of information about policy has included a systematic effort to intimidate numerous individuals whose expertise and factual presentations might undermine White House policy.

Former EPA head Christine Todd Whitman said that when she offered a different point of view on environmental policy, White House officials sought to intimidate her into silence. "In meetings, I'd ask if there were any facts to support our case," she said, according to one reporter, "and for that I was accused of disloyalty."

A former acting ambassador to Iraq, Joe Wilson, was asked by the

CIA to travel to Niger to investigate the allegations that Saddam Hussein had been seeking yellowcake uranium from that African country. He said that he found that there was no such effort, and he reported his conclusions to the agency. Much later, when he read the White House assertions that Saddam was seeking yellowcake, Wilson made efforts to ascertain what the basis of the White House's conclusion had been and found that there was no basis. He then wrote a column for *The New York Times* describing what he believed to be the truth of the situation. Immediately, the White House launched a campaign to intimidate Wilson by attacking him and, in violation of federal law, made public the identity of Wilson's wife, a CIA officer involved with undercover programs. Both Wilson and his wife, Valerie Plame, felt immediately that the motive for the personal attacks on them was to intimidate others who might disagree with the White House from coming forward.

The White House also tried to extend its efforts to manipulate the impressions of the American people with a campaign to intimidate the media into presenting a more favorable image of the administration. Shortly after the 9/11 attacks, former Bush press secretary Ari Fleischer responded to criticism of the administration's rhetoric about terrorism by warning that commentators "need to watch what they say." When the White House became upset with coverage by CBS television news, the president engaged in the theatrics of personal intimidation by staging a photo op during his on-camera walk from the Oval Office to his waiting limousine, carrying under his arm for the cameras to photograph a copy of a book by a right-wing conservative attacking CBS as biased.

Dan Rather, former CBS anchor, said that the post-9/11 atmosphere stifled journalists from asking government officials "the toughest of the tough questions." Rather went so far as to compare administration efforts to intimidate the press with necklacing in apartheid South Africa. While acknowledging it as, in his phrase, "an obscene comparison," he said, "the fear is that you will be necklaced; you will have a flaming tire of lack of patriotism put around your neck."

CNN's Christiane Amanpour said, "I think the press was muzzled, and I think the press self-muzzled. I'm sorry to say, but certainly television—and perhaps, to a certain extent, my station—was intimidated by the administration."

New York Times columnist Paul Krugman was one of the first journalists to regularly expose the president's consistent distortion of the facts. Krugman wrote, "Let's not overlook the role of intimidation. After 9/11, if you were thinking of saying anything negative about the president . . . you had to expect right-wing pundits and publications to do all they could to ruin your reputation." Bush and Cheney have purposefully spread confusion, while attempting to punish in any way they can any reporters who pose a threat to the perpetuation of that confusion.

The present executive branch has made it a practice to try to control and intimidate news organizations, from PBS to CBS to *Newsweek*. When they needed a hand at crucial moments, they routinely called on pseudo-reporter, Jeff Gannon, who had been given press credentials by the White House even though he worked for a Web site owned by a Republican Party delegate from Texas. Jeff Gannon, of course, was also a former male escort. Ironically, one of Gannon's (his real name was James D. Guckert) efforts to bail out President Bush came immediately after a question from a real reporter about payments by the Bush administration to the columnist Armstrong Williams for disguising favorable propaganda for their policies as independent and unbiased news. As the president finished his answer, he quickly pointed to Gannon and said, "Yes, sir?" Gannon then offered a scathing criticism of Democratic leaders in the House and Senate and asked the president, "How are you going to work with people who seem to have divorced themselves from reality?" Good question.

How perfect that the president's exchange with a "journalist" was in service of an effort to misdirect attention from efforts to investigate the growing corruption of the interaction of a free press and public officials. It serves as a live-action version of the counterfeit scenes in political commercials when actors pretend to be "objective citizens" expressing support for a candidate whose backers have paid for an ad. These synthetic imitations of democracy, like Gannon's portrayal of a journalist, serve to distract the public's attention from the ongoing betrayal of the real democratic process.

They also paid actors to make phony video press releases and paid cash to some commentators who were willing to take it in return for positive treatment. And almost every day, with the help of their right-wing radio allies, they unleash squadrons of digital harassers to hector any journalist who is considered critical of the president.

These tactics are all aimed at making it easier to deceive the people. As Justice Hugo L. Black once wrote in a landmark opinion, "The Press was protected so that it could bare the secrets of the government and inform the people. Only a free and unrestrained press can effectively expose deception in government. And paramount among the responsibilities of a free press is the duty to prevent any part of the government from deceiving the people. . . ."

In 2002, the Bush administration even proposed a citizen-spy program that amounted to deputizing millions of Americans to spy on their fellow citizens. Run out of the Department of Justice, the Terrorism Information and Prevention System, or "TIPS," was designed to encourage Americans—people who had access to homes, like letter carriers, utility employees, and truck drivers—to tell the government what they observed in the course of their workday. Congress shot down the program shortly after it was proposed, but some elements of it—such as eavesdropping on American citizens without a warrant—were secretly enacted anyway.

This administration is seeking to conduct its work in secret even as it demands broad unfettered access to personal information about American citizens. Under the rubric of protecting national security, administration members have obtained new powers to gather information from citizens and to keep it secret. Yet at the same time, they themselves refuse to disclose information that is highly relevant to the war against terrorism.

And it is the constricted role of ideas in the American political system today that has encouraged the White House to vigorously impose unprecedented secrecy over its activities and to attempt to control the flow of information— as a means of controlling the outcome of all important decisions that still lie in the hands of the people. Rather than accepting our traditions of openness and accountability, this administration has opted to rule by unquestioned authority.

For this administration, all too often, the truth hurts; it hurts, that is, when it is available to the American people. Consequently, they have often sought relief by depriving the American people of access to information to which they have a right.

A government of and for the people is supposed to be generally open to public scrutiny by the people—while the private information of the people themselves should be routinely protected from government intrusion. This administration has turned the fundamental presumption of our democracy on its head. And in the end, its assaults on our core democratic principles have left us less free and less secure.

CHAPTER FIVE

The Assault on the Individual

Just as the boundary line between the "economic sphere" and the "political sphere" has shifted back and forth over time, as noted in chapter 3, in the same way, the boundary between the "individual" and the "nation" has also been drawn differently in different societies and at different periods in history. The new information ecology of the printing press, which empowered individuals to wield knowledge as a source of influence, led to a new recognition of, and respect for, the role of individuals. You could say that the idea of individual dignity acquired new meaning with the new accessibility of information that arrived in the wake of the printing press. Without printed words—and the knowledge conveyed by them to the masses who became literate—there would have been no Bill of Rights in America to protect the freedom and dignity of individuals.

In much the same way that the information revolution in the last quarter of the twentieth century transformed economic output by substituting ingenuity for raw materials (the total value of everything produced in the American economy grew by 300 percent from 1950 to 2000, while the gross tonnage remained the same), the information revolution that began in the late fifteenth century progressively substituted the force of thought for force of arms in the political economy of Europe.

As soon as complex thoughts could be easily conveyed from one individual to the mass of others—and as soon as others could easily receive them and potentially agree with them—every individual suddenly had the potential for leveraging mass political power. The free flow of information therefore gave each individual more standing within society—without reference to class or fortune—to claim a measure of dignity equal to all others and empowered individuals to scrutinize the use of power by those in government.

As a result, as long as individuals had access to the public forum on terms equal to—or nearly equal to—those with wealth and power, they could exercise political power and were seen as being entitled to deference by the state. Indeed, by the time of the American Revolution, the state's power came to be seen as legitimate only when it was derived from the consent of the individuals in whose name it was exercised. It was as if every person were entitled to symbolically fly the legendary flag carried by the marines mustered by the Continental Congress in 1775: DONT TREAD ON ME.

Today, by contrast, Americans in the age of television do not have the same means of attracting the attention—and agreement—of the masses of their fellow citizens for even the most eloquently expressed opinion. Unlike the menacing snake with thirteen rattles on the flag more than two centuries ago, individual Americans in the twenty-first century no longer seem to get the same respect.

African Americans, Native Americans, and women were not included in the circle of respect two centuries ago, of course. And in reality, access to the public forum was much more freely available to educated elites than to the average person. Even though literacy rates were high in the late eighteenth century, illiteracy was a barrier for many then, as it is for many Americans still.

Nevertheless, with the dominance of television over the printing press and the continued infancy of the Internet in its development as a serious competitor to television, we have temporarily lost a common meeting place in the public forum where powerful ideas from individuals have the potential to sway the opinions of millions and generate genuine political change. What has emerged in its place is a very different kind of public forum—one in which individuals are constantly flattered but rarely listened to. When the consent of the governed is manufactured and manipulated by marketers and propagandists, reason plays a diminished role.

With each passing month, the Internet is bringing new opportunities for individuals to reassert their historic role in American democracy. Blogs, for example, are now beginning to serve as a check and balance on inaccurate information conveyed by the mass media. And the growing distribution of short video clips over the Web is creating more confidence that television will eventually be seen as a transition medium between the age of print and the age of the Internet. Nevertheless, for the time being, television is still by far the most powerful medium. And the sameness of the cleverly designed messages aimed at the mass audience—and the lack of genuine interaction—undermines and corrodes individualism. As a result, the dignity of individuals in American society has been undermined.

Moreover, the diminished role of individuals in America's national conversation has been accompanied by a diminished respect for the *rights* of individuals—especially during the Bush-Cheney administration.

For example, President Bush has declared that he has a heretofore unrecognized inherent power to seize and imprison any American citizen whom he alone determines to be a threat to our nation—without an arrest warrant, without notifying them of what charges have been filed against them, and without even informing their families that they have been imprisoned. The president claims that he can simply snatch an American citizen off the street and keep him or her locked up indefinitely—even for the rest of his or her life—and refuse to allow that citizen the right to make a phone call or talk to a lawyer—even to argue that the president or his appointees have made a mistake and imprisoned the wrong person.

All that is necessary to make this move legal, according to the president, is that he label that citizen an "unlawful enemy combatant." Those are the magic words. If the president alone decides that those words accurately describe someone, then that person can be immediately locked up and held incommunicado for as long as the president wants, with no court having the right to determine whether the facts actually justify his imprisonment. These claims have been and are being challenged in court, but so far with only modest success.

Now, if the president makes a mistake or is given faulty information by somebody working for him, and he locks up the wrong person, then it's almost impossible for that prisoner to prove his or her innocence—because he or she can't talk to a lawyer or family or anyone else. The prisoner doesn't even have the right to know what specific crime he or she is accused of committing. So a constitutional right to liberty and the pursuit of happiness that we used to think of in an old-fashioned way as "inalienable" can now be instantly stripped from any American by the president with no meaningful review by any other branch of government.

For those in federal custody who do manage to gain legal representation, the current administration has issued regulations authorizing the attorney general to monitor all conversations between the accused and his attorney if the attorney general alone suspects it is necessary. These regulations bypass procedures for obtaining prior judicial review for such monitoring in the rare instances when it was permitted in the past. Now, whoever is in federal custody has to assume that the government could be listening to their consultations with their lawyers.

In his famous book *The Trial*, Franz Kafka wrote about fictional prisoner "K.," who was put in a predicament eerily similar to the circumstances of some held in custody by the Bush-Cheney administration:

But K. should not forget that the trial would not be public, if the court deems it necessary it can be made public but there is

no law that says it has to be. As a result, the accused and his defence don't have access even to the court records, and especially
not to the indictment, and that means we generally don't
know—or at least not precisely—what the first documents need
to be about, which means that if they do contain anything of
relevance to the case it's only by a lucky coincidence. If anything
about the individual charges and the reasons for them comes out
clearly or can be guessed at while the accused is being questioned, then it's possible to work out and submit documents that
really direct the issue and present proof, but not before.
Conditions like this, of course, place the defence in a very un-
favourable and difficult position. But that is what they intend.
In fact, defence is not really allowed under the law, it's only tolerated, and there is even some dispute about whether the relevant parts of the law imply even that. So strictly speaking, there
is no such thing as a counsel acknowledged by the court, and
anyone who comes before this court as counsel is basically no
more than a barrack room lawyer. The effect of all this, of course,
is to remove the dignity of the whole procedure.

As Winston Churchill once put it, "The power of the executive to
cast a man into prison without formulating any charge known to the
law, and particularly to deny him the judgment of his peers, is in the
highest degree odious, and the foundation of all totalitarian government whether Nazi or Communist."

The Supreme Court has recently disagreed with the administration's
bizarre claim of extralegal power, but the president engaged in legal
maneuvers that have thus far prevented the Court from providing any
meaningful relief for this abuse.

This administration simply does not seem to agree that the challenge of preserving democratic freedom cannot be met by surrendering core American values. Incredibly, this administration has
attempted to compromise the most precious rights that America has

stood for all over the world for more than two hundred years: due process, equal treatment under the law, the dignity of the individual, freedom from unreasonable search and seizure, freedom from promiscuous government surveillance.

For example, when America was founded, individual citizens were protected by the Bill of Rights from unreasonable search and seizure. During America's first two centuries, if the police wanted to search your house, they had to be able to persuade an independent judge to give them a search warrant, and then (with rare exceptions) they had to bang on your door and yell, "Open up!" If you didn't quickly open up, they were then permitted to knock down the door. Also, if they seized anything, they had to leave a list explaining what they had taken. That way, if it was all a terrible mistake (as it sometimes is), you could go and get your stuff back.

But that's all changed now. Starting a few years ago, federal agents were given broad new statutory authority by the Patriot Act to "sneak and peek" in nonterrorism cases. They can secretly enter your home with no warning—whether you are there or not—and they can wait for months before telling you they were there. Such searches need not have any relationship to terrorism whatsoever. They can be triggered by any garden-variety crime. And the new law makes it very easy to get around the need for a traditional warrant; agents simply need to say that searching your house might have some connection (even a remote one) to the investigation of some agent of a foreign power. Then they can go to another court—a secret court—that has rejected only four warrant applications of the more than 18,000 filed.

In a speech at FBI headquarters, President Bush went even further and formally proposed that the attorney general be allowed to authorize these special subpoenas by administrative order, without the need for a warrant from any court.

Here's another recent change in our civil liberties: Now, if it wants to, the federal government has the right to monitor every Web site you go to on the Internet, and keep a list of everyone you send e-mail to or receive e-mail from and everyone you call on the telephone or who calls you—and it doesn't even have to show probable cause that you've done anything wrong. Nor does the government ever have to report to any court on what it's doing with the information. Moreover, there are precious few safeguards to keep the government from reading the content of all your e-mail.

As a matter of fact, the current administration also claims the right to read all the mail you receive from the U.S. Postal Service—and to listen to all your telephone calls as well—if it chooses to do so. Administration officials promise not to do it unless they have a really good reason. But they get to decide on their own what constitutes a good reason, and they don't need permission from a judge. That comes as a surprise to those who are familiar with the U.S. Constitution. The courts have always recognized an inherent presidential authority in rare emergency cases to conduct surveillance and searches that would otherwise require a warrant. What is different is that this president claims the right to break and enter, tap your phone, and read your correspondence at will—and to do so regularly, for a significant number of Americans, on a massive scale.

Whenever critics of this practice point out that it constitutes a historic weakening of the individual rights guaranteed to Americans under the Constitution, this administration accuses them of "coddling terrorists." But an increasing number of Americans in both political parties have expressed concern that the Bush policy will serve to set a precedent for future presidents to routinely violate the individual rights that are protected in the Constitution.

Many fear that if the pattern of practice begun by this administration is not challenged, it may well become a permanent part of the American system. A few principled conservatives have pointed out that granting unchecked power to this president might well mean that the next president will have unchecked power as well. And they are well aware that the next president might be someone whose values and beliefs they do not share.

The United States Congress, while it was under Republican control, passed a law that clarified the procedures that must be followed by the executive branch to protect privacy of letters delivered by the U.S. Postal Service. But the president issued a written statement at the time he signed the law emphasizing his own independent authority to order, without a warrant, that mail be opened for inspection.

As James Madison, the principal author of the Constitution, wrote, "There are more instances of the abridgement of the freedom of the people by the gradual and silent encroachments of those in power, than by violent and sudden usurpations."

Or to cite another change—and thanks to the librarians, more people know about this one—the White House has claimed the right to send the FBI into any library and ask for the records of anybody who has used the library and get a list of who is reading what, simply by claiming the information is relevant to an intelligence investigation. They have even claimed the power to compel the librarians to be silent about the request lest the librarians themselves also be imprisoned, although a court ruled that this gag order was unconstitutional, and Congress has since changed it. Similarly, the FBI can demand all the records of banks, colleges, hotels, hospitals, credit card companies, and many more kinds of companies.

The administration has also claimed the right to run credit and background checks and gather other information about anyone the government decides is "of investigatory interest"—meaning anyone the administration thinks is suspicious—even without any evidence of criminal behavior.

The administration has further authorized FBI agents to attend church meetings, rallies, political meetings, and any other citizen activity open to the public simply on the agents' own initiative, reversing a decades-old policy that required justification to supervisors that such an infiltration has a provable connection to a legitimate investigation.

As we now know, the executive branch of our government has been caught eavesdropping on huge numbers of American citizens and has brazenly declared that it has the unilateral right to continue without regard to the established law enacted by Congress to prevent such abuses. It is imperative that respect for the rule of law be restored.

Why should we be alarmed about such eavesdropping? Recall that for the last several years of his life, Dr. Martin Luther King Jr. was illegally wiretapped—one of hundreds of thousands of Americans whose private communications were intercepted by the U.S. government during this period. The FBI privately called King "the most dangerous and effective Negro leader in the country" and vowed to "take him off his pedestal." The government even attempted to destroy his marriage and allegedly tried to blackmail him into committing suicide.

This campaign continued until Dr. King's murder. In fact, it was the discovery that the FBI had conducted a long-running and extensive campaign of secret electronic surveillance designed to infiltrate the inner workings of the Southern Christian Leadership Conference, and to learn the most intimate details of Dr. King's life, that helped persuade Congress to enact new statutory restrictions on wiretapping in the first place.

The result of these and other similar abuses was the Foreign Intelligence Surveillance Act (FISA), which was enacted expressly to ensure that foreign intelligence surveillance would be presented to an impartial judge to verify that there is a sufficient cause for the surveillance. I voted for that law during my first term in Congress, and for almost thirty years the system has proven a workable and valued means of according a level of protection for private citizens while permitting foreign surveillance to continue.

Then in December of 2005, Americans suddenly awoke to the shocking news that in spite of this long-settled law, the executive branch has been secretly spying on large numbers of Americans for more than four years and eavesdropping on a huge number of telephone calls and e-mails "inside the United States" without any search warrants or new legal authority.

During the period when this eavesdropping was still secret, the president went out of his way to reassure the American people on more than one occasion that, of course, judicial permission is required for any government spying on American citizens and that, of course, these constitutional safeguards were still in place.

The president's soothing statements turned out to be knowingly false. Moreover, as soon as this massive domestic spying program was uncovered by the press, the president not only confirmed that the story was true, but also declared that he had no intention of bringing these wholesale invasions of privacy to an end.

At present, we still have much to learn about a more recent statement in the aftermath of the change in control of Congress that the White House would begin to abide by FISA. But the imposition of secrecy on all of the legal proceedings is not reassuring. And what we do know about this pervasive wiretapping leads to the unavoidable conclusion that the president of the United States has been breaking the law repeatedly and persistently.

Attorney General Gonzales wrote that the administration still believes the program is legal but that they have now gone to the FISA court and that a judge on the court has set rules that preserve "the speed and agility necessary" to battle terrorism. Neither Gonzales nor Justice Department officials disclosed details of the rules set by the court, arguing that details were classified, so it is unclear whether the administration is getting individualized approval as required by FISA or rather has received some broader authority. The presiding judge of the FISA court said she was willing to release the ruling, but the administration has objected on the grounds that the orders include classified information. The administration's handling of this issue is in keeping with its tendency to try to render controversies moot by making small concessions in their practice without conceding on the larger principle at stake.

The president's men have minced words about America's laws. The attorney general openly conceded that the "kind of surveillance" we now know they have been conducting requires a court order unless authorized by statute. FISA self-evidently does not authorize what the National Security Agency has been doing, and no one inside or outside the administration claims that it does. Incredibly, the administration claims instead that the surveillance was implicitly authorized when Congress voted to approve the use of force against those who attacked us on September 11.

This argument just does not hold water, and faces a number of embarrassing facts. First, another admission by Attorney General Alberto Gonzales: He concedes that the administration knew that the NSA project was prohibited by existing law and that it consulted with some members of Congress about changing the statute. Gonzales says that the administration was told this probably would not be possible. So it stretches credibility for the administration to subsequently claim that the Authorization for the Use of Military Force somehow implicitly authorized the NSA project all along. Second, when the authorization was being debated, the administration members did in fact seek to have language inserted in it that would have authorized them to use military force domestically—and the Congress did not agree. Senator Ted Stevens (R-AK) and Representative Jim McGovern (D-MA), among others, made statements during the authorization debate clearly restating that that authorization did not operate domestically.

It is the administration's disrespect for America's Constitution that has now brought our republic to the brink of a dangerous breach in the fabric of democracy. And the disrespect embodied in these apparent mass violations of the law is part of a larger pattern of seeming indifference to the Constitution that is deeply troubling to millions of Americans in both political parties.

Thomas Paine, whose pamphlet *Common Sense* helped ignite the American Revolution, succinctly described America's alternative. Here, he said, we intended to make certain that "the law is king." Vigilant adherence to the rule of law strengthens our democracy and strengthens America. It ensures that those who govern us operate within our constitutional structure, which means that our democratic institutions play their indispensable role in shaping policy and determining the direction of our nation. It means that the people of this nation ultimately determine its course and not executive officials operating in secret without constraint.

The rule of law makes us stronger by ensuring that decisions will be tested, studied, reviewed, and examined through the processes of government that are designed to improve policy. And the knowledge that they will be reviewed prevents overreaching and checks the accretion of power.

By the same token, whenever power is unchecked and unaccountable, it almost inevitably leads to mistakes and abuses. In the absence of rigorous accountability, incompetence flourishes. Dishonesty is encouraged and rewarded.

In January 2006, for example, Vice President Cheney attempted to defend the administration's eavesdropping on American citizens by saying that if it had conducted this program prior to 9/11, it would have found out the names of some of the hijackers.

Tragically, he apparently still doesn't know that the administration members did in fact have the names of at least two of the hijackers well before 9/11 and had available to them information that could have easily led to the identification of most of the other hijackers. Yet because of incompetence in the handling of this information, it was never used to protect the American people.

There was in fact a great deal of specific information that *was* available prior to 9/11 that probably could have been used to prevent the tragedy. A recent analysis by the Markle Foundation (working with data from a software company that received venture capital from a CIA-sponsored firm) demonstrates this point in a startling way:

- In late August 2001, Nawaf Alhazmi and Khalid Almidhar bought tickets to fly on American Airlines Flight 77 (which was flown into the Pentagon). They bought the tickets using their real names. Both names were then on a State Department/INS watch list called TIPOFF. Both men were sought by the FBI and CIA as suspected terrorists, in part because they had been observed at a terrorist meeting in Malaysia.

- These two passenger names would have been exact matches when checked against the TIPOFF list. But that would only have been the first step. Further data checks could then have begun.

- Checking for common addresses (address information is widely available, including on the Internet), analysts would have discovered that Salem Alhazmi (who also bought a seat on American Airlines Flight 77) used the same address as Nawaf Alhazmi. More important, they could have discovered that Mohamed Atta (American Airlines Flight 11, North Tower of the World Trade Center) and Marwan Al-Shehhi (United Airlines Flight 175, South Tower of the World Trade Center) used the same address as Khalid Almidhar.

- Checking for identical frequent flier numbers, analysts would have discovered that Majed Moqed (American Airlines Flight 77) used the same number as Almidhar.

- With Mohamed Atta now also identified as a possible associate of the wanted terrorist Almidhar, analysts could have added Atta's phone numbers (also publicly available information) to their checklist. By doing so, they would have identified four other hijackers (Fayez Ahmed, Mohand Alshehri, Wail Alshehri, and Abdulaziz Alomari).

- Closer to September 11, a further check of passenger lists against a more innocuous INS watch list (for expired visas) would have identified Ahmed Alghamdi. Through him, the same sort of relatively simple correlations could have led to identifying the remaining hijackers, who boarded United Airlines Flight 93 (which crashed in Pennsylvania).

This analysis from the Markle Foundation clearly demonstrates that all of the necessary raw data was available to stop the 9/11 attacks. In the next chapter, I will explain that the relevant officials at the FBI and CIA were aware of much of this information and yet were stymied in their efforts to get the White House to pay attention to it.

Not to put too fine a point on it, what is needed is better and more timely analysis. Simply piling up more raw data that is almost entirely irrelevant is not only not going to help, it may actually hurt the cause. As one of the nation's top security technologists, Bruce Schneier, said: "We're looking for a needle in a haystack here. Dumping more hay on the pile doesn't necessarily get you anywhere."

In other words, the mass collecting of personal data on hundreds of millions of people actually makes it more difficult to protect the nation against terrorists, so they ought to cut most of it out.

There have, of course, been other periods in American history when the executive branch claimed new powers that were later seen as excessive and mistaken. Our second president, John Adams, passed the infamous Alien and Sedition Acts and sought to silence and imprison critics and political opponents.

When his successor, Thomas Jefferson, eliminated the abuses he said: "The essential principles of our Government . . . form the bright constellation which has gone before us and guided our steps through an age of revolution and reformation. . . . Should we wander from them in moments of error or of alarm, let us hasten to retrace our steps and to regain the road which alone leads to peace, liberty and safety."

Our greatest president, Abraham Lincoln, suspended habeas corpus during the Civil War. Some of the worst abuses prior to those of the current administration were committed by President Woodrow Wilson during and after World War I with the notorious "Red Scare" and Palmer raids. The internment of Japanese Americans during World War II marked a low point for the respect of individual rights at the hands of the executive. Then came the McCarthy abuses of the cold war. And during the Vietnam War, the notorious COINTELPRO program was part and parcel of the abuses experienced by Dr. King and thousands of others.

But in each of these cases, when the conflict and turmoil subsided, the country recovered its equilibrium and absorbed the lessons learned. And after each of these periods of excess, we as a nation felt ashamed and tried to make up for the abuses—with monetary payments in some cases, with apologies, with new laws and new protections. And although we have not yet entered the period of regret and atonement this time around, it is already obvious that we have been for some time in one of those periods of regrettable excess.

Former Supreme Court justice William Brennan commented on this cycle once, writing, "After each perceived security crisis ended, the United States has remorsefully realized that the abrogation of civil liberties was unnecessary. But it has proven unable to prevent itself from repeating the error when the next crisis came along."

There are also reasons for concern this time around that what we are experiencing may no longer be the first half of a recurring cycle, but rather the beginning of something new. For one thing, this war is predicted by the administration to last for the rest of our lives. So we are told that the conditions of national threat that have been used by other presidents to justify arrogations of power will persist in near perpetuity. Some have expressed the view that over time it will begin to resemble the "war" against drugs—that is, it will become a more or less permanent struggle that occupies a significant part of our law enforcement and security agenda from now on. If that is the case, then when—if ever—does this encroachment on our freedoms die a natural death?

For another thing, we have for decades been witnessing the slow and steady accumulation of presidential power. In a global environment of nuclear weapons and cold war tensions, Congress and the American people accepted ever enlarging spheres of presidential initiative to conduct intelligence and counterintelligence activities and to allocate our military forces on the global stage. As Supreme Court justice Felix Frankfurter wrote in a 1952 Supreme Court case, "The accretion of dangerous power does not come in a day. It does come, however slowly, from the generative force of unchecked disregard of the restrictions that fence in even the most disinterested assertion of authority."

In that case, President Harry Truman was faced with a dispute with the owners of America's largest steel manufacturers in the midst of the worsening Korean War. In an overreach of presidential power, Truman declared that the U.S. government would simply take over operation of the steel mills. But the court prevented him from following through based on prior congressional legislation governing the matter.

A third reason to worry that what we are witnessing is a discontinuity and not another turn of the recurring cycle is that the new technologies of surveillance—long anticipated by novelists like George Orwell and other prophets of the "police state"—are now more widespread than they have ever been. They give the government a vast new capacity to sweep up and analyze enormous quantities of information and to mine it for intelligence. This adds significant vulnerability to the privacy and freedom of enormous numbers of innocent people. And they do have the potential for shifting the balance of power between the apparatus of the state and the freedom of the individual in ways both subtle and profound.

Moreover, these technologies are being widely used not only by the government, but also by corporations and other private entities. And that is relevant to an assessment of the requirements in the Patriot Act for so many corporations—especially in the finance industries—to prepare millions of reports annually for the government on suspicious activities by their customers. It is also relevant to the new flexibility corporations have been given to share information with one another about their customers.

The fourth reason for concern is that the threat of additional terror strikes is all too real, and the concerted efforts of terrorist organizations to acquire weapons of mass destruction do create a real imperative to exercise the powers of the executive branch with swiftness and agility—just as the emergence of nuclear weapons and ICBMs created a new practical imperative in the cold war that altered the balance of war-making responsibility between Congress and the president. Moreover, there is in fact an inherent power that is conferred by the Constitution to the president to take unilateral action to protect the nation from a sudden and immediate threat, and it is simply not possible to precisely define in legalistic terms exactly when that power is appropriate and when it is not. For example, if, in an isolated case— or even in a small number of cases—a president is presented with an opportunity to seize an individual he has good reason to believe is about to cause grave harm to the United States or its citizens, he has the inherent power to act quickly on that information. As vice president, I myself made that very point to President Clinton when he had the opportunity to seize an al-Qaeda operative who was planning an attack against us. And the president took my advice, though the individual we attempted to capture escaped.

But there is a big difference between the exercise of that inherent presidential power in exceptional cases and an effort to silently institute a massive and permanent new pattern that clearly oversteps the boundaries established in the Constitution. The existence of that inherent power cannot be used to justify a gross and excessive power grab lasting for years that produces a serious imbalance in the relationship between the executive and the other two branches of government.

There is a final reason to worry that we may be experiencing something more than just another cycle of overreach and regret. This administration has come to power in the thrall of a legal theory that aims to convince us that this excessive concentration of presidential authority is exactly what our Constitution intended.

That is, of course, not true. If our Founders could see the current state of their generation's handiwork and assess the quality of our generation's stewardship now, at the beginning of this twenty-first century, I am certain they would be amazed at the claims of the current administration.

There is simply no question that we continue to face new challenges in the wake of the attack of September 11 and that we must be vigilant in protecting our citizens from harm. But we do not have to break the law or sacrifice our system of government to protect Americans from terrorism. In fact, doing so makes us weaker and more vulnerable.

Moreover, it is often the case that an executive branch beguiled by the pursuit of unchecked power responds to its own mistakes by reflexively proposing that it be given still more power. Often, the request itself is used to mask accountability for mistakes in the use of power it already has made.

Some of the worst abuses of individuals by the current administration came when Arab American immigrants were rounded up in the weeks following the 9/11 attacks. This mass mistreatment actually hurt our security in a number of important ways.

But first, let's be clear about what happened: This was little more than a cheap and cruel political stunt by then attorney general John Ashcroft. More than 99 percent of the mostly Arab-background men who were rounded up had merely overstayed their visas or committed some other minor offense as they tried to pursue the American dream just like most immigrants. But they were used as extras in the administration's effort to give the impression that it had caught a large number of bad guys. And many of them were treated horribly and abusively.

Consider this example reported in depth by former *New York Times* columnist Anthony Lewis:

Anser Mehmood, a Pakistani who had overstayed his visa, was arrested in New York on October 3, 2001. The next day he was briefly questioned by FBI agents, who said they had no further interest in him. Then he was shackled in handcuffs, leg irons, and a belly chain and taken to the Metropolitan Detention Center in Brooklyn. Guards there put two more sets of handcuffs on him and another set of leg irons. One threw Mehmood against a wall. The guards forced him to run down a long ramp, the irons cutting into his wrists and ankles. The physical abuse was mixed with verbal taunts.

After two weeks Mehmood was allowed to make a telephone call to his wife. She was not at home and Mehmood was told that he would have to wait six weeks to try again. He first saw her, on a visit, three months after his arrest. All that time he was kept in a windowless cell, in solitary confinement, with two overhead fluorescent lights on all the time. In the end he was charged with using an invalid Social Security card. He was deported in May 2002, nearly eight months after his arrest.

The faith tradition I share with Ashcroft includes this teaching from Jesus: "Whatsoever you do unto the least of these, you do unto me."

And make no mistake: The disgraceful treatment suffered by many of these vulnerable immigrants at the hands of the administration has created deep resentments and hurt the cooperation desperately needed from immigrant communities in the United States and from the security services of other countries.

In what is in some ways an even more brazen move, years after the Justice Department rounded up over 1,200 individuals of Arab descent, it still refuses to release the names of the individuals who were detained, even though virtually every one of those arrested has been "cleared" by the FBI of any connection to terrorism. There is absolutely no national security justification for keeping the names secret.

War is lawful violence, but even in its midst we acknowledge the need for rules. We know that in our wars there have been dissents from these standards, often the result of spontaneous anger arising out of the passion of battle. But we count on our president to protect us from this kind of violence, not to create the framework that makes it possible.

We could look to the chief executive as the point from which redress would come and law would be upheld. That was one of the great prides of our country: humane leadership faithful to the law. What we have now, however, is the result of decisions taken by a president and an administration for whom the best law is no law, as long as law threatens to constrain their political will. And where the constraints of law cannot be prevented or eliminated, then they maneuver it to be weakened by evasion, by delay, by hair splitting, by obstruction, and by failure to enforce on the part of those sworn to uphold the law.

In 1999, Israel's highest court was asked to balance the right of individual prisoners against dire threats to the security of its people. Here is what the court declared: "This is the destiny of democracy, as not all means are acceptable to it and not all practices employed by its enemies are open before it. Although a democracy must often fight with one hand tied behind its back, it nonetheless has the upper hand. Preserving the rule of law and recognition of an individual's liberty constitutes an important component in its understanding of security. At the end of the day they strengthen its spirit and allow it to overcome its difficulties."

The constant violations of civil liberties by the Bush-Cheney administration also promote the false impression that these violations are necessary in order to take every precaution against another terrorist attack. But the simple truth is that the vast majority of the violations have not benefited our security at all; on the contrary, they hurt our security. And they have taken us much further down the road toward an intrusive "Big Brother"–style government—toward the dangers prophesied by George Orwell in his book *1984*—than anyone ever thought would be possible in the United States of America.

So what should be done? Well, to begin with, our country ought to find a way to immediately stop its policy of indefinitely detaining American citizens without charges and without a judicial determination that their detention is proper. Such a course of conduct is incompatible with American traditions and values, with sacred principles of due process of law and separation of powers.

It is no accident that our Constitution requires in criminal prosecutions a "speedy and public trial." The principles of liberty and the accountability of government, at the heart of what makes America unique, require no less. The Bush administration's treatment of American citizens it calls "enemy combatants" is nothing short of un-American.

Second, foreign citizens held in Guantánamo and elsewhere as captured combatants should be protected by the United States under Article 3 of the Geneva Conventions, which forbids murder, mutilation, cruel treatment, torture, and humiliating and degrading treatment. Article 3 also prohibits the passing of sentences and the carrying out of executions without previous judgment pronounced by a regularly constituted court affording all the judicial guarantees which are recognized as indispensable by civilized peoples. Since the conventions were adopted, that has been done in every war until this one, including Vietnam and the Gulf War.

If we don't provide this protection, how can we expect American troops captured overseas to be treated with equal respect? We owe this to our sons and daughters who fight to defend freedom in Iraq, in Afghanistan, and elsewhere in the world.

Next, our nation's greatness is measured by how we treat those who are the most vulnerable. Noncitizens whom the government seeks to detain should be entitled to some basic rights. The administration must stop abusing the so-called material witness statute. That statute was designed to hold witnesses briefly before they are called to testify before a grand jury. It has been misused by this administration as a pretext for indefinite detention without charge. That is simply not right.

The Patriot Act, along with its many excesses, contained a few needed changes in the law. And it is certainly true that many of the worst abuses of due process and civil liberties that are now occurring are taking place under the color of laws and executive orders other than the Patriot Act. Nevertheless, the Patriot Act has turned out to be, on balance, a terrible mistake and has become a kind of Gulf of Tonkin Resolution conferring Congress's blessing for this president's assault on civil liberties. Congress missed a golden opportunity when it voted to reauthorize the act, including its most objectionable features, with only minor changes—instead of replacing it with a new, smaller, and more effective law.

The politicization of law enforcement in this administration is part of its larger agenda to roll back the changes in government policy brought about by the New Deal and the Progressive movement. Toward that end, it is cutting back on civil rights enforcement, women's rights, progressive taxation, the estate tax, access to the courts, Medicare, and much more. It has even begun an effort to force the retirement of U.S. attorneys for what appear to be purely political reasons. In some cases investigated by the new Congress, U.S. attorneys who were praised by members of both parties for their high competence were replaced by individuals whose only apparent qualifications were political connections to the White House. One of those, David C. Iglesias of New Mexico, said that he was pressured to indict prominent Democrats before the 2006 midterm elections by two unnamed New Mexico Republicans. He refused to do so and the White House approved his firing.

But there has been no more bizarre or troubling manifestation of how seriously off track this president's policies have taken America than the profound shocks to our nation's conscience regarding torture. First came those extremely disturbing pictures from Abu Ghraib, which documented the strange forms of physical and sexual abuse and even torture—and even murder—committed by some of our troops against people taken as prisoners in Iraq, an estimated 70 to 90 percent of them mistakenly charged.

As a direct result of the incompetent planning and inadequate troop strength, our young men and women in uniform were put in untenable positions. For example, reservists assigned to the Iraqi prisons were called up without training or adequate supervision and then instructed by superiors from organizations not in their chain of command to break down prisoners in order to prepare them for interrogation. They were placed in a confusing situation where the chain of command was crisscrossed between intelligence gathering and prison administration and further confused by unprecedented mixing of military and civilian contractor authority. The soldiers who committed these atrocities are of course responsible for their own actions. But they're not the ones primarily responsible for the disgrace that has been brought upon the United States of America. They're not the ones who designed the policy and put it in place. Private Lynndie England did not make the decision that the United States would no longer observe the Geneva Conventions. Specialist Charles Graner was not the architect of the extensive network of U.S. facilities in multiple countries with cold, naked prisoners to be stressed, and even tortured, to force them to say things that legal procedures might not induce them to say.

The policies that laid the groundwork for these atrocities were designed and insisted upon by the Bush White House. Indeed, the president's own legal counsel briefed him specifically on the subject. His secretary of defense and the assistant secretaries of defense pushed these cruel departures from historic American standards over the objections of the uniformed military. Members of the judge advocate general's department within the Defense Department were so disturbed and so upset, and so opposed to this policy, that they took the unprecedented step of coming as a group to seek the help of a private attorney who specializes in human rights in Washington, D.C. As a group, they said to him, "There is a calculated effort to create an atmosphere of legal ambiguity, where the mistreatment of prisoners is concerned." Indeed, the secrecy of the program indicates an understanding on the part of its authors that the regular military culture and its mores would not support these activities. And neither would the American public or the world community. That's why they tried to keep it secret. Another implicit acknowledgment of violations of accepted standards of behavior is the process of farming out prisoners to countries less averse to torture and to private contractors who are accountable apparently to no one.

President Bush himself set the tone for our attitude toward suspects in his State of the Union address in 2003. He noted that more than three thousand suspected terrorists have been arrested in many countries. And then he added, "And many others have met a different fate. Let's put it this way. They are no longer a problem to the United States and our friends and our allies."

He promised to "change the tone" in Washington, and indeed he did—much for the worse. We now know that, tragically, as many as thirty-seven prisoners may have been murdered while in captivity, though the numbers are difficult to rely upon because in many of the cases involving violent death, there were no autopsies. It is outrageous for the administration to blame its misdeeds on young enlisted personnel from a reserve unit in upstate New York, and to claim that this extensive pattern is the work of a "few bad apples" among enlisted personnel.

President Bush should make amends not only for letting down the young soldiers, who are themselves culpable but who were clearly forced to wade into a moral cesspool created by the policies of the Bush White House. The perpetrators as well as the victims were both placed in their relationship to one another as a result of decisions made in Washington, D.C. Those decisions by the Bush-Cheney administration resulted in behavior that shocked the conscience of Americans and dragged the good name of our country through the mud of Abu Ghraib, Saddam Hussein's former torture prison.

Make no mistake, though. The damage done at Abu Ghraib is not only to America's reputation and America's strategic interests, but also to America's spirit. Remember how shocked each of us was when we first saw those hideous images? The natural tendency was at first to re-coil from the images and then to assume that they represented a strange and rare aberration that came about because of a few twisted minds or, as the Pentagon said, a few bad apples.

But not long thereafter, an army survey of prisoner deaths and mis-treatment in Iraq and Afghanistan showed a widespread pattern of abuse involving a significant number of military units in many dif-ferent locations. This pattern of abuse clearly did not spring from a few twisted minds at the lowest ranks of our military enlisted personnel. It came from twisted values and atrocious policies at the highest level of our government. This was done by our leaders, in our name.

These horrors were the predictable consequence of policy choices that flowed directly from this administration's contempt for the rule of law. And the dominance they have been seeking is truly not just un-worthy of America, it is also an illusory goal in its own right. Our world is unconquerable because the human spirit is unconquerable. And any national strategy based on pursuing the goal of domination is doomed to fail because it generates its own opposition and in the process creates enemies for the would-be dominator.

You'll recall the strange and perverted legal memorandum from in-side the administration that actually sought to justify torture and to somehow provide a legal rationale for the sadistic activities conducted in the name of the American people, activities that, according to any reasonable person, would be recognized as offensive to the conscience of humankind.

The uproar caused by the disclosure of this legal analysis forced the administration to claim it was throwing out the memo and to dismiss it as irrelevant and overbroad, but the administration still refuses to acknowledge that the memo's original audacious claims that the pres-ident can ignore the law are just wrong.

Congress was understandably unmoved by these disclaimers and enacted the McCain Amendment, preventing not only what the memo regards as torture but also "cruel, inhuman and degrading treatment" of detainees. Despite the threat of a veto, the legislation passed by overwhelming, veto-proof majorities in both houses. Rather than see his veto overridden, the president signed the law but simultaneously issued a signing statement indicating that he would not be bound by the new law. The statement declared that the McCain Amendment would be "construe[d]" to make it "consistent with" the president's power as head of the unitary executive and as commander in chief and also in light of the "constitutional limitations on the judicial power."

Are we still routinely torturing helpless prisoners, and if so, does it feel right that we as American citizens are not outraged by the practice? And does it feel right to have no ongoing discussion of whether or not this abhorrent, medieval behavior is being carried out in the name of the American people?

The administration must disclose all of its interrogation policies, including those used by the military in Iraq and Afghanistan and those employed by the CIA at any detention centers operated outside the United States, as well as all of the analyses related to the adoption of those policies. We deserve to know what and why it's being done in our name.

In making their analysis, the administration lawyers concluded that the president, whenever he is acting in his role as commander in chief, is largely above and immune from the rule of law. At least we don't have to guess what our Founders would have to say about that bizarre and un-American theory.

In addition, the broad analysis regarding the commander in chief's powers that they had asserted has explicitly not been disavowed. And the view of the aforementioned memo—that it was within the commander in chief's power to order any interrogation techniques necessary to extract information—most certainly contributed to the atmosphere that led to the atrocities committed against the Iraqis at Abu Ghraib. President Bush rewarded the principal author of this legal monstrosity with a seat on the U.S. Court of Appeals.

This president episodically poses as a uniter and healer. If he really had any desire to play that role, then he would have condemned Rush Limbaugh—among his strongest political supporters—who said publicly that the torture at Abu Ghraib was a brilliant maneuver and that the photos were "good old American pornography" and that the actions portrayed were simply those of people having a good time and needing to "blow some steam off."

Differences of degree are important when the subject is torture. The apologists for what has happened do have points that should be heard and clearly understood. It is a fact that every culture and every political system sometimes expresses itself in cruelty. It is also undeniably true that other countries have tortured, and do torture, more routinely and far more brutally than has ours.

George Orwell wrote in *1984* about a fictional totalitarian regime based on that of Soviet Russia and characterized life in it as a "boot stamping on a human face—forever." That was the ultimate culture of cruelty, so ingrained, so organic, so systematic, that everyone in it lived in terror, even the terrorizers. That was the nature and degree of state cruelty in Saddam Hussein's Iraq as well. We know these things, and we need not reassure ourselves and should not congratulate ourselves that our society is less cruel than some others. However, it is worth noting that many are less cruel than ours. What we do now, in reaction to documented atrocities like those committed at Abu Ghraib, will determine a great deal about who we are at the beginning of the twenty-first century.

It is important to note that just as the abuses of the prisoners flowed directly from the policies of the Bush White House, those policies, in turn, not only flowed from the instincts of the president and his advisers, they also found support in shifting attitudes on the part of some in our country in response to the outrage and fear generated by the attack of September 11. The president exploited and fanned those fears, but some otherwise sensible and levelheaded Americans expressed them as well.

I remember reading soberly written essays asking publicly whether or not the prohibitions against torture were any longer relevant or desirable. The same grotesque misunderstanding of what is really involved in torture was responsible for the tone in the memo from Alberto Gonzales, who wrote on January 25, 2002, that the attack of 9/11 "renders obsolete Geneva's strict limitations on questioning of enemy prisoners and renders quaint some of its provisions."

"Quaint"? Is progress in civilization a quaint idea? Is it truly naive to think that the United States will continue to lead that progress? Now we have long since seen the pictures, we have long since learned the news. We cannot unlearn it; it is part of us. So the important question now is: What will we do about torture in our name?

Stop it? Yes, of course, but that means demanding all of the facts, not covering them up as some now charge the administration is doing. One of the whistle-blowers at Abu Ghraib, Sergeant Samuel Provance, told the news media that he was being punished for telling the truth: "There is definitely a cover-up. I feel like I am being punished for being honest," he said.

The president himself placed the blame for the horrific consequences of his policies on the young privates and corporals and sergeants, who may well be culpable as individuals for their actions but were certainly not responsible for the policies that led to America's strategic catastrophe in Iraq.

And none of the Pentagon or White House officials responsible for this horrible and felonious betrayal of American values has yet been held accountable.

The right-wing commentator Laura Ingraham said, "The average American out there loves the show *24*. Okay? They love Jack Bauer, and they love *24*. In my mind, that's as close to a national referendum that it's okay to use tough tactics against high-level al-Qaeda operatives as we're going to get." How perfect, and how sad a comment on what happens when we no longer have a robust public forum where individuals can use the rule of reason to hold government accountable.

Our opinions on good and evil are interpreted through the Nielsen ratings.

Even worse, according to Jane Mayer of *The New Yorker,* DVDs of *24* have become widely popular among U.S. troops stationed in Iraq. Mayer quoted a former army interrogator, Tony Lagouranis, as saying, "People watch the shows and then walk into the interrogation booths and do the same things they've just seen."

The abhorrent acts at Abu Ghraib and elsewhere were a direct consequence of the culture of impunity—encouraged, authorized, and instituted by Bush and Rumsfeld in their statements that the Geneva Conventions did not apply. These kinds of horrific abuses were the logical, inevitable outcome of policies and statements from the administration. To me, just as glaring as the evidence of the pictures themselves was the revelation that it was established practice for prisoners to be moved around during the visits of the International Committee of the Red Cross so they would not be available for interviews. No one can claim *that* was the act of a few bad apples. That was policy set from above with the direct intent to violate U.S. values that the administration was claiming to uphold.

This was the kind of policy that we see and criticize in places like China and Cuba. Moreover, the administration now has also set up the men and women of our own armed forces for payback the next time they are held as prisoners. For that the administration should be held responsible.

It is now clear that the abuses of the truth and the unforgivable abuse of trust after 9/11 led to the problems in the prison, and we are now learning that there were similar problems in many other facilities constructed as part of the Bush administration's network of secret prison camps. In the prisons in Iraq, according to the Red Cross, between 70 and 90 percent of these people were mistakenly detained.

What would Thomas Jefferson think of the curious and discredited argument from our current Justice Department that the president may authorize what plainly amounts to the torture of prisoners and that any law or treaty that attempts to constrain his treatment of prisoners in time of war would itself be a violation of the Constitution?

It is deeply disturbing that the administration so frequently uses the word *dominance* to describe its strategic goals. It is disturbing because an American policy of dominance is as repugnant to the rest of the world as the ugly pictures of those helpless, naked Iraqi prisoners being so "dominated" has been to the people of our country.

Dominance is as dominance does. Dominance is not really a strategic policy or political philosophy at all. Rather, it is a seductive illusion that tempts the powerful to satiate their hunger for still more power by striking a bargain with their consciences. And as always happens sooner or later to those who shake hands with the devil, they find out too late that what they have given up in the bargain is their soul.

One of the clearest indications of the impending loss of intimacy with one's soul is the failure to recognize the existence of the soul in those over whom power is being exercised, especially if the helpless come to be dehumanized and treated as animals and degraded. It has been especially shocking and awful to see these evils perpetrated so crudely and cruelly in the name of the United States of America.

Those pictures of torture and sexual abuse came to us embedded in a wave of news about escalating casualties and growing chaos enveloping our entire policy in Iraq. But in order to understand the failure of our overall policy, I believe it is important to focus specifically on what exactly happened in Abu Ghraib prison and ask whether or not those actions were representative of who we are as Americans.

As noted, many of these captives have reportedly died while being tortured by executive branch interrogators, and many more have been broken and humiliated. In the notorious Abu Ghraib prison itself, investigators who documented the pattern of torture estimated that more than *90 percent* of the victims were innocent of any charges.

This shameful exercise of power overturns a set of principles that our nation has observed since General Washington first enunciated them during our Revolutionary War and has been observed by every president since then—until now. These practices violate the Geneva Conventions and the United Nations Convention Against Torture, not to mention our own laws against torture. In fact, following World War II, the U.S. government prosecuted foreign soldiers for water-boarding American troops.

The president has also claimed that he has the authority to deliver captives under our control for imprisonment and interrogation on our behalf by autocratic regimes in nations that are infamous for the cruelty of their techniques for torture.

Can it be true that any president really has such powers under our Constitution? If the answer is yes, then under the theory by which these acts are committed, are there any acts that can on their face be prohibited? If the president has the inherent authority to eavesdrop, imprison citizens on his own declaration, kidnap, and torture, then what *can't* he do?

After analyzing the executive branch's claims of these previously unrecognized powers, Harold Koh, dean of Yale Law School, said: "If the president has commander-in-chief power to commit torture, he has the power to commit genocide, to sanction slavery, to promote apartheid, to license summary execution."

The principal alternative to democracy throughout history has been the consolidation of virtually all state power in the hands of a single strongman or small group that together exercises that power without the informed consent of the governed.

It was in revolt against just such a regime, after all, that America was founded. When Lincoln declared at the time of our greatest crisis that the ultimate question being decided in the Civil War was "whether that nation, or any nation so conceived, and so dedicated, can long endure," he was not only saving our Union, but also recognizing the fact that democracies are rare in history. And when they fail, as did Athens and the Roman Republic upon whose designs our Founders drew heavily, what emerges in their place is another strongman regime.

The top-heavy focus on dominance as a goal for the U.S. role in the world is exactly paralleled by this administration's aspiration for the role of the president to completely dominate our constitutional system. The goal of dominance necessitates a focus on power, even absolute power.

The administration has also launched an assault on the right of the courts to review its actions, on the right of the Congress to have information on how the public's money is being spent, on the right of the news media to have information about the policies that it is pursuing, and on anyone who criticizes its excesses. This instinct, in turn, has also led them to introduce a new level of viciousness in partisan politics. It was that which led to the attacks labeling Senator Max Cleland, who lost three limbs during the Vietnam War as unpatriotic.

This same pattern characterizes virtually all of the Bush administration's policies. It resents any constraint as an insult to its will to dominate and to exercise power, and its appetite for power is astonishing. The drive to consolidate power in the name of national security is an old story, and the consequences of that drive today are all too familiar to history, as we will see in more detail in the following chapter.

CHAPTER SIX

National Insecurity

Newton's third law states, "For every action force there is an equal and opposite reaction force." National security policy is very different from physics, but the principles of logic and reason turn out to be useful and relevant there, too. And something like Newton's third law does seem to be a reality in international relations. When any nation is seen as trying to dominate others, there is a "reaction force" that pushes back.

The pursuit of "dominance" in foreign policy led the Bush administration to ignore the United Nations, to do serious damage to our most important alliances, to violate international law, and to cultivate the hatred and contempt of many in the rest of the world. The seductive appeal of exercising unconstrained unilateral power led this president to interpret his powers under the Constitution in a way that brought to life the worst nightmare of the Founders.

Any policy based on domination of the rest of the world not only creates enemies for the United States and creates recruits for al-Qaeda, but also undermines the international cooperation that is essential to defeating terrorists who wish to harm and intimidate America. Instead of "dominance," we should be seeking preeminence in a world where nations respect us and seek to follow our leadership and adopt our values.

Unilateralism, as we have painfully seen in Iraq, is often its own reward. Going it alone may indulge a political instinct, but it is dangerous to our military—even without the commander in chief taunting terrorists to "bring them on."

And the kind of unilateral power President Bush and Vice President Cheney imagine is, in any case, a strategic El Dorado. Just as their pursuit in Iraq has led to tragic consequences for our troops and the Iraqi people, the pursuit of a new interpretation of the presidency that ends up weakening the Congress, the courts, and civil society is not good for either the presidency or the rest of the nation. If the Congress becomes an enfeebled enabler to the executive and the courts become known for political calculations in their decisions, then the country suffers.

Wise generals and admirals throughout history have understood the dangers of preparing to fight "the last war" rather than the next one. Wise nations—and until recently, the United States was considered one—also understand the dangers of preparing to protect their national security only against old threats while ignoring new ones that are more dangerous. America's classic national security agenda was built upon common efforts to resist aggression and to stop armed conflict. During our first two centuries, we witnessed wars among nations and violence on the scale of war within nations, for many reasons.

Claims of religious, ideological, racial, or ethnic superiority have precipitated major conflicts throughout history. Poverty has caused the collapse of expectations and made people desperate and then open to demagogic appeals. Leaders have sometimes used aggression against their neighbors as a way of redirecting tensions inside their own countries. The lust for power has often resulted in expansion, violence, and aggression.

But while the old threats still face our global community, there are new things under the sun—new forces arising that could soon challenge international order, raising issues of peace and war. What matters is that we find one of those precious few moments in all of human history when we have a chance to cause the change we wish to see in the world—by seeking a common agreement to openly recognize a powerful new truth that has been growing just beneath the surface of every human heart: It is time to change the nature of the way we live together on this planet.

From this new vantage point, we have an opportunity to forge and follow a new agenda for national and world security. First and foremost, our security is threatened by the global environmental crisis, which could render all our other progress meaningless, unless we deal with it successfully. Already, the increase in severe droughts, severe flooding, and stronger storms is having a harsh impact.

Second, there is a looming water crisis that reflects both the sharp growth in demand for freshwater, global warming's disruption of the natural storage system of mountain snow packs and glaciers, and a decline in water quality owing to the effects of pollution and inadequate water treatment.

Third, we must conquer the global challenge presented by terrorism, magnified by a growing access to new weapons of mass destruction.

Fourth, the global challenge of defeating drugs and corruption, which now spill across our borders, has never been more serious given the growing strength and sophistication of international crime organizations.

Fifth, new pandemics like HIV/AIDS are laying waste to whole societies, a problem compounded by the emergence of new strains of old diseases that are horrifyingly resistant to the antibiotics that protected the last three generations.

We tend to think of threats to security in terms of war and peace. Yet no one can doubt that the havoc wreaked by HIV/AIDS threatens our safety. The heart of the security agenda is protecting lives— and we now know that the number of people who will die of AIDS in the first decade of the twenty-first century will rival the number that died in all the wars of the twentieth century.

When hundreds of people in sub-Saharan Africa are infected every hour of every day; when fifteen million children have already become orphans, and many must be raised by other children; when a single disease threatens everything from economic strength to peacekeeping—we clearly face a security threat of the greatest magnitude.

Our task is not merely to recognize and confront these challenges but to rise to our higher ideals. To succeed, we must create a world where people's faith in their own capacity for self-governance unlocks their potential and justifies their growing belief that all can share in an ever widening circle of human dignity and self-sufficiency.

As a world community, we must prove that we are wise enough to control what we have been smart enough to create. We must understand that the old conception of global security—with its focus almost solely on armies, ideologies, and geopolitics—has to be enlarged.

We should pursue a new and broader national security agenda with determination, adequate resources, and creative use of the new tools at the world's disposal that can be used to bring us together in successful common efforts—tools such as the Internet and the emerging global information infrastructure—which, if used imaginatively, will enable new depths of insight and cooperation by nations, nongovernmental organizations, and citizens at all levels.

We should follow a policy of "forward engagement," as professor Leon Fuerth at George Washington University has advocated, and reestablish a robust role for reason in our analysis of and early engagement with the many strategic opportunities and dangers that we must anticipate in building a safer, more secure, and more civilized world for future generations.

It is important to take hope from the large advances in human history, which we sometimes take for granted or see as having been inevitable. Slavery, for example, was once commonplace and yet now is almost universally considered abhorrent and obsolete. Although remnants of this evil practice remain in hidden portions of the world—and although the word *slavery* is attached to related abhorrent practices like the abduction of women for the sex trades—there is no longer open institutionalized enslavement of one race of people by another, on a massive scale, as there was prior to the American Civil War.

Centuries from now, many practices that we now take for granted will also be seen as having been completely self-defeating and absurd. But we are currently faced with the urgent task of accelerating our own psychological, emotional, intellectual, and spiritual evolution in order to see over the internal walls that may have served some useful purpose ages ago but are now merely obstacles that prevent us from seeing the new path we must take.

We need to show that we not only can contain aggression, prevent war, and mediate conflicts, but can work together to anticipate and respond to a new century with its new global imperatives.

At this fateful juncture in our history, it is vital that we see clearly who—and what—our enemies are and how we intend to deal with them. It is also important, however, that in the process we preserve not only the physical safety of our people, but also our dedication to the rule of law. As a nation, our greatest export has always been the hope that through the rule of law, people can be free to pursue their dreams. We have hoped that democracy can supplant repression and that justice, not power, can be society's guiding force.

With the blatant failure by the present U.S. government to respect the rule of law, we now face a great challenge in restoring America's moral authority in the world and demonstrating our commitment to bringing a better life to our global neighbors.

We have reached a point where we hardly recognize our country when we look in the mirror. How could we have come to this point? Just as major corporations have come to recognize the value of the "brands" they are marketing to customers, so we as American citizens should recognize that there is great significance and value in whatever visceral opinions people throughout the world have when they hear or read the phrase "United States of America." Our Founders understood this in different words more than two centuries ago. Thomas Jefferson once wrote, "The good opinion of mankind, like the lever of Archimedes, with the given fulcrum, moves the world."

Make no mistake, it is precisely our moral authority that is our greatest source of strength. It is precisely our moral authority that has been recklessly put at risk by the cheap calculations of this willful president. He wagered with history and put America's goodwill and good name at risk. He lost, and because our nation was made a hostage to his moral compromises, we all lost.

The same troubling pattern characterizes the Bush-Cheney administration's approach to almost all national issues. In almost every policy area, the administration's consistent goal has been to eliminate any constraints—whether by law, regulation, alliance, or treaty—on their exercise of raw power. And in the process it has caused America to be seen by the other nations of the world as holding contempt and disdain for the international community.

The disdain that this administration demonstrates in its approach to all international agreements and treaties is similar to its contempt for rational debate based on reason and evidence in our national politics and public discourse. Rather than trusting that the international public forum can produce agreements that benefit all participants, the Bush-Cheney administration has an avowed foreign policy goal of unilateralism: Power is more important than compromise, and dominance is more important than international law.

The Bush administration's objective of attempting to establish U.S. domination over any potential adversary was exactly what led to the hubristic, tragic miscalculation of the Iraq war—a painful misadventure marked by one disaster after another, based on one mistaken assumption after another. But the people who paid the price have been the American men and women in uniform trapped over there and the Iraqis themselves.

At the level of our relations with the rest of the world, the administration has willingly traded in *respect* for the United States in favor of *fear*. That was the real meaning of "shock and awe." This administration has coupled its theory of American dominance with a doctrine of preemptive strikes, regardless of whether the threat to be preempted is imminent or not. George Tenet, director of the CIA from 1997 to

2004, made it clear that the Agency never said Iraq was an imminent threat. For this administration, the threat to be preempted didn't have to be imminent.

The new doctrine called "preemption" asserts a new, uniquely American right to preemptively attack whomever the president deems a potential future threat. It is based on the idea that in the era of pro-liferating weapons of mass destruction, and against the background of a sophisticated terrorist threat, the United States cannot wait for proof of an established mortal threat. It must act fast to cut the threat short.

The problem with preemption is that in the first instance it is not needed in order to give the United States the means to act in our own defense, either against terrorism in general or against Iraq in particu-lar. But that is a relatively minor issue compared with the longer-term consequences that I think can be foreseen for this doctrine.

The doctrine is presented in open-ended terms, which means that Iraq is not necessarily the last application. In fact, the very logic of the concept suggests a string of military engagements against a succession of sovereign states: Syria, Libya, North Korea, Iran—none of them very popular in the United States, of course—but the implication is that wherever the combination exists of an interest in weapons of mass destruction together with an ongoing role as host to or participant in terrorist operations, the doctrine will apply.

It also means that the Iraq resolution created the precedent for pre-emptive action anywhere, whenever this or any future president de-cides that it is time.

The risks of this preemption doctrine stretch far beyond the disas-ter in Iraq. This policy affects the basic relationship between the United States and the rest of the world. Article 51 of the United Nations Charter recognizes the right of any nation to defend itself, in-cluding the right to take preemptive action in order to deal with im-minent threats.

If other nations asserted the broader right to preemption that the Bush administration has, however, then the rule of law would quickly be replaced by the reign of fear. Under this approach, any nation that perceives circumstances that could eventually lead to an imminent threat would be justified in taking military action against another nation. In other words, President Bush initiated one of the most fateful military doctrines in history. He abandoned what we thought was America's mission in a world in which nations are guided by a common ethic codified in the form of international law.

The consequences of an emerging national strategy that not only celebrates American strengths but also appears to glorify the notion of dominance could actually strengthen the very enemies we seek to defeat. If what America represents to the world is leadership in a commonwealth of equals in which we are preeminent, then our friends will be legion. But if what we represent to the world is empire, then it is our enemies who will be legion. Over two decades ago, the Soviet Union claimed the right to launch a preemptive war in Afghanistan. We properly encouraged and then supported Afghanistan's resistance movement, which a decade later forced the Soviet army to retreat and withdraw. Unfortunately, however, when the Russians left, we abandoned the Afghans, and the lack of any coherent nation-building program led directly to the conditions that allowed the Taliban to take control and give al-Qaeda a home and a base for their worldwide terrorist operations.

That's where they planned the 9/11 attacks. Incredibly, in spite of that vivid lesson, after defeating the Taliban rather easily, and despite pledges from President Bush that we would never again abandon Afghanistan, we have done precisely that in most of the country. Only a portion of the capital city has been secured. Predictably, the Taliban and al-Qaeda have quickly moved back in.

The issue that faced us in 2002 was whether Saddam Hussein presented such a dire and imminent threat to the United States that we would be justified in acting under the generally accepted understanding of Article 51 of the UN Charter, which reserves to states the right to act in self-defense. Because he did not present such a threat, the

United States should not have sought to precipitate an immediate confrontation, to find a cause for war, and to launch an attack.

There's no international law that can ever prevent us from taking action to protect our vital interests when it is manifestly clear that there is a choice to be made between law and our survival. Indeed, international law itself recognizes that such choices remain within the purview of all nations. I believe, however, that such a choice was not present in the case of Iraq.

Iraq was not an imminent threat, so our decision to launch an invasion was not justified by the general understanding of international law. But this administration actually seems to prefer to exist outside the realm of international law. In fact, the Bush administration seems opposed to almost any international treaty—not just the Kyoto Protocol—regardless of how much it would help our national security or how little it would limit our foreign policy decision making. When it comes to treaties, this White House is always ready to acknowledge the cost, without ever considering the benefit.

For example, the Comprehensive Nuclear Test Ban Treaty was an effort to strike a bargain between states possessing nuclear weapons and all the others who had pledged to refrain from developing them. Of course, we haven't tested a nuclear weapon in over fifteen years, and we had no plans for nuclear testing when we negotiated the CTBT. So actually the treaty didn't require us to give up anything. In exchange for our non–policy change, we could have helped build an international coalition of countries committed to stopping others like North Korea from testing nuclear weapons. The internationally renowned weapons inspector Hans Blix has stated publicly, "No single measure would today give greater encouragement to global arms control than an acceptance by all states of the Comprehensive Test Ban Treaty that was adopted in 1996."

But this administration has rejected the CTBT and now, incredibly, wants to embark on a program to build a new generation of smaller nuclear bombs to *use* to destroy underground bunkers. We already have both the most advanced nuclear "bunker busters" of any country and conventional weapons that could destroy most enemy bunkers. So again, the cost of not developing these weapons is small. But in my opinion, new nuclear testing would be utter madness. If we did start testing, our allies—and more important, states hostile to our interest—would have an incentive to conduct their own nuclear tests. As we rushed to build a new generation of nuclear weapons, China, Russia, India, Pakistan, and others would feel pressure to keep up with us, and this would cause countries around the world to feel the keen need to develop their own nuclear weapons. We might find ourselves in a world in which new states join the nuclear club much faster than in the last few decades.

The Bush White House announced in 2002 that, for the first time, the United States was making it a part of our deterrence strategy to consider using nuclear weapons in a first-strike attack against *non*-nuclear states. This radical and reckless doctrine of nuclear preemption actually creates an incentive for other nations to develop nuclear weapons as quickly as possible so that they can respond if America does launch a first strike, an active possibility according to the Bush team. Their policy, enacted in the classified *Nuclear Posture Review,* has drawn sharp criticism from leading experts in arms control. Arguably, the administration's failure to stop North Korea and Iran from moving forward in their efforts to build nuclear weapons arsenals could be seen by future historians as the worst mistake of all.

Another example of the administration's failed nonproliferation strategy is its disregard for the foundation of multilateral nuclear arms control, the Nuclear Non-Proliferation Treaty. Over 180 countries have signed the NPT, and since it entered into force in 1970, it has arguably been the most useful tool in slowing the spread of nuclear weapons. Many credit the NPT regime for pressuring countries like Egypt, Argentina, South Africa, and Ukraine to give up their nuclear weapons programs. The NPT unites the international community in its efforts to discourage states from developing nuclear weapons. Unfortunately, the Bush administration has seriously damaged our perceived commitment to the NPT through policies like its attempted nuclear deal with India, its Proliferation Security Initiative, its disregard for the CTBT, and its disastrous approach to space weapons.

Bush's weakening of the nonproliferation regime has been matched by his consistent failure to secure the loose nuclear material that would be the most likely source of a terrorist nuclear strike on the United States. Graham Allison, an expert on loose nuclear material and professor at Harvard, makes the case that preventing nuclear terrorism is actually possible, and all that it requires is understanding "a basic matter of physics: without fissile material, you can't have a nuclear bomb. No nuclear bomb, no nuclear terrorism." Allison argues that we should adopt a strategy of global cooperation, especially with Russia, to contain loose nuclear material to deny dangerous states and terrorist groups access to fissile material. How does Allison view the Bush administration's efforts in this regard? He concluded in 2004:

The list of actions not taken by the administration remains lengthy and worrisome. Bush has not made nuclear terrorism a personal priority for himself or those who report directly to him. And he has resisted proposals by Senator Richard Lugar (R-IN), former Senator Sam Nunn (D-GA), and others to assign responsibility for the issue to a single individual, who could then be held accountable. As a result, were the president today to ask his cabinet who is responsible for preventing nuclear terrorism, either a dozen people would raise their hands, or no one would. Bush has also not communicated his sense of urgency about nuclear terrorism to the presidents of Russia or Pakistan. Nor has Bush increased the pace of U.S. cooperation with Russia in securing former Soviet nuclear weapons and materials. As a result, after a decade of effort, half of the Soviet arsenal remains inadequately secured.

Moreover, Bush has demonstrated a willingness to disregard the most important treaties relating to space, and this has made the world significantly less secure. In 1967, America and other nations codified the protection of the peaceful and commercial use of space in the Outer Space Treaty. This commitment reflected the practical desire of all countries to avoid an arms race in space that could disrupt the scientific discoveries made possible by space exploration and the growth in communications and commerce made possible by the launch of satellites. But the Outer Space Treaty also stood for something more than a practical approach to the exploitation of space: It reflected the understanding that space is a common frontier for our entire species and that every nation has the right to experience the wonder and transcendence made possible by space exploration.

The 1972 Anti-Ballistic Missile Treaty, signed during the height of the cold war, reflected the same spirit. Among the many provisions of this important agreement was a restriction against space-based missile defense systems. This agreement was based on the understanding between the two rival powers that an arms race in space was in neither country's interest.

But President Bush's policy decisions appear to violate the ABM Treaty, and he seems ready to violate the Outer Space Treaty. The administration's statement of space policy, declared in 2006, is in line with its fundamental view of America's security. Security requires overall military dominance, in the administration's view, up to and including a level sufficient to inhibit competitors from even making the effort to challenge us. A corollary of this approach is antagonism to arms control or other international constraints on the development or use of military power, as a potential impediment to the maintenance of American military advantage. Abrogation of the ABM Treaty was a demonstration of this administration's preference not to be encumbered by agreements. The doctrine of preemptive strikes against potential enemies (as opposed to a last-resort action to deal with imminent threat) fits naturally into this construct. The administration has denied that its statement of policy was intended to portend development of space-based weapons. However, it is clear that figures such as former defense secretary Rumsfeld were very much in favor of such an approach. And the logic of the doctrine, as written, clearly points toward the conclusion that the administration believes America should be in a position to deny other nations access to space, if that is what is needed to protect U.S. strategic assets located there.

As a result, the international community is strongly inclined to view the administration's policy as the foundation for an American effort to unilaterally and permanently dominate space as a medium of combat. No other major state is likely to accept the Bush space policy as permanently acceptable. The administration's shocked response to China's recent test of an antisatellite ASAT system is an example of America's attitude that its predilections are substitutes for international law. It would be a nice world (for us) if we could make our desires stick. Experience suggests, however, that in the longer term we would be wiser to work with others collectively to reduce the risk that we will make outer space a militarized theater of operations.

In addition to the reasonable concern that any effort to militarize space will encourage other countries to do the same, there is the ironic fact that these weapons and defensive systems are unlikely to make us more secure. There is little credible evidence that space-based weapons or defenses are effective at stopping any attack on our country, be it a terrorist strike or a missile launch from another nation. If we did manage to develop an effective defense system, it would only encourage other countries and terrorist groups to try to develop ways of getting around the system, either through advanced technological countermeasures or through alternative tactics like suitcase bombs.

It is also ironic that this administration, which has expressed concern about the possibility of terrorist biological weapons, has been unwilling to endorse any new verification measures to support the Biological Weapons Convention. To be fair, President Bush has recommended some steps to strengthen the BWC, and at times, he seems almost to support its existence. But most experts agree that without inspection provisions, it will be impossible for countries to enforce this agreement and ensure the destruction of biological weapon stockpiles. After rejecting the international community's inspection plan, President Bush did not offer any alternative verification program.

Bush has also sabotaged the International Criminal Court. I agree with some of the Bush administration's concerns regarding the relevant treaty as it currently stands and how it would affect our men and women in uniform. But I have learned that rather than just abandoning the international dialogue when other countries don't immediately accept our position—as Bush did with the ICC—we have a better chance of getting our way *and* leading the world to an agreement that benefits our national security and global security by staying involved in the process and trusting that in the international arena, all nations can come together to use reason and logic to craft the best compromise.

But perhaps we shouldn't be surprised that Bush did not want to work to create an international court to handle war crimes, because, as I described earlier, he has done everything possible to create an atmosphere of legal ambiguity surrounding the question of whether Americans in uniform can legally use interrogation techniques that clearly amount to torture. He has urged the Congress to make America the first country to repudiate the Geneva Conventions, the international agreement supported by almost 190 countries for half a century that prohibits "outrages upon personal dignity, in particular, humiliating and degrading treatment."

As noted in chapter 5, the Geneva Conventions protect our service members. If our brave men and women in uniform are captured, they know that they are protected by international law if they choose not to answer any strategic questions. However, if the U.S. military begins to torture its captives with impunity, our troops will have to learn to expect the same treatment if they are captured.

In my religious tradition I have been taught in the book of

Matthew, "Ye shall know them by their fruits. Do men gather grapes of thorns or figs of thistle? Even so, every good tree bringeth forth good fruit but a corrupt tree bringeth forth evil fruit wherefore by their fruits ye shall know them."

The president convinced a majority of the country that Saddam Hussein was responsible for attacking us on 9/11 when in truth he had nothing to do with it. Bush planted the seeds of war and harvested a whirlwind. The corrupt "tree" of this war, waged on false premises, has brought us the evil "fruit" of Americans' torturing and sexually humiliating prisoners who are helpless in their care.

In the immediate aftermath of September 11, we had an enormous reservoir of goodwill and sympathy from all over the world. That has been squandered and replaced with great anxiety all around the world, not primarily about what the terrorist networks might do, but about what *we* might do. My point is not that other nations are right to feel that way, but that they do feel that way. Squandering all that goodwill and replacing it with anxiety is similar to what was done in turning a projected $5 trillion surplus into a projected cumulative deficit of $4 trillion.

Officials within the administration have suggested that the war on terrorism may last for the rest of our lives. I think I know what they meant by that, but the apprehensions in the world are not eased by the doctrine of preemption that was asserted by Bush. By now, the administration may have begun to realize that national and international cohesion are indeed strategic assets. But it is a lesson long delayed and clearly not uniformly and consistently accepted by senior members of the cabinet. From the outset, the administration has operated in a manner calculated to please the portion of its base that occupies the Far Right, at the expense of solidarity among all Americans and between our country and our allies.

The gross violations of human rights authorized by Bush at Abu Ghraib, Guantánamo Bay, and dozens of other locations around the world have seriously damaged U.S. moral authority and delegitimized

U.S. efforts to continue promoting human rights. As one analyst, James Zogby, put it, "Once we set a high standard for the world; now we have lowered the bar." Our moral authority is, after all, our greatest source of enduring strength in the world.

The handling of prisoners at Guantánamo has been particularly harmful to America's image. Even the nations that are arguably our closest allies—England and Australia—have criticized our departure from international law, particularly the Geneva Conventions. Our handling of captives there has been about as thoughtful as Rumsfeld's "postwar plan" for Iraq.

Indeed, many of our traditional allies have been shocked by these new practices. The British ambassador to Uzbekistan—a nation with one of the worst reputations for torture—registered a complaint to his home office about the senselessness and cruelty of the new U.S. practice: "This material is useless—we are selling our souls for dross. It is in fact positively harmful." Experts in interrogation have long known that the information gained from torture leads to false confessions and bad intelligence. Even if torture was not morally repugnant and an affront to what America stands for in the world, we should reject it.

During the presidency of Ronald Reagan, Secretary of Labor Ray Donovan was accused of corruption. When, after much publicity, the indictment was eventually thrown out by the judge, Donovan asked, "Where do I go to get my reputation back?" President Bush has now placed our whole nation in that same situation. Where do we—the United States of America—go to get our reputation back? And unlike those against Secretary Donovan, many of the accusations against us are *not* false.

One of the most tragic consequences of these official crimes is that it will be very hard for any of us as Americans to effectively stand up for human rights elsewhere and criticize other governments when our policies have resulted in our soldiers' behavior. This administration has shamed America and has deeply damaged the cause of freedom and human rights everywhere, thus undermining the core message of America to the world.

The abandonment of the rule of reason by the current administration in preference for the temptations of raw power not only creates a sense of strangeness in America, but also creates a disorienting effect for the world as a whole. Without a positive example from the United States, the rest of the world is more likely to move in the wrong direction. For example, the abrupt reversal of progress toward political and economic freedom in Russia might not have occurred had the United States not abandoned its own commitment to these values.

President Bush offered a brief and halfhearted apology to the Arab world, but he should make amends to the American people for abandoning the Geneva Conventions and to the United States Army, Air Force, Navy, and Marine Corps for sending troops into harm's way while ignoring the best advice of their commanders.

Perhaps, most important of all, he owes an explanation to all of those men and women throughout our world who have held high the ideal of the United States as a shining goal to inspire in their land their own efforts to bring about justice and the rule of law.

Of course, a sincere apology requires an admission of error and a willingness to accept responsibility and to hold people accountable. President Bush seems to be not only unwilling to acknowledge error, but thus far has seemed unwilling to hold anyone in his administration accountable for the worst strategic and military miscalculations and mistakes in our entire history.

Ironically, the administration has had no problem ignoring all of its didactic messages to the world about how democracies don't invade other nations. If we had behaved as a democracy, we would not have invaded Iraq. We can effectively defend ourselves abroad and at home without dimming our core principles. Indeed, our success in defending ourselves depends precisely on not giving up what we stand for. Our top priority should be preserving what America represents and stands for in the world and winning the war against terrorism first.

The Bush White House has asked us to concentrate exclusively on this threat. Tragically, however, they completely failed to protect us against the worst terrorist attack in American history.

Most Americans have tended naturally to give the Bush-Cheney administration the benefit of the doubt when it came to its failure to take action in advance of 9/11 to guard against an attack. After all, everyone knows from experience that hindsight casts a harsh light on mistakes that should have been visible at the time they were made.

But now, years later, with the benefit of investigations that have been made public, it is no longer clear that the administration deserves this act of political grace from the American people.

It is useful and important to examine the warnings that the administration ignored—not to "point the finger of blame," but in order to better determine how our country can avoid such mistakes in the future. When leaders are not held accountable for serious mistakes, they and their successors are more likely to repeat those mistakes.

In the last chapter, I documented how the information that might possibly have been used to prevent the attacks of 9/11 was available at the time and how that information was ignored by the Bush administration. I do not for one second believe they intentionally ignored it with the awareness that it would enhance the odds of a successful terrorist attack. Of course not! Instead, I believe they ignored the data because of their unjustified tendency to assume that they already knew everything they needed to know and thus had no need to react with alarm to the warnings of experts and government professionals. Their behavior, in my opinion, was reckless, but the explanation for it lies in hubris, not in some bizarre conspiracy theory.

For example, we now know from his testimony to the 9/11 Commission that acting FBI director Thomas J. Pickard was repeatedly asking the chief law enforcement officer appointed by President Bush to be in charge of counterterrorism, John Ashcroft, to *pay attention* to the many warning signs that were being picked up by the FBI throughout the summer of 2001. Pickard testified under oath that Ashcroft angrily told him he did not want to hear this information anymore and that Ashcroft shut down the discussion. (Ashcroft denied his accusation in his testimony to the 9/11 Commission.)

It is worth remembering that among these reports that Ashcroft ordered the FBI not to show him anymore was an expression of alarm in one field office that the nation ought immediately to check on the possibility that Osama bin Laden was having people trained in commercial flight schools around the United States. At the same time, an FBI field agent e-mailed his supervisors on August 19, 2001, that flight-school attendee Zacarias Moussaoui was "an Islamic extremist preparing for some future act in furtherance of radical fundamentalist goals."

The CIA was also picking up unprecedented warnings that an attack on the United States by al-Qaeda was imminent. Indeed, George Tenet wrote that the entire warning system was "blinking red." We also know from Bob Woodward's reporting, and from confirming evidence, that CIA head George Tenet was frantically trying to communicate the same warnings in June and July 2001 to Bush's national security adviser, Condoleezza Rice, and that he was blown off.

These affirmative and repeated refusals to listen to clear warnings constitute behavior that goes beyond simple negligence. At a minimum, it represents a reckless disregard for the safety of the American people.

Of course, it was in the same time frame, *after* all the other "blinking red" warnings had been not only ignored but angrily dismissed, that the president himself was personally presented with a CIA report that carried a headline more alarming and more pointed than any I saw in eight years of six-days-a-week CIA briefings: "Bin Laden determined to strike in U.S."

The only warnings of this nature that I recall remotely resembling the one given to George Bush were about the so-called millennium threats predicted for the end of the year 1999 and somewhat less specific warnings about the dangers that might face the Olympics in

Atlanta in 1996. In both cases, these warnings in the President's Daily Brief (PDB) were followed immediately, on the same day, by the beginning of urgent daily meetings in the White House with representatives from the agencies and offices involved in preparing our nation to prevent the threatened attack.

I personally participated in, and sometimes convened and chaired, these meetings. And neither President Clinton nor I felt that we were going above and beyond our duties to the nation. These meetings were simply based on a commonsense response to dire warnings, of the kind that any police chief in America would recognize as part of the job. It is what any "reasonable person" would do in a similar situation if responsibility were his or hers.

By contrast, when President Bush received this fateful and historic PDB, he did not convene the National Security Council. He did not bring together the FBI and CIA and other agencies with responsibility to protect the nation. He did not even ask follow-up questions about the warning. He *did*, however, dismiss his CIA briefer with a comment. "All right. You've covered your ass now," Bush said, according to journalist Ron Suskind.

The bipartisan 9/11 Commission summarized, in its unanimous report, what happened. "We have found no indication of any further discussion before September 11th between the president and his advisors about the possibility of a threat of al-Qaeda attack in the United States."

The commissioners went on to report that in spite of all the warnings to different parts of the administration, the nation's "domestic agencies never mobilized in response to the threat. *They did not have direction* and did not have a plan to institute. The borders were not hardened. Transportation systems were not fortified. Electronic surveillance was not targeted against a domestic threat. State and local law authorities were not marshaled to augment the FBI's efforts. The public was not warned." (Italics added.)

Terrorism has actually been on the rise. It is true that we have not suffered another terrorist attack inside the United States since September 11, 2001, and it is only fair to assume that one of the reasons has to do with the many changes the president and the Congress have made in the aftermath of the attack. However, in April 2006, the National Counterterrorism Center released its annual *State Department Country Reports on Terrorism.* It showed that terrorist attacks worldwide increased nearly fourfold in 2005. Six months later, in September, a series of leaks forced Bush to release portions of the National Intelligence Estimate that painted just how grim the terror picture had become. "The Iraqi jihad is shaping a new generation of terrorist leaders and operatives," the report read. "Perceived Jihadist success there would inspire more fighters to continue the struggle elsewhere. . . . If this trend continues, threats to U.S. interests at home and abroad will become more diverse, leading to increasing attacks worldwide."

There was then, there is now, and there would always have been, regardless of what President Bush did, a threat of terrorism that we would have to deal with. But instead of making it better, he has made it worse. We are less safe because of his policy. He has created more anger and righteous indignation against us than any leader of our country in all the years of our existence as a nation.

Part of the explanation for the increased difficulty in gaining cooperation in fighting terrorism is Bush's attitude of contempt for any person, institution, or nation that disagrees with him. He has exposed Americans abroad and Americans in every U.S. town and city to a greater danger of attack because of his arrogance and willfulness, in particular his insistence upon stirring up a hornets' nest in Iraq. Compounding the problem, he has regularly insulted the religion, the culture, and the tradition of people in other countries throughout the Muslim world.

He has also pursued policies that have resulted in the deaths of thousands of innocent men, women, and children, all of it done in our name. President Bush has said repeatedly that the war in Iraq is the central front in the war on terror. It was *not*, of course, the central front, but it has unfortunately *become* the central recruiting office for terrorists.

The unpleasant truth is that President Bush's failed policies in both Iraq and Afghanistan have made the world a far more dangerous place. It is unfortunate, but it is true. The International Institute for Strategic Studies reported, "The Iraq conflict has arguably focused the energies and resources of al-Qaeda and [bin Laden's] followers, while diluting those of the global counter-terrorism coalition." The IISS said that in the wake of the war on Iraq, al-Qaeda now has more than eighteen thousand potential terrorists scattered around the world.

Our friends in the Middle East, including most prominently Israel, have been placed in greater danger because of the policy blunders and sheer incompetence with which the civilian Pentagon officials have conducted this war. The prestigious Jaffe think tank in Israel released a devastating indictment of how this misadventure in Iraq has been a deadly distraction from the crucial war on terror. This report has been corroborated and supported by similar studies from the United States and around the world. It is nearly a consensus view.

The war in Iraq has become a recruiting bonanza for terrorists who use it as their most damning indictment of the United States and of U.S. policy. The massive casualties suffered by civilians in Iraq, shown routinely and constantly on Arab television stations throughout the Middle East, have been a propaganda victory for Osama bin Laden beyond his wildest dreams. This is tragic, and it was avoidable.

The Iraq war plan was incompetent in its rejection of advice from military professionals. And the analysis of the intelligence was incompetent in its conclusion that our soldiers would be welcomed with garlands of flowers and cheering crowds. That mistaken assumption was one of the reasons the Pentagon did not respect the so-called Powell doctrine of using overwhelming force.

Luckily, there was a high level of competence on the part of our men and women in uniform, even though they were denied the tools and the numbers they needed for their mission. But what a disgrace that their families have had to hold bake sales to buy discarded Kevlar vests so the troops can stuff them into the floorboards inside the Humvees they often have to ride around in without adequate armor. Bake sales for body armor. What kind of policy is that?

In early 2007, the secretary of the army, Francis Harvey, was forced to resign because of the squalor, bureaucratic chaos, and insensitivity with which wounded U.S. veterans of the Iraq war were being treated at Walter Reed Army Medical Center. Even though some in the administration had apparently known of the scandalous conditions for months, nothing was done until *The Washington Post* printed a series of major investigative stories.

General Joseph Hoar, former head of the U.S. Marine Corps, told Congress, "I believe we are absolutely on the brink of failure. We are looking into the abyss." When a senior military leader like Joe Hoar uses the word *abyss,* then the rest of us had better sit up and listen. Here's what he means: more American servicemen and -women dying, Iraq slipping into more chaos and violence, no end in sight, with America's influence and moral authority seriously damaged. Retired U.S. Marine Corps general Anthony Zinni, the former four-star general in charge of Central Command, said recently that our nation's current course in Iraq is "headed over Niagara Falls."

Zinni, named by President Bush as his personal emissary to the Middle East in 2001, offered this view of the situation in a recent book: "In the lead-up to the Iraq war and its later conduct, I saw at a minimum true dereliction, negligence and irresponsibility; at worse, lying, incompetence and corruption. False rationales presented as a justification; a flawed strategy; lack of planning; the unnecessary alienation of our allies; the underestimation of the task; the unnecessary distraction from real threats; and the unbearable strain dumped on our overstretched military. All of these caused me to speak out ... I was called a traitor and a turncoat by Pentagon officials."

I remember watching White House spokesman Dan Bartlett being asked on television about these scathing condemnations by generals involved in the highest levels of the Pentagon. And he dismissed them because they came from retired military officials.

But then even active duty military officers began speaking out against President Bush's policy. For example, a senior general at the Pentagon was quoted as saying, "The current office of the secretary of defense refused to listen or adhere to military advice." The commander of the Eighty-second Airborne Division, Major General Charles Swannack Jr. was asked whether he believed the United States was losing the war in Iraq. "I think strategically, we are," he said. Colonel Paul Hughes, who directed strategic planning for the occupation authority in Baghdad, compared what he saw in Iraq with what happened in the Vietnam War, where he lost his brother. "I promised myself, when I came on active duty," he said, "that I would do everything in my power to prevent that from happening again." He noted the pattern in Vietnam of winning battles but losing the war. Hughes added, "Unless we ensure that we have coherence in our policies, we will lose strategically." Another general said, "Like a lot of senior army guys, I'm quite angry with Rumsfeld and the rest of the administration." He listed two reasons. He said, "I think they're going to break the army." And he said what really gets him mad is "I don't think they care."

Those generals who disagreed with the White House policy were undercut and sidelined. Those who supported it enthusiastically were promoted—even though it has been a catastrophic failure at every turn. Future management gurus may eventually write about a "W Deviation" to the Peter Principle: When someone has clearly been promoted to the level at which his incompetence is on flamboyant display, present him or her with a Medal of Freedom and assign him or her even more responsibilities.

For five years, there has been a growing tension between President Bush's portrait of the situation in which we find ourselves and the real facts on the ground. In fact, his entire agenda collapsed around his ankles. What is left of the Iraqi state is also collapsing, with a growing

U.S. casualty rate and a multisided civil war, with the attendant chaos and risk of an Islamic fundamentalist state or "failed state" that breeds terrorism for years to come. The conservative talk show host Tucker Carlson said about Bush's Iraq policy, "I think it is a total nightmare and disaster, and I am ashamed that I went against my own instincts in supporting it."

Doug Bandow, a senior fellow at the Cato Institute, a veteran of both the Heritage Foundation and the Reagan White House, wrote in September 2004, "Serious conservatives must fear for the country. . . . Conservatives should choose principles over power." He seemed most concerned about Bush's unhealthy habits of mind. "He does not appear to reflect on his actions," Bandow wrote, "and seems unable to concede even the slightest mistake. Nor is he willing to hold anyone else responsible for anything." Bandow continued, "It is a damning combination." He described the Bush foreign policy as "a shambles, with Iraq aflame and America increasingly reviled by friend and foe alike."

William F. Buckley Jr., widely acknowledged as the founder of the modern conservative movement, wrote of the Iraq war, "If I knew then what I know now about what kind of situation we would be in, I would have opposed the war."

One of the central points of this book is that we as Americans should have "known then what we know now"—not only about the invasion of Iraq but also about the climate crisis, and what would happen if the levees failed to protect New Orleans during Hurricane Katrina, and about many other fateful choices that have been made on the basis of flawed and even outright false information. We *could* have known and we should have known, because the information was readily available. We should have known years ago about the potential for a global HIV/AIDS pandemic. And the larger explanation for this crisis in American decision making is that reason itself is playing a diminished, less respected role in our national conversation.

The war against terrorism manifestly requires a multilateral approach. It is impossible to succeed against terrorism unless we have secured the continuing, sustained cooperation of many nations. And here's one of my central points: Our ability to secure that kind of multilateral cooperation in the war against terrorism was severely damaged by the way we went about undertaking unilateral action against Iraq.

The 9/11 attacks prompted most Americans to wrestle with the question of what our country needs to do to defend itself. At the earliest signs of what President Bush and his national security team had in mind for Iraq, I argued that an invasion would only weaken America's security. We should have focused our efforts first and foremost against those who attacked us and who thus far have gotten away with it. I never believed that we should allow ourselves to be distracted simply because tracking down Osama bin Laden was more difficult than anyone predicted. Great nations persevere and then prevail. They do not jump from one unfinished task to another.

Once we pushed the Taliban out of power, I believe that we should have had a force of up to thirty-five thousand international troops to come into Afghanistan as we did in Bosnia and say, in effect, "There's a new sheriff in town. Calm down." And after a while, their blood pressure would have gone down and their general expectation of violence and conflict would have been replaced with a general expectation of cooperation. That was not done in Afghanistan, even though many in our military were in favor of it.

Back in 1991, I was one of a handful of Senate Democrats to vote in favor of the resolution endorsing the Persian Gulf War. I felt betrayed by the first Bush administration's hasty departure from the battlefield even as Saddam began to renew his persecution of the Kurds in the north and the Shiites in the south—groups that we had encouraged to rise up against Saddam. After a brilliant military campaign, our decision to abandon prematurely the effort to destroy Saddam's offensive military capability allowed him to remain in power. This precedent should have been debated and discussed by the Congress in 2002. The Congress should have required, as part of any resolution regarding the proposed invasion of Iraq, explicit guarantees relating to the aftermath of a military victory.

I first spoke against the regime of Saddam Hussein in the fall of 1988, soon after he used poison gas against a minority within his own people. My father's older brother had been the victim of poison gas in World War I. Because of that, my family's oral history has always emphasized the horror of those weapons. The World War I generation impressed that same lesson on peoples around the world. We went through all of World War II without poison gas, save some horrible experiments in the Far East. When Saddam became the first to break the taboo, it set off alarm bells.

It is instructive to look at the differences between the decision to expel Iraq from Kuwait in 1991 and the decision to invade Iraq in 2002. To review a few of the differences briefly: In 1991, Iraq had crossed an international border, invading a neighboring sovereign nation and annexing its territory. By contrast, in 2002, Iraq had not invaded a neighbor. On the contrary, we were the ones who crossed an international border. The difference in the circumstances had profound implications for the way the rest of the world viewed our policy.

Another difference: In 1991, the United Nations passed a resolution supporting our response to Saddam. In 2002, we went to the United Nations to ask for a resolution supporting our invasion but were not successful in getting it.

In 1991, the first President Bush patiently and skillfully put together a broad international coalition. His task was easier than the one that confronted his son, in part because Saddam had invaded another country. For whatever reason, most Arab nations, except Jordan— which is in Iraq's shadow next door—supported our military efforts and were a part of the international coalition, and some of them supplied troops. Virtually all of our allies in Asia and Europe supported the coalition, materially or vocally.

In 2002, however, most of our allies in Europe and Asia openly opposed what President Bush did, and most of the few who did encourage us initially conditioned their support on the passage of a new UN resolution. Even had President Bush been correct about his contention that Saddam Hussein had weapons of mass destruction, his approach to dealing with it was the wrong one. As I said before the war, in 2002, a successful invasion would have required an international coalition. If you're going after Jesse James, you ought to organize the posse first, especially if you're in the middle of a gunfight with somebody else at the same time.

Fourth, the coalition assembled in 1991 paid the vast majority of all of the significant costs of the war. This time, the American taxpayers have shouldered the cost of $700 billion and counting.

Fifth, back in 1991, President George H. W. Bush purposely waited until after the midterm elections of 1990 in order to push for a vote at the beginning of the new Congress in 1991. President George W. Bush pushed for a vote in the fall of 2002, immediately before the midterm congressional elections.

The second President Bush was demanding, in a high political season, that Congress speedily affirm that he had the necessary authority to proceed immediately against Iraq, regardless of subsequent developments or emerging circumstances. The timing of this sudden burst of urgency to take up this new cause as America's top priority, displacing our former top priority, the war against Osama bin Laden, was explained innocently by the White House chief of staff in his now well-known statement: "From a marketing point of view, you don't introduce new products in August."

Rather than making efforts to dispel concerns at home and abroad about the role of politics in the timing of his policy, the president was on the campaign trail two and three days a week, often publicly taunting Democrats with the political consequences of a no vote. The Republican National Committee ran prepackaged advertising based on the same theme—all of this apparently in accord with a political strategy explicitly described in a White House aide's misplaced computer disk. The strategy advised Republican operatives that their principal game plan for success in the election a few weeks away was to "focus on the war." Vice President Cheney, meanwhile, indignantly described suggestions of any such thing as reprehensible and then quickly took this exact discussion of the war to *The Rush Limbaugh Show.*

I believe this foreshortening of deliberation in the Congress robbed the country of the time it needed for careful analysis of exactly what lay in front of it. Such consideration was all the more important because the administration failed to lay out an assessment of how it thought the course of a war would run—even while it gave free rein to persons both within and close to the administration to suggest at every opportunity that this would be an easy matter. The administration did not say much of anything to clarify its idea of what would follow a regime change or the degree of engagement that it was prepared to accept for the United States in the months and years after a regime change.

The brazen use of the war vote in the midterm elections raised many doubts about the role that politics played in the calculations of some in the administration. And because they were raised, this became a problem for our country's effort to build a national consensus and an international coalition. To cite just one example, the German election campaign revealed a profound and troubling change in the attitude of the German electorate toward the United States. We also saw our most loyal ally, Tony Blair, fall into serious trouble with his electorate, in part because of similar doubts raised about his decision to join the invasion.

When I and others asked the Bush administration what they planned to do in the aftermath of a speedy victory in the initial invasion of Iraq, Secretary Rumsfeld said that he wasn't certain we would have any responsibility at all. "That's for the Iraqis to come together and decide," Rumsfeld said. At that very moment, we now know, he was attempting to shut down the program at the U.S. Army War

College that was focused on postinvasion stabilization. He was also excluding from postwar planning the State Department team that was focused on nation building.

This should not have come as a total surprise. I vividly remember that during one of the campaign debates in 2000, moderator Jim Lehrer asked then governor George Bush whether or not America, after being involved in military action, should engage in any form of nation building. Bush's answer was, "I don't think so. I think what we need to do is convince people who live in the lands they live in to build the nations. Maybe I'm missing something here. We're going to have kind of a nation-building corps in America? Absolutely not."

We faced a choice about nation building in a much larger context at the end of World War II. America's power in comparison with the rest of the world was even greater than it is now. The choice we made then was to become a cofounder of what we now think of as the postwar era, based on the concepts of collective security and defense, manifested first and foremost in the United Nations. Through all the dangerous years that followed, we never abandoned our belief that what we were struggling to achieve was not bounded by our physical security, but extended to the unmet hopes of humankind.

The absence of any enlightened nation building after World War I led directly to the conditions that made Germany vulnerable to fascism and the rise of Adolf Hitler and made all of Europe vulnerable to his evil designs. By contrast, after World War II, there was an enlightened vision embodied in the Marshall Plan, the UN, NATO, and all of the other nation-building efforts that in turn led directly to the conditions that fostered prosperity and American leadership throughout the world. It is no longer reasonable to expect any similar enlightened vision from the current administration, but it is not too late for subsequent administrations to return America to the long-standing mainstream of its position in relation to the rest of the world. The damage to be undone is vast, but the cost of continuing to perpetuate that damage is literally incalculable.

CHAPTER SEVEN

The Carbon Crisis

Our policies on the climate crisis and our overdependence on fossil fuels—especially foreign oil—illustrate what can happen to a great nation when reason is replaced by the influence of wealth and power. Indeed, all of the pathologies that have been explored earlier in this book—deception, secrecy, the politics of fear, the appeal of a "crusade," and the substitution of raw power for knowledge and logic—are on vivid display in our energy and environmental policies.

The energy crisis and the climate crisis are inextricably linked—both in their causes and in their solutions. In order to deal with the planetary emergency caused by the rapid accumulation of man-made carbon dioxide (CO_2) in the earth's atmosphere, we must quickly address its principal cause—which is, of course, our civilization's tragic overdependence on burning massive quantities of carbon-based fuels.

There are, in fact, multiple reasons why the United States should undertake a massive strategic effort to solve the climate crisis and the fossil fuel dependency crisis simultaneously. They are the same crisis. And the fact that we still have our heads in the sand is perhaps the single best example of how the decline of reason in our national discourse blinds us to our own self-interest.

Coal and oil are especially harmful to the earth's climate because of their high carbon content relative to each unit of energy derived from them. The CO_2 produced as waste in the burning of fossil fuels—seventy million tons of it every day—traps part of the infrared energy reradiated by the earth into space.

And coal is much worse than oil. Moreover, the other dirty carbon-based fuels found in large quantities in North America—tar sands and oil shale—are the worst of all. Any significant use of these CO_2-laden deposits would make the climate crisis infinitely more difficult to solve. And the energy-intensive processing of coal, shale, and tar sands into liquid and gaseous forms would further complicate any effort to use them as alternatives to oil and natural gas.

In the case of oil, the concentration of the largest source of cheaply recoverable reserves in what is arguably the least stable region of the world—the Persian Gulf—has led a growing number of Americans to the conclusion that renewable sources of energy should be developed quickly in order to avoid the disruptive consequences of suddenly losing access to affordable oil supplies.

Actually, the largest supplier of oil to the United States is now Canada, and our second largest supplier is Mexico. Saudi Arabia is only our third largest supplier. (The fourth largest is Venezuela.) But the Persian Gulf still dominates the top of the list of world suppliers—and since the market for oil is largely integrated globally, any disruption of oil supplies or prices originating in the Persian Gulf would quickly have a cascading impact on the world market for oil—and on the U.S. economy.

By keeping world oil prices high, our steadily increasing consumption of oil also ensures the continued flow of petrodollars into the coffers of states like Iran, which are hostile to our interests, and Saudi Arabia, where significant sums have apparently been diverted to train and support terrorists.

Our current excessive dependence on oil endangers not only our national security and the earth's environment, but also our economic security. Anyone who believes that the international market for oil is a "free market" is seriously deluded. It does have many characteristics of a free market, but it is also subject to periodic manipulation by the group of nations controlling the largest recoverable reserves (the Organization of Petroleum Exporting Countries, or OPEC)— sometimes in concert with the small group of companies that dominate the global production, refining, and distribution network.

It is extremely important for us to be clear among ourselves that these episodic manipulations have not one objective, but two. First of all, these producing nations naturally seek to maximize profits. But more significant, they also seek to manipulate our political will. And for the last thirty years, they have paid careful attention to the need for price reductions every time the West comes close to recognizing the wisdom of developing adequate supplies of our own independent sources of renewable fuels.

We need to face the fact that our dangerous and unsustainable consumption of oil from a highly unstable part of the world is similar in its consequences to other forms of self-destructive behavior. The longer it continues, the greater the harm and the more serious the risk.

By now, it is pretty obvious to most Americans that we have had one too many wars in the Persian Gulf, where our troops have been sent for the second time in a dozen years—at least partly to ensure our continued access to oil. And it is equally obvious that we need an urgent effort to develop environmentally sustainable substitutes for fossil fuels and a truly international effort to stabilize the Persian Gulf and rebuild Iraq.

Since oil became the key source of energy for industrial economies and militaries a century ago, ensuring access to the largest reserves has been a key factor in strategic planning by the United States and other great powers—in peacetime and especially in wartime. As documented in chapter 4, many feel that one of the hidden reasons for launching the war in Iraq in early 2003 was the oft-stated and long-held opinion of Vice President Dick Cheney and others that ensuring continued U.S. access to the easily recoverable oil reserves of the Persian Gulf is so important as to justify even the extraordinary cost and reckless risk to America's reputation of invading another country on false pretenses.

The same instinct for deception that everyone now realizes was a prominent part of the launching of the war in Iraq was also obvious in the way the Bush White House removed the climate crisis from its agenda of problems to address, immediately after the inauguration. In fact, we now know that during the first weeks of the administration, Vice President Cheney began meeting with his infamous Energy Task Force and secretly advised lobbyists for polluters that the White House would take no action on global warming. He then asked for their help in designing a totally meaningless "voluntary" program.

In an effort to explain why they should waste time on the seemingly irrelevant voluntary program, one of the utility industry's top air pollution lobbyists, Quin Shea of the Edison Electric Institute, made unguarded comments to a coal industry group. "Let me put it to you in political terms," Shea said in April 2001, unaware that his comments were being transcribed. "The president needs a fig leaf. He's dismantling Kyoto, but he's out there on a limb."

A fig leaf.

Bush's solemn promise to the American people during the 2000 campaign that CO_2 would be regulated as a polluting greenhouse gas was instantly abandoned only days after the inauguration. He replaced it with a promise to the largest polluters that CO_2 would not be regulated at all.

Similarly, his seemingly heartfelt declaration to the American people during the campaign that he genuinely believed global warming was a real problem was replaced immediately after the inauguration by a dismissive expression of contempt for all of the careful, peer-reviewed work by the Environmental Protection Agency scientists who had presented for his review the plain facts about the dangers of the climate crisis. "I read the report put out by the bureaucracy," Bush responded when reporters asked him in the Oval Office about the report. Although the president finally used the phrase "climate change" in his

2007 State of the Union address, the slight rhetorical shift has not been accompanied by any real policy change—at least not yet.

In the same way, the promise by candidate Bush in 2000 to conduct a "humble" foreign policy and avoid any effort at "nation building" was transformed in the first days of the Bush presidency—according to newly available evidence from eyewitnesses—into a methodical secret search for any excuse to invade Iraq at the earliest opportunity.

Later, during the invasion itself, even as looters were carrying off many of Iraq's priceless antiquities from museums designed to commemorate the "cradle of civilization," only one government building was protected by American troops: the petroleum ministry. In 2007, even as Iraq was disintegrating into sectarian violence, the Bush administration was carefully crafting legal documents—while the United States was still the occupying power—guaranteeing preferential access to the enormous profits expected from production of Iraq's vast oil reserves for ExxonMobil, Chevron, BP, and Shell.

Critics like Greg Muttitt of the human rights and environmental group Platform, which monitors the oil industry, described the proposed law as a terrible deal for Iraqis and regional citizens, who were totally cut out of the process. "The draft went to the U.S. government and major oil companies in July [2006]," Muttitt said in January 2007, "and to the International Monetary Fund in September. Last month I met a group of twenty Iraqi MPs in Jordan, and I asked them how many had seen the legislation. Only one had."

Many Americans are realizing the folly of borrowing huge amounts of money from China to buy huge amounts of oil from the Persian Gulf and to make huge amounts of pollution that destroy the planet's climate. Increasingly, most Americans believe that we have to change every part of that equation.

Imported oil represents the largest single category of our enormous trade deficit—in 2006, more than 40 percent of the total deficit came from the purchase of foreign oil. When I visit port cities like Seattle, New Orleans, or Baltimore, I find the same sad story. Many massive ships, running low in the water, heavily burdened with foreign cargo or foreign oil, arrive by the thousands. These same cargo ships and tankers depart riding high with only ballast water to keep them from rolling over. Instead of goods, we send money, electronically, in the appropriate direction.

One-way trade is destructive to our economic future. We can change this by inventing and manufacturing new solutions to stop global warming right here in America. I still believe in good old-fashioned American ingenuity. We need to fill those ships with new products and technologies that we create to turn down the global thermostat. But we must begin by winning the first battle against inertia and the fear of change. And that means we have to understand exactly what we're up against.

More than a quarter century ago, when I was still in the U.S. House of Representatives, I began an intensive study of nuclear arms control and in the process spent a lot of time with military theorists and experts on nuclear strategy. One of the many insights they shared with me had to do with the typology of military conflicts. All conflicts fall, generally speaking, into one of three basic categories: local battles that may or may not have some larger strategic significance but are largely confined to a small area; regional conflicts or wars that range across a larger area and typically involve the crossing of multiple geopolitical boundary lines; and strategic or global conflicts that—while far less common—can significantly alter the course of history.

Later, I came to see that environmental challenges also fall naturally into three similar categories, each requiring a different way of thinking and responding. Most of the environmental issues people deal with are essentially local in nature: water pollution, air pollution, toxic waste dumps.

In the last several decades, as environmental awareness expanded, we began to focus on a newly recognized class of regional environmental threats: "acid rain" originating largely from midwestern smokestacks and affecting the entire northeastern United States; an enormous "dead zone" affecting a huge portion of the Gulf of Mexico and caused by the runoff of agricultural chemicals from the nation's breadbasket that are carried south by the Mississippi River past New Orleans; and the rapid and unsustainable depletion of underground freshwater supplies in the Ogallala Aquifer, which lies underneath eight states in the High Plains between the Mississippi basin and the Rocky Mountains.

Then there is the relatively rare but potentially devastating category of environmental threats that are strategic or global in nature.

The Bush administration has abandoned its responsibility to protect the environment in all three of these categories and has essentially given control of environmental policy to the largest polluters and other special interests, many of whom have tried for decades to weaken or gut environmental standards.

Take, for example, the Bush administration's handling of mercury, an extremely toxic pollutant causing severe developmental and neurological defects in fetuses. Even Bush's own Food and Drug Administration issued warnings about the consumption of mercury in tuna, swordfish, halibut, and other long-lived deepwater fishes that "bioconcentrate" mercury.

We know that the principal unregulated source of mercury pollution is coal-fired power plants. But the Bush administration has gutted the protections of the Clean Air Act that used to limit mercury, by modifying the Clean Air Act to allow polluters to avoid actually having to reduce mercury. They are, of course, extremely hazardous—but the coal and utility industries persuaded the Bush White House to pretend that they aren't and then to overrule the scientists.

To take another example, the cleanup of toxic waste dumps has come to a virtual halt. The Superfund, which I helped to establish in 1980 when I was in the Congress, was designed to provide funding for the protection of those affected by hazardous dumps. But the Bush administration has allowed the fund to dwindle from $3.8 billion to a shortfall of $175 million. The result—as predicted—is fewer cleanups, slower cleanups, and a toxic mess left for our children. That's because the Bush administration has let its industry friends off the hook; the tax these polluters used to pay to support the Superfund has been eliminated, so taxpayers are left holding the bill.

We have also seen a radical change in the stewardship of America's national parks. Although the president requested an increase in money for parks in the 2008 budget, many feel it is too little too late—especially since his policies have allowed harmful exploitation of the parks. A coalition of more than one hundred retired career National Park Service employees wrote a letter not long ago saying that the mission of the Park Service to protect parks' natural resources has been changed in favor of focusing instead on commercial and special-interest use of parks. To mention only one example, we've seen Bush and Cheney work tirelessly to allow their friends to drill in the Arctic National Wildlife Refuge.

These are not small shifts in policy—they are radical changes that reverse a century of American commitments to protect our natural resources. Yellowstone Park was created in 1872, in part to preserve its forest, mineral, and geothermal resources. Theodore Roosevelt in 1906 championed this philosophy, setting aside millions of acres of forest reserves, national monuments, and wildlife refuges. The Clinton-Gore administration protected just as much land. This balanced approach, combining the use of needed resources in the short term with conservation for future generations, has been honored by every president since Roosevelt, on down the line. Until this one.

When it comes to enforcing environmental laws, the Bush administration consistently chooses special interests over its obligation to protect the American people from pollution. It regularly ignores scientific evidence in favor of unproven assertions by large polluters that are among its supporters. A recent review of contributions to the Bush campaign from utility industry executives, lawyers, and lobbyists showed that ten Bush Pioneers—those who raised at least $100,000 for the Bush campaign—came from these industries and their trade associations.

The Bush administration has also frequently sought to slash enforcement personnel levels at the EPA. Enforcement offices have also been warned not to pursue certain cases. The Bush administration announced in 2006 that it was dropping the investigations of fifty power plants for violating the Clean Air Act—a move that Senator Chuck Schumer said "basically announced to the power industry that it can now pollute with impunity." Rich Biondi, a veteran EPA official, quit after concluding that he was being prevented from doing his job effectively. "The rug was pulled out from under us," Biondi said.

The best-known and by far most serious of the strategic environmental threats is the climate crisis. For me, this issue is in a special category because of what I believe is at stake. I am particularly concerned because the vast majority of the most respected environmental scientists from all over the world have sounded a clear and urgent alarm. The international community—including the United States—began a massive effort several years ago to assemble the most accurate scientific assessment of the growing evidence that the earth's environment is sustaining severe and potentially irreparable damage from the unprecedented accumulation of pollution in the global atmosphere.

In essence, these scientists are telling the people of every nation that global warming caused by human activities has become a serious threat to our common future and must be confronted. I am also troubled that the Bush-Cheney administration does not seem to hear the warnings of the scientific community in the same way that most of us do.

In spite of the clear evidence available all around us, there are many who still do not believe that global warming is a problem at all. And it's no wonder, because they are the targets of a massive and well-organized campaign of disinformation pushed by the administration and lavishly funded by polluters who are determined to prevent any action to reduce the greenhouse gas emissions that cause global warming, out of a fear that their profits might be affected if they have to stop dumping so much pollution into the atmosphere.

Wealthy right-wing ideologues have joined with the most cynical and irresponsible companies in the oil, coal, and mining industries to contribute large sums of money to finance pseudoscientific front groups that specialize in sowing confusion in the public's mind about global warming. They issue one misleading "report" after another, pretending that there is significant disagreement in the legitimate scientific community in areas where there is actually a broad-based consensus.

The techniques they use were pioneered years earlier by the tobacco industry in its long campaign to create uncertainty in the public's mind about the health risks caused by tobacco smoke. Indeed, some of the very same scientific camp followers who took money from the tobacco companies during that effort are now taking money from coal and oil companies in return for their willingness to say that global warming is not real.

In early 2007, just as the new international scientific report by the Intergovernmental Panel on Climate Change (IPCC) was being released, one of these front groups financed by ExxonMobil offered $10,000 for each pseudostudy or paper disputing the findings of the scientific community. This strategy has been followed for decades by the largest polluters.

In a candid memo about political strategy for Republican leaders, pollster Frank Luntz expressed concern that voters might punish candidates who supported more pollution, but he offered advice on the key tactic for defusing the issue: "Should the public come to believe that the scientific issues are settled, their views about global warming will change accordingly. Therefore, you need to continue to make the lack of scientific certainty a primary issue in the debate. . . ."

The Bush administration has gone far beyond Luntz's recommendations, however.

In the case of the global climate crisis, Bush has publicly demeaned scientists in his own administration who author official reports that underscore the extreme danger facing the United States and the world. Instead, he has preferred a self-interested and deeply flawed analysis financed by the largest oil company on the planet, ExxonMobil. He even went so far as to censor elements of an EPA report dealing with global warming and substitute in the official government report language from the ExxonMobil document. The consequences of accepting ExxonMobil's advice—to do nothing to counter global warming—are almost unthinkable.

ExxonMobil has been particularly influential with the current administration and has been more active than any other polluter in its brazen efforts to try to manage public perceptions of the reality and seriousness of the climate crisis. Numerous organizations devoted to scientific integrity have blown the whistle on ExxonMobil's disgraceful practices, but thus far with little effect.

The Royal Society—the U.K.'s equivalent of the National Academy of Sciences—formally renewed its request that ExxonMobil stop disseminating to the public "very misleading" and "inaccurate" information that is "not consistent" with what is accepted in the scientific community about the climate crisis. The Royal Society also called upon ExxonMobil to stop paying millions of dollars per year to organizations that "misrepresented the science of climate change, by outright denial of the evidence that greenhouse gasses are driving climate change, or by overstating the amount and significance of uncertainty in knowledge, or by conveying a misleading impression of the potential impacts of anthropogenic climate change."

Another organization of scientists, the U.S.-based Union of Concerned Scientists (UCS), prepared a lengthy report in 2006 showing that "ExxonMobil has funneled nearly $16 million between 1998 and 2005 to a network of 43 advocacy organizations that seek to confuse the public on global warming science."

"ExxonMobil has manufactured uncertainty about the human causes of global warming just as tobacco companies denied their product caused lung cancer," said Alden Meyer, UCS director of strategy and policy. "A modest but effective investment has allowed the oil giant to fuel doubt about global warming to delay government action just as big tobacco did for over forty years."

Two United States senators, Republican Olympia Snowe from

Maine and Democrat Jay Rockefeller from West Virginia, also joined in the growing effort to persuade ExxonMobil to behave ethically. The two senators said that ExxonMobil's brazen and outrageous effort to spread ignorance and confusion about the climate crisis "has damaged the United States' reputation." Saying that ExxonMobil's ongoing misrepresentation of the science is not honest, they protested "ExxonMobil's 'significant and consisten financial support of this pseudo-scientific, non-peer reviewed echo chamber.'"

ExxonMobil's motive for engaging in this extraordinary and ongoing effort at mass deception is certainly not mysterious. In early 2007, the company announced the largest annual profit for the preceding year, 2006, of any corporation in U.S. history.

The company directors have long since concluded that efforts to solve the climate crisis and the energy crisis are not in their best interest. They have also lavishly rewarded their executives for suppressing any qualms they might have experienced at being so dishonest. Former CEO Lee Raymond was given a retirement package worth $400 million. He was then promptly named by President Bush as the chair of a committee to lead a key study examining America's alternative energy future. Indeed, it seems at times as if the Bush-Cheney administration is wholly owned by the coal, oil, utility and mining companies.

The problem is that our world is now confronting a five-alarm fire that calls for bold moral and political leadership from the United States of America.

As the human population quadrupled in the previous century (from 1.6 billion in 1900 to 6.6 billion today), and as new technologies multiplied the average impact of each person on the earth's environment thousands of times over, the fundamental relationship between the human species and planet Earth was radically altered. Our "footprint" can now be measured not only by the impact of all the CO_2 we are pumping daily into the earth's atmosphere, but also by our careless destruction of one football field's worth of forest on the surface of the planet every second of every day. It can be measured also in the destruction of ocean fisheries and the pending threat of human-caused extinctions—at current rates of exploitation—for virtually every important ocean species in less than a half century.

One of the first crises in the strategic category of global environmental threats was the depletion of the stratospheric ozone layer, a global crisis of the atmosphere caused by the sudden increase of man-made chlorine compounds in the course of a few decades that led to a 600 percent increase in the concentration of chlorine atoms in the entire atmosphere of the planet. The most serious manifestation of this crisis was the appearance of a U.S.-size "ozone hole" in the stratosphere high above Antarctica every astral fall (September through November), but the thinning of the ozone layer occurred (and is still occurring) worldwide.

What stratospheric ozone depletion shares in common with global warming is that in both cases, the chemical substance causing the problem is invisible and produces its threatening consequences in the global dimension.

What the strategic environmental threats have in common with strategic or global military conflicts is the necessity of an all-out global mobilization as the only means of ensuring that the outcome brings a positive future for human civilization.

In order to conquer our fear and walk boldly forward on the path that lies before us, we have to insist on a higher level of honesty in America's political dialogue. When we make big mistakes in America, it is usually because the people have not been given an honest accounting of the choices before us. It also is usually because too many leaders in both parties who knew better did not have the courage to do better.

Our children have a right to hold us to a higher standard when their future—indeed, the future of all human civilization—is hanging in the balance. They deserve better than the spectacle of censorship of the best scientific evidence about the truth of our situation and harassment

of honest scientists who are trying to warn us about the looming catastrophe. They deserve better than politicians who sit on their hands
and do nothing to confront the greatest challenge that humankind has
ever confronted—even as the danger bears down on us.

In 2006 and 2007, scientists reached a newer and stronger consensus that global warming is increasing the destructive power of hurricanes by as much as one-half of one full category on the 1 to 5 scale
typically used by forecasters. So in Florida, a hurricane hitting in the
future that would have been a category 3 in the past will on average
become a category 4 hurricane. Scientists around the world are also
alarmed by what appears to be an increase in the rate of CO_2 buildup
in the atmosphere, a development that if confirmed in subsequent
years could potentially signal the beginning of an extremely dangerous runaway greenhouse effect.

Another respected scientific team reported that under the "business
as usual" scenario, the entire Arctic ice cap could melt and be completely gone in summer within as little as thirty-four years. (Even
though I have studied this crisis for more than forty years, I still am
shocked by some new findings. That is one of them.) Yet President
Bush continues to rely for his scientific advice on global warming on
the one company that most stands to benefit by delaying a recognition of reality.

In 2006, new information showed dramatic increases in the burning of forests throughout the American West, a trend that has increased
decade by decade as warmer temperatures have dried out soils and
vegetation. All these findings came at the end of a summer with record-
breaking temperatures and the hottest year ever recorded in the United
States, with persistent drought in vast areas of our country.

Many scientists are now warning that we are moving closer to several "tipping points" that could—within as little as ten years—make it
impossible for us to avoid irretrievable damage of the planet's habitability for human civilization. In this regard, another group of scientists reported on the surprisingly rapid increases in the release of carbon

and methane emissions from frozen tundra in Siberia, now beginning to thaw because of human-caused increases in global temperature.

Similarly, in 2006, yet another team of scientists reported that the previous twelve months saw thirty-two glacial earthquakes on Greenland that measured between 4.6 and 5.1 on the Richter scale—a disturbing sign that a massive destabilization could well be under way deep within the second largest accumulation of ice on the planet, capable of raising sea level twenty feet worldwide if it broke up and slipped into the sea.

Each passing day brings yet more evidence that we are now facing a planetary emergency—a climate crisis that demands immediate action to sharply reduce carbon dioxide emissions worldwide in order to turn down the earth's thermostat and avert catastrophe. In the lead article in its special issue on global warming in September 2006, *Scientific American* offered the following simple conclusion: "The debate on global warming is over."

Even though the earth is of such vast size, the most vulnerable part of the global environment is the atmosphere—because it is surprisingly thin, like a coat of varnish on a globe, as the late Carl Sagan used to say.

There is no longer any credible basis for doubting that the earth's atmosphere is heating up because of global warming. Global warming is real. It is happening already, and the anticipated consequences are unacceptable.

The one event in recent years that probably did more than anything else to convince Americans to look differently at the climate crisis was the catastrophic damage inflicted by Hurricane Katrina.

As we all watched the tragedy of Hurricane Katrina unfold, we all had a lot of different thoughts and feelings. But all those feelings were mixed in with puzzlement at why there was no immediate response and why there was not an adequate plan in place. We were told that this was not a time to point fingers, even as some of those saying "Don't point fingers" were themselves pointing fingers at the victims of the tragedy, who did not—many of whom could not—evacuate the city of New Orleans because they didn't have automobiles and they did not have adequate public transportation.

We were told this was not a time to hold our national government accountable because there were more important matters that confronted us. But this is not an either/or choice. They are linked together. As our nation belatedly found effective ways to help those who were so hard hit by Hurricane Katrina, it was important to learn the right lessons from what happened, lest we were spoon-fed the wrong lessons. After all, if we do not absorb the right lessons from history, we are, in the historian's phrase, doomed to repeat the mistakes that have already been made.

All of us know that our nation failed the people of New Orleans and the Gulf Coast when Hurricane Katrina was approaching them and when it struck. When the corpses of American citizens are floating in toxic floodwaters five days after a hurricane strikes, it is time not only to respond directly to the victims of the catastrophe, but to hold the processes of our nation accountable, and the leaders of our nation accountable, for the failures that have taken place.

Four years before Katrina, in August 2001, President Bush received a dire warning: "Al-Qaeda determined to strike inside the US." No meetings were called, no alarms were sounded, and no one was brought together to say, "What else do we know about this imminent threat? What can we do to prepare our nation for what we have been warned is about to take place?"

If members of the administration had been prepared, they would have found a lot of information collected by the FBI, the CIA, and the National Security Agency—including the names of most of the terrorists who flew those planes into the World Trade Center and the Pentagon and the field in Pennsylvania. They would have discovered that various FBI field offices had issued warnings of suspicious characters getting flight training without expressing any curiosity about the part of the training that has to do with landing. They would have found directors of FBI field offices in a state of agitation about the fact that there was no terrorism plan in place and no effective preparations for a response. Instead, it was vacation time, not a time for preparation. Or protecting the American people.

Four years later, there were dire warnings, three days before Hurricane Katrina hit New Orleans, that if it followed the path it was then on, the levees would break, and the city of New Orleans would drown, and thousands of people would be at risk.

It was once again vacation time. And the preparations were not made, the plans were not laid, the response was not forthcoming.

I believe that the very fact that there has been no accountability for the horrendous misjudgments and outright falsehoods that laid the foundation for the horrible tragedy that we have ongoing in Iraq is one of the principal reasons there was no fear of being held accountable for a cavalier, lackluster, mistaken, and inadequate response to the onrushing tragedy in New Orleans. After all, it was clearly visible for those who were watching television and for those who were reading the news. What happened was not only knowable, it was *known*—in advance, in great and painstaking detail. Emergency management officials had even done tabletop planning exercises and identified exactly what would take place, according to the scientific evidence. But members of the administration ignored all of that.

Where there is no vision, the people perish.

It's not only that there was no vision; it's that there has been a misguided vision. The Bush administration has appeared to be determined to weaken and diminish the ability of the federal government to do its job. After all, there had been warnings three years before Katrina hit New Orleans, from James Lee Witt, director of the Federal Emergency Management Agency (FEMA) in the Clinton-Gore administration, that FEMA was being rendered weak and helpless and would be unable to respond in the event of a catastrophe unless adequate resources were restored to it. But administration officials didn't listen. The budget was cut and the resources were sent elsewhere, mainly back to wealthy taxpayers in the form of disproportionate tax cuts.

Carl Pope, executive director of the Sierra Club, said he was *embarrassed* by the horror in New Orleans. *Embarrassed* is a tricky word when it comes to describing the feelings of Americans about the policies and actions of our government. I'm not sure that any single word is entirely adequate to describe the feelings that many had after the invasion of Iraq when they saw American soldiers holding dog leashes attached to helpless prisoners, 99 percent of whom were innocent of any connection to terrorism or violence against our troops; they were innocent prisoners who were being tortured in our name. What did you feel?

I don't know the words to describe my own feelings. But I would like all Americans to draw a line connecting the feelings they had when they saw the visual images of our soldiers, acting in our name, with our authority, torturing helpless people—and it was a matter of policy, even though the White House pointed fingers at the privates and corporals and said it was all their responsibility—with the emotions they felt during Hurricane Katrina when they saw those corpses in the water, people without food, water, medicine—our fellow citizens left helpless.

And of course in both cases the story is complex and many factors are involved, but I want people to draw a line connecting the feelings they had in both situations. And then I want them to draw another line connecting those responsible for both unbelievable tragedies that embarrassed our nation in the eyes of the world. Connect those who ignored the warnings about Katrina and then bungled the aftermath with those who ignored the warnings not to invade Iraq and then bungled the aftermath, and the line makes a small circle.

In the middle of that circle is President George W. Bush.

There are scientific warnings now of another onrushing catastrophe. We were warned of an imminent attack by al-Qaeda; we didn't respond. We were warned the levees would break in New Orleans; we didn't respond. Now, the scientific community is warning us of the worst catastrophe in the history of human civilization.

Two thousand scientists in a hundred countries, engaged in the most elaborate, well-organized scientific collaboration in the history of humankind, have long since produced a consensus that we will face a string of terrible catastrophes unless we act to prepare ourselves and deal with the underlying causes of global warming. In February 2007, this group—the IPCC—further strengthened its consensus to say there is a 90 percent probability that humans are responsible for global warming.

It is important to learn the lessons of what happens when scientific evidence and clear authoritative warnings are ignored—in order to induce our leaders not to do it again, not to ignore the scientists and leave us unprotected in the face of those threats that are facing us right now.

The president says that he is not sure humans are responsible for the threat of global warming. He is not ready to do anything meaningful to prepare us for a threat that he's not certain is real. He tells us that he believes the science of global warming is in dispute. This is the same president who said after the devastation of New Orleans, "Nobody could have predicted that the levees would break."

It's important to establish accountability in order to make our democracy work. All the uncertainty and lack of resolution, the willful misunderstanding of what the scientific community is saying, the preference for what a few of his supporters in the coal and oil industries (far from all, but a few) want him to do—ignore the science have created a serious problem.

While New Orleans was still waiting for a White House response, the president went to an event in California designed to build support for his policy in Iraq and drew an analogy between his decision to invade and Franklin Roosevelt's handling of World War II. Let me offer another analogy to World War II. When the storm was gathering over continental Europe, Winston Churchill provided warnings of what was at stake. He said this about the government then in power in England, which wasn't sure that the threat was real: "They go on in strange paradox, decided only to be undecided, resolved to be irresolute, adamant for drift, solid for fluidity, all powerful to be impotent. The era of procrastination, of half measures, of soothing and baffling expedients, of delays, is coming to a close. In its place, we are entering a period of consequences."

The warnings about global warming have been extremely clear for a long time. We are facing a global climate crisis. It is deepening. We are entering a period of consequences.

Churchill said something else, directed at the people of his country who were looking for any way to avoid having to really confront the threat he was warning of and asking them to prepare for. He said that he understood why there was a natural desire to deny the reality of the situation and to search for vain hope that it wasn't as serious as some claimed it was. But he said they should know the truth. And after the appeasement by Neville Chamberlain, he said: "This is only the beginning of the reckoning. This is only the first sip, the first foretaste of a bitter cup which will be proffered to us year by year—unless by a supreme recovery of moral health and martial vigor, we arise again and take our stand for freedom. . . ."

It is time now for us to recover our moral health in America and stand again for freedom, demand accountability for poor decisions, missed judgments, lack of planning, lack of preparation, and willful denial of the obvious truth about serious and imminent threats that are facing the American people. And we must reject the false lessons being offered to us as explanations for the horrendous tragedy of Hurricane Katrina.

Some (including some in the current administration) are now saying that the pitiful response by government proves that we cannot ever rely on the government. Yet FEMA worked extremely well during the previous administration. The fact that this administration can't manage its own way out of a horse show doesn't mean that all government programs should be abolished.

They have in the past proposed more unilateral power for themselves as the solution to a catastrophe of their own creation. But we should not give them more power to abuse and misuse, the way they have so recently done. We should hold them accountable. And we should demand that they acknowledge the scientific evidence and respect the rule of reason.

A hundred years ago, Upton Sinclair wrote, "It is difficult to get a man to understand something when his salary depends upon his not understanding it." Here's what I think we understand about Hurricane Katrina and global warming: Yes, it is true that no single hurricane can be blamed on global warming. Hurricanes have come for a long time and will continue to come in the future. Yes, it is true that the science does not definitively tell us that global warming increases the frequency of hurricanes—because, yes, it is true there is a multidecadal cycle, a cycle of twenty to forty years, that profoundly affects the number of hurricanes that come in any single hurricane season. But it is also true that the science is extremely clear now, that warmer oceans make the average hurricane stronger: not only make the winds stronger, but dramatically increase the moisture evaporating from the oceans into the storm—thus magnifying its destructive power—and make the intensity of the hurricane stronger.

The newscasters told us after Hurricane Katrina went over the southern tip of Florida that there was a particular danger for the Gulf Coast of the hurricane's becoming much stronger because it was passing over unusually warm waters in the gulf. And indeed, the waters in the gulf have been unusually warm. The oceans generally have been getting warmer. And the pattern is exactly consistent with what scientists have predicted for twenty years. They now say that the average hurricane will continue to get stronger because of global warming. A scientist at MIT published a study well before this tragedy showing that since the 1970s, hurricanes in both the Atlantic and the Pacific have increased in duration, and in intensity, by about 50 percent.

The scientists are telling us that what the science tells them is that unless we act quickly and dramatically, this is indeed, in Churchill's phrase, only "the first sip . . . of a bitter cup which will be proffered to us year by year" until there is a supreme recovery of moral health.

We also have to connect the dots. When the Superfund sites aren't cleaned up, we get a toxic gumbo in a flood. When there is not adequate public transportation for the poor, it is difficult to evacuate a city. When there is no ability to give medical care to poor people, it is difficult to get hospitals to take refugees in the middle of a crisis. When the wetlands are turned over to the developers, the storm surges from the ocean threaten the coastal cities more. When there is no effort to restrain the global warming pollution gases, then global warming gets worse, with all of the consequences that the scientific community has warned us about.

Abraham Lincoln once said, "The occasion is piled high with difficulty and we must rise with the occasion. As our case is new, we must think anew and act anew. We must disenthrall ourselves and then we shall save our country." And so must we disenthrall ourselves from the sound-and-light show that has diverted the attentions of our great democracy from the important issues and challenges of our day. We must disenthrall ourselves from the Michael Jackson trial and the Aruba search and the latest sequential obsession with celebrity trials or whatever relative triviality dominates the conversation of democracy instead of making room for us as free American citizens to talk with one another about our true situation—and then save our country.

The refugees we have seen in our own country could well be the first sip of that bitter cup, because sea-level rise in countries around the world will create millions of environmental refugees.

This is a moral moment. This is not ultimately about any scientific debate or political dialogue. Ultimately, it is about who we are as human beings and whether or not we have the capacity to transcend our own limitations and rise to this new occasion. It is about whether or not we can see with our hearts, as well as our heads, the unprecedented response that is now called for; whether or not we can—in Lincoln's phrase—disenthrall ourselves, shed the illusions that have been our accomplices in ignoring the warnings that have been clearly given, and to hear clearly the ones that are being given now.

At another moment of supreme challenge, Lincoln told us that the question ultimately facing the people of the United States of America was whether or not this government of the people, by the people, and for the people—conceived in liberty and dedicated to freedom—or any government so conceived—would perish from this earth.

Where there is no vision, the people perish.

But there is another side to this moral challenge. Where there *is* vision, the people prosper and flourish, and the natural world recovers, and our communities recover. The good news is we know what to do. The good news is we have everything we need now to respond to the challenge of global warming. We have all the technologies we need, though more and better ones are being developed, and as they become available and become more affordable when produced in scale, they will make it easier to respond. We have everything we need—save perhaps political will. And in our democracy, political will is a renewable resource.

We are now at a true fork in the road. And in order to take the right path, we must choose the right values and adopt the right perspective. This is the time for those who see and understand and care and are willing to work to say, "This time the warnings will not be ignored. This time we will prepare. This time we will rise to the occasion. And we will prevail."

This is not a political issue. This is a moral issue. It affects the survival of human civilization. It is not a question of Left vs. Right; it is a question of right vs. wrong. Put simply, it is wrong to destroy the habitability of our planet and ruin the prospects of every generation that follows ours.

What is motivating millions of Americans to think differently about the climate crisis is the growing realization that this challenge is bringing us unprecedented opportunity. I have spoken in public about the way the Chinese express the concept of crisis. They use two symbols, the first of which—by itself—means danger. The second, in isolation, means opportunity. Put them together and you get "crisis." Our single word conveys the danger but doesn't always communicate the presence of opportunity in every crisis.

In this case, the opportunity presented by the climate crisis is not only the opportunity for new and better jobs, new technologies, new opportunities for profit, and a higher quality of life. It gives us an opportunity to experience something that few generations ever have the privilege of knowing: a common moral purpose compelling enough to lift us above our limitations and motivate us to set aside some of the bickering to which we as human beings are naturally vulnerable.

America's so-called greatest generation found such a purpose when they confronted the crisis of global fascism and won a war in Europe and in the Pacific simultaneously. In the process of achieving their historic victory, they found that they had gained new moral authority and a new capacity for vision. They created the Marshall Plan and lifted their recently defeated adversaries from their knees and assisted them to a future of dignity and self-determination. They created the United Nations and the other global institutions that made possible many decades of prosperity, progress, and relative peace. In recent years, we have squandered that moral authority, and it is high time to renew it by taking on the highest challenge of our generation.

In rising to meet this challenge, we too will find self-renewal and transcendence and a new capacity for vision to see other crises in our time that cry out for solutions: twenty million HIV/AIDS orphans in Africa alone, civil wars fought by children, genocides and famines, the rape and pillage of our oceans and forests, an extinction crisis that threatens the web of life, and tens of millions of our fellow humans dying every year from easily preventable diseases. And by rising to meet the climate crisis, we will find the vision and moral authority to see all these not as political problems, but as moral imperatives. It is therefore an opportunity for bipartisanship and transcendence, an opportunity to find our better selves and create a brighter future.

CHAPTER EIGHT

Democracy in the Balance

The relationship between checks and balances on the one hand and the reliance on the rule of reason on the other is the *Da Vinci Code* of American democracy.

The astonishing sophistication of our Founders' understanding of human nature included a penetrating insight into the vulnerability we all have to make reason itself a slave to ego. Though this Freudian concept obviously did not exist two centuries ago, our Founders understood it nevertheless. In Federalist No. 10, James Madison wrote, "As long as the reason of man continues fallible, and he is at liberty to exercise it, different opinions will be formed. As long as the connection subsists between his reason and his self-love, his opinions and his passions will have a reciprocal influence on each other; and the former will be objects to which the latter will attach themselves."

In other words, reason must be separated from the "self-love" of the individuals using it, and focused instead on the public good—by ensuring that no individual or small group can exercise power without entering into a negotiation with others who must be convinced that the proposed exercise of power meets the test of reason.

As much as our Founders relied on a "well-informed citizenry" to exercise the rule of reason and free expression to safeguard American democracy, they believed that reason alone was not enough to ensure the survival of the Republic. Madison argued in Federalist No. 51, "A dependence on the people is, no doubt, the primary control on the government; but experience has taught mankind the necessity of auxiliary precautions."

The "auxiliary precautions" he had in mind were the checks and balances that our Founders used in their design of the Constitution in order to prevent the unhealthy concentration of too much power in the hands of a few—and thereby to force those in authority to justify their views to one another by applying the rule of reason. When those in power are forced into a process of deliberation, then and only then will reason play its necessary central role. The separation of powers and the system of checks and balances are therefore essential to create the virtual space within which reason operates in American democracy.

That is why for more than two centuries, America's freedoms have been protected against the unhealthy accumulation of too much power in the hands of one person by our Founders' wise decision to divide the aggregate power of our federal government into three coequal branches, each of which serves to check and balance the power of the other two. But many of our Founders continued to worry about one particular scenario that they felt would remain especially dangerous: In wartime, the president would enjoy a politically enhanced position in his role as commander in chief. During their debates in Philadelphia, they identified the potential accumulation of power in the hands of the executive as a serious threat to the Republic. They worried that the president's suddenly increased political power during times of war might spill over its normal constitutional boundary and upset the delicate checks and balances so crucial to the maintenance of liberty.

That is precisely why they took extra care to parse the war powers in the Constitution, assigning the command of the troops to the president but retaining for the Congress not only the crucial power of deciding whether or not and when our nation might decide to go to war but also significant powers to define the nature and scope of the mission. These powers include the power to raise and support armies and navies and the power to make rules for the government and regulation of the land and naval forces among numerous others. These limitations on the power of the executive to make war were seen as crucially important. James Madison wrote in a letter to Thomas Jefferson these words: "The Constitution supposes what the History of all Governments demonstrates, that the executive is the branch of power most interested in war and most prone to it. It has accordingly with studied care vested the question of war in the Legislature."

During the Korean War, one of our most eloquent Supreme Court justices, Robert Jackson, wrote that the president should be given the "widest latitude" in wartime, but he warned against the "loose and irresponsible use" of phrases such as "inherent powers, implied powers, incidental powers, plenary powers, war powers and emergency powers" as an excuse for discharging the executive branch from the rules that govern our Republic. Jackson continued, "No penance would ever expiate the sin against free government of holding that a President can escape control of executive powers by law through assuming his military role." Jackson based this conclusion on the belief that our government has ample authority under the Constitution to take those steps which are genuinely necessary for our security. At the same time, our system demands that government act only on the basis of measures that have been the subject of open and thoughtful debate in Congress and among the American people, and that invasions of the liberty or equal dignity of any individual are subject to review by courts which are open to those affected and independent of the government which is curtailing their freedom.

In more recent decades, of course, the emergence of new, modern weapons that virtually eliminate the period of time between the decision to go to war or the declaration of war and the actual waging of war has naturally led to a reconsideration of the exact nature of the executive's war-making power. During the most dangerous decades of the nuclear standoff with the former Soviet Union, Americans had to adapt to the possibility that a devastating act of war against our nation might be commenced with as little as fifteen minutes' warning. Naturally, practical adjustments were made in our thinking that included the assumption that the president would use his inherent powers as commander in chief to respond immediately by waging all-out war. Uniformed military officers began following the president wherever he went with a mobile command apparatus (what became known as "the nuclear football"). Inevitably, the nation's awareness of the president's commander-in-chief persona played a more prominent role in its perceptions of him.

The more recent fear that terrorist groups may acquire a nuclear weapon has further enhanced the pragmatic imperatives many feel should increase the discretion allowed to the president to take unilateral action to protect the nation without waiting for Congress to play a role.

But the practicalities of modern nuclear warfare and counterterrorism, both of which do necessarily lead to increased war powers for the president at the expense of Congress, do not thereby render moot the concerns our Founders had so long ago that the making of war by the president, when added to his other powers, carries with it the potential for unbalancing the careful design of our Constitution—and, in the process, threatening our liberties.

When President Bush was forced to accept Congress's compromise Authorization Use of Military Force, which did not give him the full power he had sought, he secretly assumed it anyway, as if congressional authorization were a useless bother. But as Justice Felix Frankfurter once wrote: "To find authority so explicitly withheld is not merely to disregard in a particular instance the clear will of Congress. It is to disrespect the whole legislative process and the constitutional division of authority between President and Congress."

I am convinced that our Founders would counsel us today that one of the greatest challenges facing our Republic, in addition to terrorism—as serious as that threat is—is how we react to terrorism and how we manage our fears and achieve security without losing our freedom. I am also convinced that they would warn us that democracy itself is in grave danger if we allow any president to use his role as commander in chief to rupture the careful balance between the executive, legislative, and judicial branches of government.

Our Founders were greatly influenced far more than we can imagine by a careful reading of the history and human drama surrounding the democracies of ancient Greece and the Roman Republic. They knew, for example, that democracy disappeared in Rome when Caesar crossed the Rubicon in violation of the Roman Senate's long prohibition against a returning general entering the city while still in command of military forces. Though the Senate lingered in form and was humored for decades, when Caesar impolitically combined his military commander role with his chief-of-state role, the Roman Senate, and with it the Roman Republic and the dream of democracy, withered away; and for all intents and purposes, democracy disappeared from the face of the earth for seventeen centuries, until its rebirth in our land.

Our current president has gone to war and has symbolically marched back into "the city" wearing his commander-in-chief persona and has declared that our nation is—until further notice—in a permanent state of war, which will likely last for the rest of our lives. He implies that this permanent state of war justifies his unilateral reinterpretation of the Constitution in ways that increase his power as president at the expense of Congress, the courts, and every individual citizen. Indeed, he has even partially militarized domestic law enforcement by ordering uniformed military personnel to commence surveillance within the country on American citizens, businesses, and civic organizations that, in the view of the military, might pose some threat to our nation. In times past, this was unthinkable, but it has been met with very little protest.

In other words, President Bush has determinedly conflated his role of commander in chief with his roles of head of government and head of state. And in doing so, he has maximized the power he has been given by Americans who are fearful of being attacked and are eager to receive his promises of protection. We must surrender some of our traditional American freedoms, he tells us, so that he may have sufficient power to protect us against those who would do us harm.

And indeed, public fear of an attack remains at unusually high levels almost six years after we were viciously attacked on September 11, 2001. Of course, we have been constantly reminded of that attack in almost every speech by the president since it occurred, and we have been told that it is the justification for almost everything he has done.

Even though we are now attuned to "elevated" orange alerts and the potential for terrorist attacks, our Founders would almost certainly caution us that the biggest threat to the future of the America we love is still the endemic challenge that democracies have always faced whenever they have appeared in history, a challenge rooted in the inherent difficulty of self-governance and the vulnerability to fear that is part of human nature. Indeed, we have already witnessed some serious erosion of the checks and balances that have always maintained a healthy democracy in America.

President Bush is not the first president to press the boundaries of these new possibilities for exercising enhanced executive power. When the Soviet nuclear threat had freshly emerged, President Truman pushed the limits of his power during the Korean War by seizing control of several steel mills, as mentioned in chapter 5.

In the case that struck down Truman's seizure, Justice Robert Jackson eloquently restated the concerns about too much power concentrated in the executive branch that our Founders had understood by reference to King George III, and Jackson updated their insights by reference to the new twentieth-century guise of strongman rule embodied in both Hitler, who had just been defeated, and Stalin, who was even then posing a deadly threat: "The example of such unlimited executive power that must have most impressed the forefathers was the prerogative exercise by George III, and the description of its evils in the Declaration of Independence leads me to doubt that they created their new executive in his image. And if we seek instruction from our own times," he continued, "we can match it only from the executive governments we disparagingly describe as totalitarian."

Respect for our president is important. But even more important is respect for our Constitution. In that regard, it is crucial to emphasize that our ingrained American distrust of concentrated power has very little to do with the character or persona of the individual who wields that power; it is the power itself that must be constrained, checked, dispersed, and carefully balanced to ensure the survival of freedom. The limitations on the reach of executive power that are spelled out in the Constitution almost always take more specific form as laws enacted by Congress that presidents bent on expanding their power are tempted to ignore or violate.

A president who breaks the law is a threat to the very structure of our government. Our Founding Fathers were adamant that they had established a government of laws and not men. Indeed, they recognized that the structure of government they had enshrined in our Constitution—our system of checks and balances—was designed with a central purpose of ensuring that it would govern through the rule of law. As John Adams said: "The executive shall never exercise the legislative and judicial powers, or either of them, to the end that it may be a government of laws and not of men."

Our Founders were keenly aware that the history of the world proves that republics are fragile. In the very hour of America's birth in Philadelphia, Benjamin Franklin was asked, "Well, doctor, what have we got? A Republic or a Monarchy?" He replied cautiously, "A Republic, if you can keep it."

The survival of freedom depends upon the rule of law. The rule of law depends in turn upon the respect each generation of Americans has for the integrity with which our laws are written, interpreted, and enforced.

President Bush has repeatedly violated the law for six years. In spite of the fact that the only judicial decision to have reached the question of legality has ruled comprehensively against the president's massive and warrantless surveillance program, both the Justice Department and the

Congress have failed to take any action to enforce the law. There has been no request for a special prosecutor, and there has been no investigation by the FBI. There has been deafening silence. But the consequences to our democracy of silently ignoring serious and repeated violations of the law by the president of the United States are extremely serious.

Once violated, the rule of law is in danger. Unless stopped, lawlessness grows. The greater the power of the executive grows, the more difficult it becomes for the other branches to perform their constitutional roles. As the executive acts outside its constitutionally prescribed role and is able to control access to information that would expose its actions, it becomes increasingly difficult for the other branches to police it. Once that ability is lost, democracy itself is threatened and we become a government of men and not laws.

An executive who arrogates to himself the power to ignore the legitimate legislative directives of the Congress or to act free of the check of the judiciary becomes the central threat that the Founders sought to nullify in the Constitution. In the words of James Madison, "The accumulation of all powers, legislative, executive, and judiciary, in the same hands, whether of one, a few, or many, and whether hereditary, self-appointed, or elective, may justly be pronounced the very definition of tyranny."

What would Benjamin Franklin think of President Bush's assertion that he has the inherent power, even without a declaration of war by the Congress, to launch an invasion of any nation on earth, at any time he chooses, for any reason he wishes, even if that nation poses no imminent threat to the United States? How long would it take James Madison to dispose of our current president's claim, in Department of Justice legal opinions, that he is largely above the rule of law so long as he is acting in his role as commander in chief?

I think it is safe to say that our Founders would be genuinely concerned about these recent developments in American democracy and that they would feel that we, here, are now facing a clear and present danger with the potential to threaten the future of the American experiment. Shouldn't we be equally concerned, and shouldn't we ask ourselves how it is that we have come to this point?

In the name of security, this administration has attempted to relegate the Congress and the courts to the sidelines and replace our democratic system of checks and balances with an unaccountable executive. And all the while, it has constantly angled for new ways to exploit the sense of crisis for partisan gain and political dominance.

This effort to rework America's carefully balanced constitutional design into a lopsided structure dominated by an all-powerful executive branch with a subservient Congress and judiciary is an extremely dangerous threat to the survival of liberty. As a result of its unprecedented claim of new unilateral power, the executive branch has now put our constitutional design at grave risk.

One of President Bush's most contemptuous and dangerous practices has been his chronic abuse of what are called "signing statements." These are written pronouncements that the president issues upon signing a bill into law. Throughout our history, these statements have served a mainly ceremonial function, extolling the virtues of the legislation and thanking those figures responsible for the enactment. On occasion, these statements have also included passages in which the president raises constitutional concerns with some provisions of the new law. What presidents have always avoided is delineating those provisions that the president simply disagrees with and announcing that the president will not comply with them. Obviously, such a device would be unconstitutional on its face.

The Constitution gives the president the choice of signing a law, vetoing a law—in which case the law does not go into effect unless a supramajority in both the House and the Senate override the veto—or refraining from signing a law—in which case it goes into effect without his signature after ten days (unless the Congress goes out of session during those ten days, in which case the law is negated by what is called a "pocket veto"). But those are the only options laid out in the Constitution. The president must either sign or veto each law that is presented to him by the Congress. The president is not a member of the legislative branch and therefore is not entitled to pick apart all of the provisions of each law and decide for himself which provisions he will accept and which he will reject. Once the law has been passed by the Congress, he must either accept it or reject it in its entirety, as it is.

As with some other abuses by the current administration, Bush is not the first president to attempt an expansion of executive authority, but his abuses are so far beyond those of any of his predecessors that they represent a difference of kind as well as degree.

President Bill Clinton issued signing statements covering 140 laws over the eight years of his presidency, as compared with his predecessor, George H. W. Bush, who objected to 232 laws during his four years in office. President George W. Bush, by contrast, has issued more signing statements than all of his predecessors combined—challenging the constitutionality of more than 1,000 laws during his first six years in office.

The difference between the practice of President Clinton and that of President George W. Bush is not simply one of volume—though that alone is striking, particularly given that President Clinton faced a hostile and adversarial Congress dominated by the opposing political party while President Bush for the first six years faced a docile and supportive Congress. President Clinton's signing statements were based on well-settled principles of constitutional law and were guided by a desire to allow the judiciary to resolve issues of constitutional interpretation. President Bush's signing statements, however, rest on legal theories regarding his own power that are extreme and lacking in judicial support. In fact, his theory of his own power is so vast that, in practice, it amounts to an assertion of power that is so obviously unconstitutional—a power to simply declare what provisions of law he will and will not comply with.

Many legal scholars have sounded alarms about this practice. One of them, law professor David Golove from New York University, says that Bush's assertions call into question "the whole idea that there is a rule of law." Bruce Fein, who served as a deputy attorney general in the Reagan administration when Ed Meese and Samuel Alito recommended expanding the use of signing statements, now says that it "eliminates the checks and balances that keep the country a democracy." He added, "There is no way for an independent judiciary to check his assertions of power, and Congress isn't doing it, either. So this is moving us toward an unlimited executive power."

For example, after the administration dishonored and embarrassed the country by torturing large numbers of helpless prisoners, an overwhelming bipartisan majority passed legislation sponsored by three Republican senators—John McCain, John Warner, and Lindsey Graham—outlawing torture. Bush could have vetoed the law, but Congress almost certainly would have overridden his veto. Instead, he signed the law but announced that he did not, and would not, have to abide by it. This helps to explain why Bush has vetoed only one bill during his entire term in office. Why bother, if he can simply decide on his own whim which provisions of a law apply to him and which ones he will simply ignore?

In numerous other cases, the president has bargained with the Congress to sway their votes in favor of a particular law by agreeing to support the inclusion of certain provisions that various members of the House and Senate insisted upon as a condition for their support. This practice, common in democracies, is known as "compromise." In these cases, however, the president has turned around and announced in his signing statements that he would not enforce or accept as valid those portions of the law that had been put into the proposal by members of Congress as a condition of securing the support of a majority.

To take another example, a bipartisan majority in Congress recently passed a law covering the U.S. Postal Service (as noted in chapter 5) that explicitly reinforced the terms of the Fourth Amendment in the Bill of Rights and made it against the law for the president to open citizens' mail without a warrant. But the president issued a signing statement at the time he signed the law emphasizing his own independent authority to order, without a warrant, that mail be opened for inspection.

Should we amend all of the textbooks in America to explain to schoolchildren that what has been taught for more than two centuries about checks and balances is no longer valid? Should we teach them instead that the United States Congress and the courts are merely advisory groups that make suggestions to the president on what the law should be, but that the president is all-powerful and now has the final say on everything? Should we teach them that we are a government of men, not laws? Should we teach them that we used to be a democracy but now we only pretend to be?

The abusive use of signing statements to circumvent the Founders' design of checks and balances is part of a broader effort by the administration to concentrate virtually all power in the hands of the executive branch. Indeed, the current administration came to power in the thrall of a legal theory that aims to convince us that this excessive concentration of presidential authority is exactly what our Constitution intended.

This legal theory, which its proponents call "the unitary executive" but is more accurately described as "the unilateral executive," threatens to expand the president's powers until the contours of the Constitution that the Founders actually gave us become obliterated beyond all recognition. Under this theory, the president's authority when acting as commander in chief or when making foreign policy cannot be reviewed by the judiciary or checked by Congress.

President Bush has pushed the implications of this idea to its maximum by continually stressing his role as commander in chief, invoking it as frequently as he can, and conflating it with his other roles, domestic and foreign. When added to the idea that we have entered a perpetual state of war, the implications of this theory stretch as far into the future as we can imagine. These claims must be rejected and a healthy balance of power restored to our Republic. Otherwise, the fundamental nature of our democracy may well undergo a radical transformation.

In yet another abuse justified by the unitary executive doctrine, the

White House declared in early 2007 that all the rules and policy statements developed by government agencies will now undergo vetting and implementation by political appointees, providing another means through which political pressure can be brought to bear on the agencies that should be enforcing our health, safety, and environmental laws without political distortion.

It is important to remember that in addition to the president's authority to "faithfully execute the laws" that is derived from Article II of the Constitution, he exercises other power that is specifically delegated to him by the Congress in statutory laws that often include numerous safeguards designed to ensure that laws and policies are enforced in a careful and fair manner. Often, these requirements are explicitly designed to prevent wealthy and powerful special interests from seizing control of the processes designed to protect the public from the abuses of those same special interests.

In the current administration, the president's new initiative to bend all executive branch policy making to the president's political agenda is part of this same power-seeking strategy. One disillusioned former official in the White House, John DiIulio, blew the whistle on this ubiquitous pattern when he left as adviser in charge of "faith-based initiatives." DiIulio said, "What you've got is everything, and I mean everything, being run by the political arm. It's the reign of the Mayberry Machiavellis."

Bush found intellectual underpinning for an aggressive presidency when, in 1999, Karl Rove assigned the Texas governor a book called *Energy in the Executive: The Case for the Strong Presidency,* by Terry Eastland. Based on Alexander Hamilton's assertion in the *Federalist Papers* that "energy in the executive is a leading character in the definition of good government," Eastland's book, published in 1992, spelled out for conservatives an argument for a strong, unilateral presidency that they believed had been lost to post-Watergate reforms.

One of the principal advocates of this bizarre unitary executive theory is the same Samuel Alito who was the first advocate of the abusive expansion of signing statements during the Reagan administration. Alito has been a longtime supporter of the so-called unitary executive and is not likely to serve as an effective check on the expansion of executive power. Likewise, Chief Justice Roberts has made plain his deference to the expansion of executive power through his support of judicial deference to executive agency rule making. Indeed, the president's judicial appointments, taken as a whole, are clearly designed to ensure that the courts will not serve as an effective check on executive power.

The weakest and most vulnerable of the three branches, our Founders generally agreed, was the judicial branch. The power of judging was seen—at least before Chief Justice John Marshall expanded the power of the Supreme Court in the early 1800s—as being nothing compared with the power of the purse or the sword.

That inherent inequality of power, as Alexander Hamilton wrote in Federalist No. 78, "proves incontestably, that the judiciary is beyond comparison the weakest of the three departments of power; that it can never attack with success either of the other two; and that all possible care is requisite to enable it to defend itself against their attacks. . . . It is in continual jeopardy of being overpowered, awed, or influenced by its co-ordinate branches."

Hamilton went on to caution, however, that if the power of the judiciary were ever combined with the power of either the executive or the legislative branch, then liberty itself "would have everything to fear."

For that reason, it was especially important to protect the independence of the judiciary—both from influence by the passions of a temporary majority in the legislative branch and from the inevitable hunger for consolidated power by the executive branch. Montesquieu, one of the most influential of the Enlightenment thinkers often cited by our Founders, wrote, "There is no liberty, if the power of judging be not separated from the legislative and executive powers."

In a properly functioning system, the judicial branch serves as the constitutional umpire to ensure that the branches of government observe their proper spheres of authority, observe civil liberties, and adhere to the rule of law. When James Madison introduced the Bill of Rights for consideration, he explained that the courts would be the guardians of our rights, "an impenetrable bulwark against every assumption of power in the legislature or executive."

Unfortunately, the current administration has tried hard to thwart the ability of the judiciary to call balls and strikes by keeping controversies out of its hands—for example, those challenges to the administration's ability to detain individuals without legal process. It has done so by appointing judges (like Alito and Roberts) who are likely to be deferential to its exercise of power and by its support of assaults on the independence of the third branch.

President Bush is hardly the first president to seek control over the federal judiciary. Indeed, the struggle between John Adams and Thomas Jefferson was partly about whether the Federalists or the anti-Federalists would control the majority of the judges. And Franklin Delano Roosevelt tried unsuccessfully to expand the size of the Supreme Court and "pack" it with justices who would support his New Deal agenda.

Rarely in prior American history, however, has there been anything like the assault on the independence of the judiciary that we have seen during the Bush-Cheney years. Moreover, the administration has supported the assault on judicial independence that has been conducted by Republicans in Congress who have undertaken legislative efforts to curtail the jurisdiction of courts in matters ranging from habeas corpus to the Pledge of Allegiance. In short, the administration has demonstrated its contempt for the judicial role and sought to evade judicial review of its actions at every turn.

A spokesman for James Sensenbrenner, former Republican chairman of the House Judiciary Committee, said "There does seem to be this misunderstanding out there that our system was created with a completely independent judiciary."

Misunderstanding?

Some on the radical Right have even engaged in outright threats and intimidations against federal judges with whose philosophy they disagreed, even after a judge was murdered in Atlanta while presiding in his courtroom; even after the husband and mother of a federal judge were murdered in Chicago in retaliation by a disgruntled party to a failed lawsuit. Even after such acts, the then Republican leader of the House of Representatives, Tom DeLay, could respond to rulings in the Terri Schiavo case by saying ominously, "The time will come for the men responsible for this to pay for their behavior."

When the outrage following this comment worsened, Representative DeLay claimed that his words had been chosen badly, but in the very next breath he issued new threats against the same court when he said, "We seat the courts, we can unseat the courts. We have the power of the purse."

Moreover, a host of prominent Republicans have been making similar threats on a regular basis. Republican congressman Steve King from Iowa said, "If we pass a law, a specific law, and they reject that law, then the authority that they will begin to understand is when their budget starts to dry up, we'll get their attention. That's not my preferred method. My preferred method is to have them respect the Constitution and the law. But they are counterproductive to this country and if we're going to preserve our Constitution, we must get them in line."

United States Senator John Cornyn, a Republican from Texas, directly connected what he calls the state of courthouse violence to his view that unpopular decisions might be the explanation: "I wonder whether there may be some connection between the perception in some quarters, on some occasions, where judges are making political decisions yet are unaccountable to the public, that it builds up and builds up to the point where some people engage in, engage in violence, certainly without any justification, but that is a concern I have." What a disgraceful, inflammatory, and dangerous comment.

Michael Schwartz, the chief of staff for Republican senator Tom Coburn from Oklahoma, cried for mass impeachment by using the bizarre right-wing theory that the president can simply declare that any particular judge is no longer exhibiting good behavior in the president's judgment: "Then the judge's term has simply come to an end," this official said.

The elected and appointed Republican officials who made these dangerous statements are reflecting an even more broadly held belief system on the part of some grassroots right-wing organizations that have made the destruction of judicial independence the centerpiece of their political agenda. Tony Perkins, head of the Family Research Council, said, "There's more than one way to skin a cat, and there's more than one way to take a black robe off the bench." Perkins has claimed that he's had meetings with Republican leaders during which they discussed openly stripping the funding from certain courts whose rulings they didn't like. "What they're thinking of is not only the fact of just making these courts go away and re-creating them the next day, but also defunding them," Perkins went on to say of the Republican leaders. Congress could use its appropriations authority, he said, to "just take away the bench, all of his staff, and he's just sitting out there with nothing to do." Another influential right-wing spokesman, James Dobson, who heads the group Focus on the Family, focused his anger on the Ninth Circuit Court of Appeals. He said, "Very few people know this, but the Congress can simply disenfranchise a court. They don't have to fire anybody or impeach them or go through that battle, all they have to do is say the Ninth Circuit doesn't exist anymore and it's gone." Through such threats, many Republicans are creating an atmosphere in which judges might well hesitate to exercise their independence for fear of congressional retribution.

These views are completely at odds with the spirit of the U.S. Constitution. There have been times in America's past when the independence of the courts has been threatened by political maneuvers, but over time the appreciation for protecting the independence of the judicial branch has grown steadily.

Alexander Hamilton warned:

The independence of judges is equally requisite to guard the Constitution and the rights of individuals from the effects of those ill humors, which the arts of designing men, or the influence of particular conjunctures, sometimes disseminate among the people themselves, and which, though they speedily give place to better information, and more deliberate reflection, have a tendency, in the meantime, to occasion dangerous innovations in the government, and serious oppressions of the minor party in the community.

Conservative pressure on the federal bench began in earnest in 1982, when a few conservative law students gathered at the Yale and University of Chicago law schools, nurtured by law professors such as Robert Bork and Antonin Scalia. They dubbed themselves the Federalist Society, a group largely populated by the ranks of young Reagan administration officials set on nothing short of seeding the judiciary with jurists who, like themselves, believed in a view of individual rights and federal power that was a good deal narrower than the status quo. To this new society, the courts were mistakenly adapting the Constitution to the times rather than hewing close to the intent of its eighteenth-century drafters. Among the members of the group: future Supreme Court justice Samuel Alito.

Funded by the John M. Olin, Lynde and Harry Bradley, Sarah Scafe, and Charles G. Koch foundations, the group was angered and energized five years into its existence when Congress rejected Judge Robert Bork's Supreme Court nomination. Federalist Society branches spread across all of the country's major law schools. Their first big victory was beating back the attack on Justice Clarence Thomas's nomination, and soon their members were dominating the Senate Judiciary Committee. Most recently, the Federalist Society has been credited with the rise of Justices Roberts and Alito.

In the wake of the controversy surrounding the disgraced lobbyist Jack Abramoff and the all-expenses-paid lobbying trips for members of Congress, the new House of Representatives that took office in January 2007 has outlawed such congressional junkets and the Senate is soon expected to do the same. But there has been startlingly little attention paid to similar corporate junkets for the federal judiciary. Special-interest groups have started hosting education seminars for federal judges at expensive resorts to teach these judges their conservative ideologies. Often these groups spend thousands of dollars on entertainment, travel, and other hospitality expenses for every judge in attendance. Some of these gatherings are more genuinely balanced than others, and some appear to have a principal focus on a genuine philosophical exchange of ideas. But on more than a few occasions, the "curriculum" presented has been greatly weighted toward right-wing ideology, leavened with a minimum representation of alternative views to maintain the ruse that it is not a heavily biased presentation.

These groups argue that in the modern world of constantly changing technology, judges need to seek the most up-to-date information on a series of technical issues in order to make informed decisions. Of course, Congress created the nonpartisan Federal Judicial Center for the express purpose of providing the best information to judges on whatever issues they want to research. But some of these special-interest groups are less interested in providing dispassionate postgraduate education for judges and are mainly interested instead in persuading judges to adopt their point of view.

The watchdog group Community Rights Counsel (CRC) has conducted extensive research into which groups have been sponsoring these events, which judges have attended, and how their decisions have consistently supported the corporate groups that provide their "education." The results of this research are unsurprising but alarming, given our Founders' desire to create an independent judiciary.

CRC has found that the number of educational trips for judges has increased substantially—by over 60 percent—between the mid-1990s and 2004. In some years, over 10 percent of federal judges have attended such events. While many of these seminars are actually intended to provide education and information, the percentage that are sponsored by "the Big Three"—the Foundation for Research on Economics and the Environment, George Mason University's Law & Economics Center (LEC), and the Liberty Fund—has also increased dramatically.

These three organizations have an avowedly conservative approach to the law, and particularly toward environmental law and regulations. They stress that environmental laws should be repealed in favor of property protections for corporate polluters. And the judges they invite to attend their training seminars are predictable: In total, 68 percent of the attendees to Big Three conferences between 2002 and 2004 were Republican appointees, and at Liberty Fund events during this same period, 97 percent of attendees were Republican-appointed judges.

CRC documented that those judges who return to these conferences multiple times are generally responsible for writing the most radical pro-corporate, antienvironmental, and activist decisions. Of course, it would be impossible to prove that attending these conferences changes a judge's opinions. But CRC reports that "an LEC newsletter proudly proclaims that many judges report that the program 'totally altered their frame of reference for cases involving economic issues.' "

These groups are not providing unbiased judicial education. They are giving multithousand-dollar vacations to federal judges to promote their radical right-wing agenda at the expense of the public interest. Over time, this effort has had a pronounced effect. It is one more example of how wealth has replaced reason at the center of our representative democracy—this time in the heart of the judicial branch of government. Our Founders understood that neither intelligence nor education provided insulation from the temptations and frailties that are inherent in human nature.

Some argue that the remedy for this problem is simply to encourage environmental and other public interest groups to host their own "education" seminars for federal judges—but the classic problem facing advocates of a broad and effuse public interest who rely mainly on the force of argument and the rule of reason is that they simply do not have access to the same supplies of concentrated wealth that are often available to advocates of narrow special interests whose continued income is vitally affected by the decisions of the courts, the Congress, and the executive branch. But even if they did have such resources, it would be just as wrong for advocates of particular outcomes in cases before the court to be sponsoring and designing "educational" programs for judges induced to attend them by offers of free vacations.

If our Founders believed that the judicial branch, described in Article III of the Constitution, was by far the weakest of the three branches, it is also true that they intended for the legislative branch, described in Article I of the Constitution, to be the strongest. Although some of them disagreed, the vast majority felt that the legislative branch would be the most important guarantee against the emergence of an abusive concentration of power in the executive.

The most serious—and most surprising—failure of checks and balances in the last several years has been the abdication by Congress of its role as a coequal branch of government. Following the elections of 2006, the new Democratic leadership of the Congress has begun an overdue effort to recoup the standing of the legislative branch.

But serious damage was done by the obsequious majority that controlled the House during the previous twelve years and the Senate for most of that time—and especially from January 2001 until January 2007. In that span, the Republican leadership was so deferential to the president that they abandoned the practice of holding oversight hearings and allowed the executive branch to almost completely control the operations of the Congress.

The need for constant fund-raising to purchase television commercials makes the Congress highly vulnerable to the influence of special-interest groups that concentrate on providing campaign contributions. And in the Republican Party, the fund-raising process has been nationalized in a way that gives an incumbent president of the same party enormous influence over who gets contributions in House and Senate races and who does not.

It is the pitiful state of our legislative branch that primarily explains the failure of our vaunted system of checks and balances to prevent the dangerous overreach by our executive branch, which now threatens a radical transformation of the American system.

I was elected to Congress in 1976 and served eight years in the House and eight years in the Senate, and I presided over the Senate for eight years as vice president. As a young man, I saw the Congress firsthand as the son of a U.S. senator. My father was elected to Congress in 1938, ten years before I was born, and left the Senate in 1971.

The Congress we have today is unrecognizable compared with the one in which my father served. There are many distinguished senators and congressmen serving today. But the legislative branch of government under its former leadership operated as if it were entirely subservient to the executive branch. Moreover, too many members of the House and Senate now feel compelled to spend a majority of their time not in thoughtful debate of the issues, but raising money to purchase thirty-second TV commercials.

The executive branch, time and again, has co-opted Congress's role, and often Congress has been a willing accomplice in the surrender of its own power. Look, for example, at the congressional role in "overseeing" this massive four-year eavesdropping campaign that on its face seemed so clearly to violate the Bill of Rights. The president says he informed Congress, but what he really means is that he talked with the chairman and ranking member of the House and Senate intelligence committees and the top leaders of the House and Senate. The members of this small group, in turn, claimed that they were not given the full facts, though at least one of the intelligence committee leaders handwrote a letter of concern to Vice President Cheney and placed a copy in his own safe.

In any event, these leaders were briefed in secret and could not divulge the contents of their briefings to other members or even to their own staffs—that is why the note to Vice President Cheney had to be handwritten. Thus the briefings could not have led to congressional deliberation over the wisdom of the surveillance program and trade-offs it made between liberty and security.

Though I sympathize with the awkward position in which these men and women were placed, I cannot disagree with the Liberty Coalition when it said that Democrats as well as Republicans in the Congress must share the blame for not taking action to protest and seek to prevent what they consider a grossly unconstitutional program.

There are many members of Congress now serving who have never had the experience of actually conducting an oversight hearing. In the 1970s and 1980s, the oversight hearings in which my colleagues and I participated held the feet of the executive branch to the fire—no matter which party was in power. During my first two terms in the House of Representatives, for example, I joined with my Democratic colleagues in holding hard-hitting and often adversarial oversight hearings on the conduct of the executive branch of Democratic president Jimmy Carter—not because of any lack of respect for him, but simply because we felt that was part of our job as members of the legislative branch of government. Yet oversight virtually disappeared during the first six years of the Bush-Cheney administration, because the party loyalty of the Republican congressional leaders outweighed their respect for the independent role that the legislative branch is supposed to play in our constitutional system.

The role of authorization committees has declined for decades, at times into insignificance. Many annual appropriation bills never actually pass. Everything is lumped into a single giant measure that is not even available for members of Congress to read before they vote on it. More recently, members of the Democratic Party were routinely excluded from conference committees, and amendments were routinely not allowed during floor consideration of legislation. In the United States Senate, which used to pride itself on being "the greatest deliberative body in the world," meaningful debate was a rarity.

The Republican leaders of the House and Senate even started blocking Democrats from attending conference committee meetings, where legislation takes its final form; instead, they let the president's staff come to the meetings to write key parts of the laws for them.

Moreover, the ability of voters to hold members of Congress responsible for this abdication of their responsibility has been too often muted by the increasingly pro forma nature of most congressional reelection campaigns. The drawing of district lines to favor incumbents of both parties, the large taxpayer-funded budgets for computerized mass mailings, newsletters, video press releases, and airplane travel back and forth every weekend to their districts, and the ability to raise large sums of money to buy television advertising are all factors that combine to ensure that the vast majority of incumbents are reelected no matter what.

In the House of Representatives, the number who face a genuinely competitive election contest every two years is typically less than 15 percent, and the number of seats that actually change hands every two years is very small. Every so often, there is a larger shift in the public mood—as there was in 1994 and in 2006—when control of the Congress changes from one party to the other. But too many incumbents have come to believe that the key to continued access to the money for reelection is to stay on the good side of those who have the money to give; and, in the case of the Republican Party, the whole process is controlled largely by the incumbent president and his political organization.

More and more, general elections are turning into a formality, especially in the U.S. House of Representatives. The framers of the Constitution had in mind specific roles for the two chambers of Congress. The House contained the unruly youngsters, reactive to the passions of the day thanks in part to an imposition of two-year terms. Senators, on the other hand, would hold office for six-year terms and serve to check the House with a deliberativeness that longevity in office afforded. Until recently, it followed that House seats turned over more frequently than Senate seats.

In recent years, that juxtaposition has flipped. In the four elections of the new millennium, House members have been reelected an average of 96 percent of the time, compared with Senate members, who have been reelected only 85 percent of the time, according to Rhodes Cook, an expert on election statistics. It is now statistically easier for a House member to be reelected three times in succession than it is for a senator to be reelected once. As a result, the Founders' intention that House members would be on a shorter "leash" and more responsive to the public than the Senate, has been stood on its head. Of course, the more fundamental change in the nature of the Senate came with the Seventeenth Amendment to the Constitution, ratified in 1913, which provided for the direct election of senators. And indeed, in keeping with this new electoral reality, anecdotal evidence suggests that the Senate is actually now more skittish than the House of Representatives.

Moreover, in contrast with the courageous Ninety-third Congress that helped to save our country from Richard Nixon's sinister abuses, the last Congress, controlled by the president's party, virtually abdicated its constitutional role to serve as an independent and coequal branch of government. Instead, this Republican-led Congress was content, for the most part, to take orders from the president on what to vote for and against.

Fortunately for our country, President Nixon was forced to resign before he could implement his outlandish interpretation of the Constitution, but not before his defiance of the Congress and the courts created a serious constitutional crisis. The two top Justice Department officials under President Nixon, Elliot Richardson and William Ruckelshaus, turned out to be men of great integrity. And even though they were loyal Republican partisans, they were more loyal to the Constitution, and they resigned on principle rather than implement what they saw as abuses of power by Nixon. Then Congress, also on a bipartisan basis, bravely resisted Nixon's abuses of power and launched impeachment proceedings. Some of our Congress's proudest hours in recent decades came in that trial, in that struggle.

The decline and lack of independence shown by the last Congress would shock our Founders more than anything else, because they believed that the power of the Congress was the single most important check and balance against the unhealthy exercise of too much power by the executive branch.

As James Madison envisioned, ours is a deliberative democracy. Indeed, its deliberative nature is fundamental to the integrity of our social compact, because the essential alchemy of democracy whereby just power is derived from the consent of the governed can occur only in a process that is genuinely deliberative.

Moreover, it is the unique role of the United States Senate, much more than the House of Representatives, to provide a forum for deliberation and to give adequate and full consideration to the strongly held views of the minority. And it is no accident that our Founders gave the Senate the power to pass judgment on the fitness of nominees to the judicial branch, because they knew that respect for the law also depends upon the perceived independence and integrity of our judges. They wanted those qualities to be reviewed by the more reflective of our two bodies of Congress.

As discussed in chapter 2, the Republican assault on the judiciary included a threat by the Republican majority in the Senate to permanently change the rules of the Senate to eliminate the right of the minority to engage in extended debate of the president's judicial nominees.

I was genuinely dismayed and deeply concerned by the actions and statements of some Republican leaders to undermine the rule of law by demanding that the Senate be stripped of its right to unlimited debate where the confirmation of judges is concerned.

Our Founders gave no role to the House of Representatives in confirming federal judges. If they had believed that only a simple majority was needed to safeguard the nation against unwise choices for the judiciary by a partisan president, they might well have given the House as well as the Senate the power to vote on judges. But they gave the power instead only to the Senate, a body of equals, each of whom was given a term of office three times longer than that of a representative precisely to encourage a reflective frame of mind, a distance from the passions of the voters, and a capacity for deliberative consideration.

They knew that the judges sent to the Senate would, if confirmed, serve for life and that therefore their confirmation should follow a period of advice and consent in which the Senate served as an equal partner with the executive.

The Senate's tradition of unlimited debate has been a controversial weapon in America's arsenal of democracy. For decades, it was used to frustrate the efforts of the majority to pass civil rights laws and has often been used for petty purposes by individual senators. Nevertheless, it has also frequently served to push the Senate and the nation as a whole toward a compromise between conflicting points of view, to breathe life into the ancient advice of the prophet Isaiah to "come let us reason together."

In fact, under the procedures used by Republicans during the Clinton-Gore administration, far fewer than the forty-one senators necessary to sustain a filibuster were able to routinely block the Senate from voting on judges nominated by the president, by insisting on conducting a filibuster for even the least controversial among the nominees. A filibuster, of course, is a device used in the United States Senate to prevent the Senate from closing debate on a pending question and moving to an actual vote. Sixty senators out of the one hundred must vote in favor of shutting down the debate in order to allow a vote to take place. Therefore, a bare minimum of forty-one senators can obstruct the ability of the majority to proceed to take a vote. During the period when Republicans controlled the Senate, the majority leader routinely refused to bring nominations to the floor if a much smaller number of senators objected.

To put the matter in perspective, when President Clinton and I left office, there were more than one hundred vacant judge seats—owing largely to the passionate obstruction of the confirmation process by partisan Republicans. Ironically, near the end of the Clinton-Gore administration, Orrin Hatch, the Republican chairman of the Senate Judiciary Committee, said, "There is no vacancy crisis. And a little perspective clearly belies the assertion that 103 vacancies represent a systemic crisis."

Comically, soon after President Bush took office, when a number of vacancies had already been meaningfully reduced, Hatch sounded a shrill alarm. "The filibusters used to block such votes have mired the judicial-confirmation process in a political and constitutional crisis that undermines democracy, the judiciary, the Senate, and the Constitution."

I listened with real curiosity to some of the statements made during the recent debate about Republican efforts to do away with the filibuster debate. For example, I heard the former Senate majority leader Bill Frist, who's from my home state and didn't know better, say, "Every judicial nominee who cleared the Senate's committee process received the courtesy of [an up or down] vote. Sometimes nominees were rejected on the floor, but they always received a vote."

But I vividly remember. I witnessed the dozens of nominees sent to the Senate by President Clinton who were denied a vote and filibustered by various means, and I also remember in 1968 when my father was the principal sponsor of another Tennessean, Abe Fortas, who was nominated to be Chief Justice of the United States by President Lyndon Johnson. Fortas was filibustered and denied an up or down vote; the cloture vote took place on October 1, 1968. It failed 45 to 43. President Johnson was forced by the filibusters to withdraw the nomination. Never before in history?

Saying that doesn't make it so. My father's Senate colleague and friend from Tennessee Howard Baker said during that filibuster, "On any issue, the majority of any given moment is not always right."

That is precisely why our Founders established a system of checks and balances—to prevent the accretion of power in any one set of hands, in either an individual or a group, because they were wary of what Madison famously called "the mischief of factions." Yet a group of radical Republicans threatened a fundamental break with a system that has served us well for 230 years and served as a model for the rest of the world. In the words of columnist George Will, "The filibuster is an important dissent of minority rights, enabling a democratic government to measure and respect not merely numbers but also intensity in public controversy. Filibusters enable intense minorities to slow down the governmental juggernaut. Conservatives who do not think Government is sufficiently inhibited should cherish this blocking mechanism."

Senator John McCain echoed George Will's sentiments, reminding his conservative colleagues that they won't always be in the majority. And he added, "Do we want a bunch of liberal judges approved by the Senate of the United States with 51 votes if the Democrats are in the majority?" The rules and traditions of the Senate all derive from the desire to ensure that the voice of the minority can be heard. The filibuster has been at the heart of this position for more than two centuries and yet never before has anyone felt compelled to eliminate it.

Now that control of the Senate has changed hands, there may well be the traditional shift in positions on the filibuster by members of both parties. But I am convinced that our nation has a greater need to reestablish the effectiveness of checks and balances and to rehabilitate the deliberative nature of congressional proceedings, especially in the Senate, which is intended to be the more reflective legislative body. Ultimately, however, the efficacy of checks and balances, and the continued viability of the United States Constitution itself, will depend upon a much more rigorous involvement of the American people in breathing life back into our Founders' design. To do so, the American people must have access to a free flow of information about the operations of the executive branch.

The fact that our normal safeguards have thus far failed to contain this unprecedented expansion of executive power is deeply troubling. This failure is due in part to the fact that the executive branch has followed a determined strategy of obfuscating, delaying, withholding information, appearing to yield but then refusing to do so, and dissembling in order to frustrate the efforts of the legislative and judicial branches to restore our constitutional balance. After all, the other branches can't check an abuse of power if they don't know it is happening.

This administration has not been content simply to reduce the Congress to subservience. By closely guarding information about their own behavior, they are dismantling a fundamental element of our system of checks and balances. A government for the people and by the people should be transparent *to* the people. Yet the Bush administration seems to prefer making policy in secret, based on information that is not available to the public and in a process that is insulated from any meaningful participation by Congress or the American people. When Congress's approval is required under our current Constitution, it is to be given without meaningful debate. As Bush said to one Republican senator in a meeting, "Look, I want your vote—I'm not going to debate it with you."

When reason and logic are removed from the process of democracy—when there is no longer any purpose in debating or discussing the choices we have to make—then all the questions before us are reduced to a simple equation: Who can exercise the most raw power? The system of checks and balances that has protected the integrity of our American system for more than two centuries has been dangerously eroded in recent decades, and especially in the last six years.

In order to reestablish the needed balance, and to check the dangerous expansion of an all-powerful executive branch, we must first of all work to restore the checks and balances that our Founders knew were essential to ensure that reason could play its proper role in American democracy. And we must then concentrate on reempowering the people of the United States with the ability and the inclination to fully and vigorously participate in the national conversation of democracy. I am convinced this can be done and that the American people can once again become a "well-informed citizenry." In the following chapter I outline how.

CHAPTER NINE

A Well-Connected Citizenry

As a young lawyer giving his first significant public speech at the age of twenty-eight, Abraham Lincoln warned that a persistent period of dysfunction and unresponsiveness by government could alienate the American people and that "the strongest bulwark of any government, and particularly of those constituted like ours, may effectively be broken down and destroyed—I mean the *attachment* of the people."

Many Americans now feel that our government is unresponsive and that no one in a position of power listens to or cares what they think. They feel disconnected from democracy. They feel that one vote makes no difference, and that they, as individuals, now have no practical means of participating in America's self-government.

And unfortunately, they are not entirely wrong. Voters are now often viewed mainly as targets for easy manipulation by those seeking their "consent" to exercise power. What passes for a national "conversation" today is usually a television monologue consisting of highly sophisticated propagandistic messages. Indeed, in the elections of November 2006, candidates in both political parties whom I asked about their campaign budgets told me they spent more than two-thirds of them on thirty-second television advertisements.

By using focus groups and elaborate polling techniques, those who design these messages—the heirs to Edward Bernays—are able to derive the only information they're interested in receiving *from* citizens—feedback useful in fine-tuning their efforts at manipulation. Over time, the lack of authenticity becomes painfully obvious and takes its toll in the form of cynicism and alienation. And the more Americans who disconnect from the democratic process, the less legitimate it becomes.

Having a TV—which gives you the ability to receive information—fails to establish any capacity for *sending* information in the opposite direction. And the odd one-way nature of the primary connection Americans now have to our national conversation has a profound impact on their basic attitude toward democracy itself. If you can receive but not send, what does that do to your basic feelings about the nature of your connection to American self-government?

"Attachment theory" is an interesting new branch of developmental psychology that sheds light on the importance of consistent, appropriate, and responsive two-way communication—and why it is essential for an individual's feeling empowered.

First developed by John Bowlby, a British psychiatrist, in 1958, attachment theory was further developed by his protégée Mary Ainsworth and other experts studying the psychological development of infants. Although it applies to individuals, attachment theory is, in my view, a metaphor that illuminates the significance of authentic free-flowing communication in any relationship that requires trust.

By using this new approach, psychologists were able to discover that every infant learns a crucial and existential lesson during the first year of life about his or her fundamental relationship to the rest of the world. An infant develops an attachment pathway based on different patterns of care and, according to this theory, learns to adopt one of three basic postures toward the universe:

1. In the best case, the infant learns that he or she has the inherent ability to exert a powerful influence on the world and

evoke consistent, appropriate responses by communicating signals of hunger or discomfort, happiness or distress. If the caregiver—more often than not the mother—responds to most signals from the infant consistently and appropriately, the infant begins to assume that he or she has inherent power to affect the world.

2. If the primary caregiver responds inappropriately and/or inconsistently, the infant learns to assume that he or she is powerless to affect the larger world and that his or her signals have no intrinsic significance where the universe is concerned. A child who receives really erratic and inconsistent responses from a primary caregiver, even if those responses are occasionally warm and sensitive, develops "anxious resistant attachment." This pathway creates children who feature anxiety, dependence, and easy victimization. They are easily manipulated and exploited later in life.

3. In the worst case, infants who receive *no* emotional response from the person or persons responsible for them are at high risk of learning a deep existential rage that makes them prone to violence and antisocial behavior as they grow up. Chronic unresponsiveness leads to what is called "anxious avoidance attachment," a life pattern that features unquenchable anger, frustration, and aggressive, violent behavior.

The feelings of powerlessness are an adaptive function. The child adopts behavior that sets himself or herself up for more of the same. He or she becomes antisocial and stops evoking a feeling of warmth in other people, thus reinforcing the notion of powerlessness. Children then stay on the same pathway. These courses are not set in stone, but the longer a child stays on one course, the harder it is to move on to another.

By studying the behavior of adults in later life who had shared this experience of learning powerlessness during infancy, the psychologists who specialize in attachment theory have found that an assumption of powerlessness, once lodged in the brains of infants, turns out to be difficult—though not impossible—to unlearn. Those who grow into adulthood carrying this existential assumption of powerlessness were found to be quick to assume in later life that impulsive and hostile reactions to unmet needs were the only sensible response. Indeed, longitudinal studies conducted by the University of Minnesota over more than thirty years have found that America's prison population is heavily overrepresented by people who fell into this category as infants.

The key difference determining which lesson is learned and which posture is adopted rests with the pattern of communication between the infant and his or her primary caregiver or caregivers, not with the specific information conveyed by the caregiver. What matters is the openness, responsiveness, and reliability, and two-way nature of the communication environment.

I believe that the viability of democracy depends upon the openness, reliability, appropriateness, responsiveness, and two-way nature of the communication environment. After all, democracy depends upon the regular sending and receiving of signals—not only between the people and those who aspire to be their elected representatives but also among the people themselves. It is the connection of each individual to the national conversation that is the key. I believe that the citizens of any democracy learn, over time, to adopt a basic posture toward the possibilities of self-government.

If democracy seems to work, and if people receive a consistent, reliable, and meaningful response from others when they communicate their opinions and feelings about shared experiences, they begin to assume that self-expression in democracy matters. When they can communicate with others regularly, in ways that produce meaningful changes, they learn that democracy matters.

If they receive responses that seem to be substantive but actually are not, citizens begin to feel as if they were being manipulated. If the messages they receive from the media feed this growing cynicism, the decline of democracy can be accelerated.

Moreover, if citizens of a country express their opinions and feelings over an extended period of time without evoking a meaningful response, then they naturally begin to feel angry. If the flow of communication provides little opportunity for citizens to express themselves meaningfully, they naturally begin to feel frustration and powerlessness. This has happened all too often to minority communities who suffer prejudice and are not given a fair hearing by the majority for complaints.

My generation learned in our youth to expect that democracy would work. Our frustration with the ineptitude and moral insensitivity of our national leaders in the last several years is balanced by the knowledge we gained in an earlier time and is influenced by the basic posture we adopted during our first experiences as citizens. Although many in my generation became disillusioned with self-government, most of us still believe that democracy works—or can work—and that communication and participation are the keys to making it work well.

In the United States of America, the torch of democracy—to use John F. Kennedy's metaphor—is regularly passed from one generation to the next. But what happens if the torch is passed to a generation that has learned to adopt a different posture toward democracy and to assume that their opinions are not likely to evoke an appropriate, much less consistent, response from the broader community?

Many young Americans now seem to feel that the jury is out on whether American democracy actually works or not. In contemporary America, we have created a wealthy society with tens of millions of incredibly talented and resourceful individuals who play virtually no role whatsoever as citizens. Compare this with when our country was founded and only a handful of people had the modern equivalent of a college education—but when so many were vitally engaged in the historic task of bringing forth into the world an ingenious republic that embodied a new form of representative democracy.

In the early days of America's democracy, education and literacy were the prerequisites for establishing a connection to the body politic. In a world where communication was dominated by the printed word, those who learned to read also learned to write. Gaining the ability to receive ideas was automatically accompanied by the ability to send ideas, expressing your own thoughts in the same medium through which you took in the thoughts of others. The connection, once established, was two-way.

As Thomas Jefferson wrote, "The art of printing secures us against the retrogradation of reason and information."

In practice, the use of the printing press was mainly by the elites in America's early decades, and the scurrilous, vitriolic attacks of that age certainly rivaled the worst of any modern political attacks. Nevertheless, the easy accessibility to the printed word opened up avenues of participation in the dialogue of democracy for people like Thomas Paine, who had neither family wealth nor political influence—other than what he gained with the eloquence of his writing.

The age of printed pamphlets and political essays has long since been replaced by television—a distracting and absorbing medium that seems determined to entertain and sell more than it informs and educates. If the information and opinions made available in the marketplace of ideas come only from those with enough money to pay a steep price of admission, then all of those citizens whose opinions cannot be expressed in a meaningful way are in danger of learning that they are powerless as citizens and have no influence over the course of events in our democracy—and that their only appropriate posture is detachment, frustration, or anger.

Our political system today does not engage the best minds in our country to help us get the answers and deploy the resources we need to move into the future. Bringing these people in—with their networks of influence, their knowledge, and their resources—is the key to creating the capacity for shared intelligence that we need to solve the problems we face, before it's too late. Our goal must be to find a new way of unleashing our collective intelligence in the same way that markets have unleashed our collective productivity. "We the people" must reclaim and revitalize the ability we once had to play an integral role in saving our Constitution.

The traditional progressive solution to problems that involve a lack of participation by citizens in civic and democratic processes is to redouble their emphasis on education. And education is, in fact, an extremely valuable strategy for solving many of society's ills. In an age where information has more economic value than ever before, it is obvious that education should have a higher national priority. It is also clear that democracies are more likely to succeed when there is widespread access to high-quality education.

Education alone, however, is necessary but insufficient. A well-educated citizenry is more likely to be a well-informed citizenry, but the two concepts are entirely different, one from the other. It is possible to be extremely well educated and, at the same time, ill informed or misinformed. In the 1930s and 1940s, many members of the Nazi Party in Germany were extremely well educated—but their knowledge of literature, music, mathematics, and philosophy simply empowered them to be more effective Nazis. No matter how educated they were, no matter how well they had cultivated their intellect, they were still trapped in a web of totalitarian propaganda that mobilized them for evil purposes.

The Enlightenment, for all of its liberating qualities—especially its empowerment of individuals with the ability to use reason as a source of influence and power—has also had a dark side that thoughtful people worried about from its beginning. Abstract thought, when organized into clever, self-contained, logical formulations, can sometimes have its own quasi-hypnotic effect and so completely capture the human mind as to shut out the leavening influences of everyday experience. Time and again, passionate believers in tightly organized philosophies and ideologies have closed their minds to the cries of human suffering that they inflict on others who have not yet pledged their allegiance and surrendered their minds to the same ideology.

The freedoms embodied in our First Amendment represented the hard-won wisdom of the eighteenth century: that individuals must be able to fully participate in challenging, questioning, and thereby breathing human values constantly into the prevailing ideologies of their time and sharing with others the wisdom of their own experience.

As Jefferson wrote in a letter to Charles Yancey: "The functionaries of every government have propensities to command at will the liberty and property of their constituents. There is no safe deposit for these but with the people themselves, nor can they be safe with them without information. Where the press is free, and every man able to read, all is safe."

In the age of our Founders, this human impulse to demand the right of co-creating shared wisdom accounted for the ferocity with which the states demanded protection for free access to the printing press, freedom of assembly, freedom to petition the government, freedom of religion, and freedom of speech. General George Washington, in a speech to officers of the army in 1783, said, "If men are to be precluded from offering their sentiments on a matter which may involve the most serious and alarming consequences that can invite the consideration of mankind, reason is of no use to us; the freedom of speech may be taken away, and dumb and silent we may be led, like sheep to the slaughter."

But the twentieth century brought its own bitter lessons. The new and incredibly powerful electronic media that began to replace the printing press—first radio and film and then television—were used to indoctrinate millions of Germans, Austrians, Italians, Russians, Japanese, Chinese, and others with elaborate abstract ideologies that made many of them deaf, blind, and numb to the systematic leading of tens of millions of their fellow human beings "to the slaughter."

Nazism, fascism, and communism were belief systems adopted passionately by millions of well-educated men and women. Taken together, all of the totalitarian ideologies were self-contained and delivered through a one-way flow of propaganda that prevented the people who were enmeshed in the ideology from actively participating in challenging its lack of human values.

Unfortunately, the legacy of the twentieth century's ideologically driven bloodbaths has included a new cynicism about reason itself—because reason was so easily used by propagandists to disguise their impulse to power by cloaking it in clever and seductive intellectual formulations.

In an age of propaganda, education itself can become suspect. When ideology is so often woven into the "facts" that are delivered in fully formed and self-contained packages, people naturally begin to develop some cynicism about what they are being told. When people are subjected to ubiquitous and unrelenting mass advertising, reason and logic often begin to seem like they are no more than handmaidens for the sophisticated sales force. And now that these same techniques dominate the political messages sent by candidates to voters, the integrity of our democracy has been placed under the same cloud of suspicion.

Many advocacy organizations—progressive as well as conservative—often give the impression that they already have exclusive possession of the truth and merely have to "educate" others about what they already know. Resentment toward this attitude is also one of the many reasons for a resurgence of the traditional anti-intellectual strain in America.

When people don't have an opportunity to interact on equal terms and test the validity of what they're being "taught" in the light of their own experience, and share with one another in a robust and dynamic dialogue that enriches what the "experts" are telling them with the wisdom of the groups as a whole, they naturally begin to resist the assumption that the experts know best.

If well-educated citizens have no effective way to communicate

their ideas to others and no realistic prospect of catalyzing the forma-
tion of a critical mass of opinion supporting their ideas, then their education is for naught where the vitality of our democracy is concerned.

The remedy for what ails our democracy is not simply better education (as important as that is) or civic education (as important as that
can be), but the reestablishment of a genuine democratic discourse in
which individuals can participate in a meaningful way—a conversation of democracy in which meritorious ideas and opinions from individuals do, in fact, evoke a meaningful response.

And in today's world, that means recognizing that it's impossible
to have a well-informed citizenry without having a well-*connected* citizenry. While education remains important, it is now connection that
is the key. A well-connected citizenry is made up of men and women
who discuss and debate ideas and issues among themselves and who
constantly test the validity of the information and impressions they receive from one another—as well as the ones they receive from their
government. No citizenry can be well informed without a constant
flow of honest information about contemporary events and without
a full opportunity to participate in a discussion of the choices that the
society must make.

Moreover, if citizens feel deprived of a meaningful opportunity to
participate in the national conversation, they can scarcely be blamed
for developing a lack of interest in the process. And sure enough, numerous surveys and studies have documented the erosion of public
knowledge of basic facts about our democracy.

For example, from the data compiled by the National Election
Studies on one recent election, only 15 percent of respondents could
recall the name of even one of the candidates in the election in their
district. Less than 4 percent could name two candidates. When there
are so few competitive races, it's hard to blame them. Two professors,
James Snyder and David Stromberg, found that knowledge of candidates increased in media markets where the local newspaper covered
the congressional representative more. Very few respondents claimed

to learn anything at all about their congressional elections from television news.

Similarly, according to a survey conducted by FindLaw.com, only 43 percent of Americans could name a single Supreme Court justice. In the survey, respondents incorrectly identified George W. Bush and Arnold Schwarzenegger as Supreme Court justices. Moreover, this survey, released in January 2006, was conducted immediately after two new vacancies appeared on the courts. According to the 2000 National Election Studies survey, only 11 percent could identify Supreme Court chief justice as the post held by William Rehnquist.

The alienation of Americans from the democratic process has also eroded knowledge of the most basic facts about our constitutional architecture of checks and balances. When the Annenberg Public Policy Center at the University of Pennsylvania conducted a broad survey on our Constitution, released in September 2006, they found that more than a third of the respondents believed the executive branch has the final say on all issues and can overrule the legislative and judicial branches. Barely half—53 percent—believed that the president was required to follow a Supreme Court decision with which he disagreed. Similarly, only 55 percent of those questioned believed that the Supreme Court had the power to declare an act of Congress unconstitutional. Another study found that the majority of respondents did not know that Congress—rather than the president—has the power to declare war.

The Intercollegiate Studies Institute conducted a study in 2005 of what our nation's college students knew about the Constitution, American government, and American history that provoked the American Political Science Association Task Force on Civic Education to pronounce that it is "axiomatic that current levels of political knowledge, political engagement, and political enthusiasm are so low as to threaten the vitality and stability of democratic politics in the United States."

The study found that less than half of college students "recognized that the line 'We hold these truths to be self-evident, that all men are created equal' is from the Declaration of Independence." They also found that "an overwhelming majority, 72.8 percent, could not correctly identify the source of the idea of 'a wall of separation' between church and state."

When the John S. and James L. Knight Foundation conducted a survey of high school students to determine their feelings toward the First Amendment, they found that "after the text of the First Amendment was read to students, more than a third of them (35 percent) thought that the First Amendment goes too far in the rights it guarantees. Nearly a quarter (21 percent) did not know enough about the First Amendment to even give an opinion. Of those who did express an opinion, an even higher percentage (44 percent) agreed that the First Amendment goes too far in the rights it guarantees." The survey revealed that "nearly three-fourths" of high school students "either don't know how they feel about [the First Amendment] or they take it for granted."

Thomas Jefferson once wrote that "whenever the people are well-informed, they can be trusted with their own government; that, whenever things get so far wrong as to attract their notice, they may be relied on to set them right." He also said: "If a nation expects to be ignorant and free, in a state of civilization, it expects what never was and never will be."

But we are right now in a period of great vulnerability. As noted earlier, when television became the primary source of information in the United States, the "marketplace of ideas" changed radically. Most communication was in only one direction, with a sharp decline in participatory democracy.

During this period of vulnerability for American democracy—while traditional television is still the dominant source of information and before the Internet is sufficiently developed and secured as an independent, neutral medium—there are other steps that can and should be taken to foster more connectivity in our self-government.

For example, the Congress—both House and Senate—has failed to make the best use of television, radio, and the Internet to connect with the citizens of each state and congressional district. The executive branch long ago adapted skillfully to television in order to maximize the impact of the president in communicating with the American people—and with other audiences—over electronic media. The Congress, by contrast, has seen individual members of the House and Senate maximize the use of electronic media, but the institution as a whole has not. The incumbent reelection rate has soared, but the respect for the legislative branch has plummeted.

I was involved in the effort to open congressional sessions to live radio and television coverage in the late 1970s and later, when I moved to the Senate, was involved in opening the Senate sessions to broadcasting coverage as well. But both the House and Senate have insisted upon requirements that the camera focus only on the individual members speaking.

That was a necessary limitation to convince the congressional leadership to allow coverage at all, but as a result of that decision, there is no penalty for leaving one's seat empty and no penalty for the institution as a whole when virtually all of the seats are empty. It is one of the reasons why debates on the floor of the Congress are almost always poorly attended and almost never compelling anymore.

Until recently, the scheduling of important debates in Congress was driven mainly by the convenience of the individual members, who routinely worked only three to four days a week in Washington and traveled back to their districts and states for nearly constant campaigning and to locations around the country for fund-raising. The new leadership is experimenting with needed changes, but a priority should be placed on reconnecting the American people to the substance of the deliberative process.

The most important and compelling debates should be scheduled for prime time. There is no doubt in my mind that many more Americans would pay careful attention to the arguments made during congressional debates if the House and Senate established a pattern of using the most convenient hours during weekday evenings for the most interesting debates.

Another urgent task during this window of vulnerability is to try new approaches to limit the influence of large financial contributions to candidates for elected office. I am skeptical that any reform measures will be very effective so long as the principal means of communicating with voters is through expensive thirty-second television advertisements. However, I have long supported full and robust public financing of all federal elections—with provisions that encourage all candidates to accept the funding and, in return, to agree to a prohibition on private financing of campaigns. I realize that the possibility of such law's being enacted is not high, but it is worth advocating nonetheless because of the severe damage being done to our democracy by the dominance of wealthy contributors.

Paid disinformation—in support of candidates and ballot initiatives—is polluting America's democratic discourse. So long as it is politically impossible to simply prohibit such funding, we should pursue the next best option—increasing the transparency of all contributions to make it clear where the funding is coming from. Another revision would require full transparency in the funding of nonprofit organizations.

To take one example of why such measures are necessary, consider the recent experience of California, when advocates of renewable energy sources pursued a public-interest initiative, Proposition 87. The largest oil companies provided virtually all of the financing for television advertisements opposing the initiative and outspent supporters by more than thirty million dollars, according to conservative estimates. However, when the voters went to the polls, many may have had no idea that the oil industry was principally responsible for the massive television campaign that persuaded the majority to vote no on the proposition.

Some Californians have now proposed a requirement for complete disclosure of who is financing television advertisements during such campaigns so that the public will know which industry, trade, or political grouping is for—or against—a specific ballot initiative. Had this been law in 2006, the oil industry ads against Proposition 87 would have been prominently tagged "Principal funding against this initiative is from the oil industry." The same language would appear in voter pamphlets and on the ballot itself. Similar disclosure would be required for radio and print advertising.

I am skeptical about the wisdom of ballot initiatives in general because of the potential for stripping the democratic process of its necessary deliberative elements. Nevertheless, this kind of transparency would disarm this particular assault on reason and restore the initiative system to a semblance of democracy.

Ultimately, however, no reform measures will save American democracy until and unless we find a way to restore the central role of a well-informed citizenry. The revolutionary departure on which the idea of America was based was the audacious belief that, as Thomas Jefferson said, "An informed citizenry is the only true repository of the public will."

Our Founders knew that people who are armed with knowledge and the ability to communicate it can govern themselves and responsibly exercise the ultimate authority in self-government. They knew that democracy requires the open flow of information both to and, more important, *from* the citizenry.

That means it is past time for us to examine our role as citizens in allowing and not preventing the dangerous imbalance that has emerged with the efforts by the executive branch to dominate our constitutional system and reverse the shocking decay and degradation of our democracy.

Fortunately, we now have the means available to us by which the people of America can reestablish a robust connection to a vibrant and open exchange of ideas with one another about all of the issues most relevant to the course of our democracy. The Internet has the potential to revitalize the role played by the people in our constitutional framework.

Just as the printing press led to the appearance of a new set of possibilities for democracy, beginning five hundred years ago—and just as the emergence of electronic broadcasting reshaped those possibilities, beginning in the first quarter of the twentieth century—the Internet is presenting us with new possibilities to reestablish a healthy functioning self-government, even before it rivals television for an audience.

In fact, the Internet is perhaps the greatest source of hope for reestablishing an open communications environment in which the conversation of democracy can flourish. It has extremely low entry barriers for individuals. The ideas that individuals contribute are dealt with, in the main, according to the rules of a meritocracy of ideas. It is the most interactive medium in history and the one with the greatest potential for connecting individuals to one another and to a universe of knowledge.

An important distinction to make is that the Internet is not just another platform for disseminating the truth. It's a platform for *pursuing* the truth, and the decentralized creation and distribution of ideas, in the same way that markets are a decentralized mechanism for the creation and distribution of goods and services. It's a platform, in other words, for reason.

But just as it is important to avoid romanticizing the printing press and the information ecosystem it created, it is also necessary to keep a clear-eyed view of the Internet's problems and abuses. It is hard to imagine any human evil that is not somehow abundantly displayed somewhere on the Internet. Parents of young children are often horrified to learn what obscene, grotesque, and savage material is all too easily available to children whose Web-surfing habits are not supervised or electronically limited. Teen suicides, bullying, depravity, and criminal behavior of all descriptions are described and—some would argue—promoted on the Internet. As with any tool put at the disposal of humankind, it can be, and is, used for evil as well as good purposes. And as always, it is up to us—particularly those of us who live in a democracy—to make intelligent choices about how and for what we use this incredibly powerful tool.

But the Internet must be developed and protected, in the same way we develop and protect markets—through the establishment of fair rules of engagement and the exercise of the rule of law. The same ferocity that our Founders devoted to protect the freedom and independence of the press is now appropriate for our defense of the freedom of the Internet. The stakes are the same: the survival of our Republic.

The rapid growth in the importance of the Internet in consumer markets for goods and services and the rapid adoption of Internet-advertising strategies by business clearly imply that it may be only a matter of time before the Internet plays a much larger role in fostering the conversation of democracy.

The challenge is to accelerate that process and shape its evolution in ways that are conducive to the reemergence of a fully functional democracy, because this outcome is far from inevitable.

We must ensure that the Internet remains open and accessible to all citizens without any limitation on the ability of individuals to choose the content they wish regardless of the Internet service provider they use to connect to the World Wide Web. We cannot take this future for granted. We must be prepared to fight for it, because of the threat of corporate consolidation and control over the Internet marketplace of ideas. Far too much is at stake to ever allow that to happen. We must ensure by all means possible that this medium of democracy's future develops in the mold of the open and free marketplace of ideas that our Founders knew was essential to the health and survival of freedom.

There are several technological and political obstacles that we, collectively, as a nation, will have to determine how to overcome.

As one of the founders of the Internet, Vinton G. Cerf, testified before Congress in early 2006: "The vibrant ecosystem of innovation that lies at the heart of the Internet creates wealth and opportunities for millions of Americans. That ecosystem—based upon a neutral open network—should be nourished and promoted."

In fact, it is precisely this goal that many hope the Internet can accomplish: to create a connected or "wired" democracy. And there have been some promising signs that the Internet will resuscitate and revitalize our democratic discourse.

The easy accessibility individuals have to publish ideas on the Internet has led to the emergence of a new meritocracy of ideas that is similar in some ways to the public forum that existed during the time of America's founding. The Internet has several structural characteristics that make it particularly useful and powerful as a tool for reinvigorating representative democracy.

One of the features of Internet communication that makes it so accessible to individuals is its heavy reliance on text. Anyone who learns to read text also learns to write text. For most people, publishing a text message on the Internet is even easier today than publishing a printed pamphlet was in the late eighteenth century. Moreover, in contrast to radio and television broadcasting, there is no inherent limitation on the number of entryways to the public forum as it exists on the Internet.

It is also a nearly ideal medium for individuals with common perspectives and concerns to find one another and form communities around their shared interests. Already, online organizing has become a very powerful new feature of America's democracy.

Online political communities like MoveOn.org and Right March.com are bringing more people into the political process by using the Internet to foster participation. They use the Internet not only as an online organizing tool but also to organize meetings offline, like house parties. Their e-mail lists are used to alert their members to new political and societal developments that may be of interest to them and about which they might not otherwise know anything.

In my own experience, I have used algore.com to connect with hundreds of thousands of people to communicate about the climate crisis. MoveOn.org joined with algore.com to host twelve thousand people last year when the DVD version of *An Inconvenient Truth* was released by Paramount. During the same period, by the way, RightMarch.com was among the many Web sites on the right of the spectrum that were attacking me for my views about climate change.

The power of online organizing has also begun to create hope for many that America's current system of financing political campaigns—now dominated by special interests—might eventually be replaced by the millions of small donations collected online outweighing the smaller number of larger contributions from big donors.

The relatively recent development and growth of blogging is also a promising sign for our national conversation. Generally speaking, bloggers are concerned citizens who want to share their ideas and opinions with the rest of the public.

Some have genuinely interesting things to say, while others do not, but what is most significant about blogging may be the process itself. By posting their ideas online, bloggers are reclaiming the tradition of our Founders of making their reflections on the national state of affairs publicly available.

And they do so in a new way. As Larry Lessig, law professor at Stanford Law School and founder of the Center for Internet and Society, wrote, "People post when they want to post, and people read when they want to read. . . . Blogs allow for public discourse without the public ever needing to gather in a single public place." As a result, blogging is becoming a major institutional force capable of influencing national politics.

In addition to text, individuals are now also expressing themselves on the Internet with video and flash animation. The rapid decline in the cost of digital videocameras and laptop video-editing programs—and the simultaneous improvement in the quality of both—have now made it possible for millions of people to create short videos and share them with the world by means of the Internet.

Video streaming is becoming more common over the Internet, and cheap storage of streamed video is making it possible for many television viewers to engage in what the industry calls "time shifting" to personalize their television-watching habits. Moreover, as higher bandwidth connections continue to replace smaller information pipelines, the Internet's capacity for carrying television will continue to dramatically improve.

The Internet does not yet approach the television medium as a dominant source of information, largely because its basic architecture and its reliance on many smaller, as well as larger, bandwidths prevents the mass distribution of full-motion video in real time. For the remainder of this decade, it is television delivered over cable and satellite that will almost certainly continue to be the dominant medium of communication in America's democracy.

That is one of the reasons why I have worked over the last six years, with my partner, Joel Hyatt, to innovate a new business model that empowers individuals to join the democratic discourse in the language and medium of television.

Current TV relies on video streaming over the Internet as the means by which individuals send us what we call "viewer-created content," or VC2. We rely on the Internet for the two-way conversation that we have every day with our viewers, enabling them to participate in the decisions on programming our network. We also offer, free of charge, at www.current.tv, what I believe to be the world's best online training program in how to make high-quality television content. I hope that increased and widespread familiarity with the mechanisms by which television is made can serve to demystify it, at least to some extent, and in the process weaken its quasi-hypnotic power.

More important, I believe Current TV is demonstrating that democratizing television can facilitate widespread participation in our national discourse. We are trying to work within the medium of television to re-create a multiway conversation that includes individuals and operates according to a meritocracy of ideas. There is a high degree of untapped creativity, intelligence, and talent, especially among young adults. We invite our viewers—and the public at large—to tell their stories on video and submit them to air on the network. Our goal is not political or ideological.

The point is to foster a cornucopia of points of view and fresh perspectives that force people in rigid frameworks to reassess everything. Connecting individuals to the conversation of democracy over the medium that is by far the most important is a way of opening up this medium so individuals can get back into the conversation with whatever points of view they wish to bring to it.

Another remarkable development that could strengthen our democracy is the unbelievably rapid explosion of "wikis," most prominently Wikipedia. Wikis are Web sites that compile public information about particular areas of knowledge or, in the case of Wikipedia, about almost everything. The idea behind wikis is that, in general, people as a group know more than any one individual. Anyone is allowed to contribute information to a wiki, though some subjects are patrolled and checked regularly to make sure that misinformation or disinformation does not distort the aggregation process. Wikis are sometimes abused. In fact, my friend and mentor in journalism years ago, John Seigenthaler, has been one of the most thoughtful critics of Wikipedia. But wikis are steadily improving in quality, reliability, and relevance.

Another example of Internet applications that have enormous democratic potential is the emergent phenomenon of Web 2.0 social networks. While many think of Web sites such as Facebook.com and MySpace.com as opportunities for socializing and maintaining social networks, others have very effectively used these tools for overtly political purposes. And because they are completely decentralized, their potential for fostering participation is almost limitless.

But for all the promise of the Internet, there is a serious threat to its potential for revitalizing democracy. The danger arises because there is, in most markets, a very small number of broadband network operators, and this may not change in the near future. These operators have the structural capacity to determine the way in which information is transmitted over the Internet and the speed with which it is delivered. And the present Internet network operators—principally large telephone and cable companies—have an economic incentive to extend their control over the physical infrastructure of the network to leverage control of Internet content. If they went about it in the wrong way, these companies could institute changes that have the effect of limiting the free flow of information over the Internet in a number of troubling ways.

If that was the result, it would violate the Federal Communications Commission's long history of a policy of "nondiscrimination," which has guided the development of the Internet since its inception. In the 1990s, Congress and the Clinton-Gore administration made the deliberate choice to impose very few regulations on the Internet to encourage innovation, business, and political activity. Today, this long-established policy of "nondiscrimination" has been redubbed "net neutrality."

In many ways, it is this principle that has been responsible for the trillions of dollars of economic growth spurred by the Internet. The greatest success stories among Internet businesses have been ideas pursued by small entrepreneurs who were not part of established businesses—including my friends Larry Page and Sergey Brin, who were graduate students in computer science at Stanford when they started Google.

Moreover, just as home computers have become faster, more efficient, and much cheaper than they were a few years ago, so have virtually all of the components that make up the infrastructure of the Internet, including high-speed switches and servers. These technological improvements have lowered the network operators' cost to transport each "bit" of information—the fundamental digital building block of all Internet content. And because the cost of transporting bits has dropped, those providing Internet content using bits can do much more at a lower cost, such as flash animation, live audio and video streams, and high-quality telephone calls. This sharp decline in the cost of transporting bits has also greatly increased the value the network represents to consumers, who, naturally, as a result, have increased demand for Internet access.

But network operators such as AT&T and Verizon have not been able to capture as much of the increased value of the Internet as they would like. Innovators at the edges of the network are bringing the new products to the Internet, and the network operators have had difficulty increasing their rates for connecting to the Internet because of competition from other access providers and consumer resistance to higher fees for access.

As a result, the operators have a powerful incentive to look for new opportunities to capture what economists call "rents" on the increased value of the network. Because of the difficulty they encounter in charging consumers higher fees to connect to the network, these operators are proposing to impose brand-new fees on Web companies and others who put high volumes of content on the network and create two tiers of content providers.

Those Web companies that refused to pay money to the network operators might find that their sites and applications stopped running quickly for Internet users. As a result, these Web companies would lose business and consumers might lose easy access to their favorite online services. Moreover, some of the Web companies that would be charged the new fees offer online services that compete with similar services provided by the same companies that operate the networks.

In making their case for a "tiered Internet"—with first-class and second-class citizens on the Web—the network operators argue that they need to charge Web companies and other content providers in order to pay for the cost of expanding broadband networks.

But everyone who uses the Internet is *already* helping to pay for it. Everyone who has a Web site, from Google to the smallest blog, pays to upload their content. And everyone connected to the Internet pays for access to it. Both consumers and producers of Internet content pay whatever rates the market allows.

What the network operators are proposing is that they be given a new right to impose potentially discriminatory charges that would allow them to make exclusive deals with those Internet content companies that pay for the fast lane while slowing down those who cannot pay extra. Network operators could prioritize the transmission of some content—their own, for example—over other material produced by competitors.

If this was to be allowed, Web companies would lose revenues that they could otherwise devote to improvements in old products and innovations in new ones. Worse yet, the smaller content producers who can now capitalize on the two-way nature of the Internet—whether online stores or forums for democratic discourse—might be unable to secure quality service online.

There is a legitimate need to preserve adequate incentives for investments in the expansion of network capacity. But if, in the 1990s, network operators had exercised the kind of control they are now seeking, companies like Google, Yahoo, Amazon, and others might never have appeared. I serve as a senior adviser to Google and still have a financial interest in its continued success—but I also have an interest in the continued success of several of the network operators who are business partners of Current TV.

So I have seen this controversy from both sides, and I truly believe that the most important factor is the preservation of the Internet's potential for becoming the new neutral marketplace of ideas that is so needed for the revitalization of American democracy. My overriding concern is that the creation of a tiered Internet would seriously limit that potential by giving the largest, wealthiest, and most established organizations and companies a dominant role on the Internet, to the disadvantage of individuals and smaller companies and organizations. Network neutrality rules could easily be crafted to protect the free market and free speech online while making allowances for adequate investment incentives.

When the first skirmishes over net neutrality were fought in 2006, many in the Internet community who agree with the point of view I share mobilized and used the tools they had available on the Internet to defend its independence. In the months leading up to the congressional vote on the 2006 telecom bill, more than one and a half million citizens contacted Congress and more than eight hundred organizations joined the Save the Internet Coalition, organized by the upstart media reform organization Free Press, using innovative online mobilization tactics. The many citizens who made up the grassroots opposition movement were joined by the leaders of many established Internet-based corporations and small-business leaders who shared their concerns. In addition, a great many citizens who supported freedom of speech also joined the movement.

The result, in the words of Ben Scott, the policy director for the Save the Internet Coalition, "was a grand moment for supporters of a democratic Internet." However, this triumph for net neutrality should not be seen as the ultimate victory for defenders of the Internet. Congress is the appropriate venue for action. For one thing, Congress is in the process of a long review of the Telecommunications Act of 1996, which is going to be revised and updated to suit the broadband world. This is a critical juncture in which the future of the Internet will be determined through a reformulation of the public regulations governing essential communications systems. We are moving out of a world in which telephone, video, and data were all different services and into a converged platform where everything is a stream of digital bits.

As we make the new underlying law for the broadband future, it is proper and fitting that the neutrality debate occur in this context. In fact, neutrality should be the central tenet that will set us on a path toward an open, democratic Internet where free speech and free markets are encouraged. This is a decision worthy of congressional attention, and it is too important to be left to an agency.

The public is finally involved in the debate about the future of the Internet and many are organizing to shape that debate. This critical juncture will see the first mass mobilization of public actors in a debate over the nature, scope, and implementation of the twenty-first century's central disruptive technology. People are not only fighting for free speech online, but they are also working to keep the Internet a decentralized, ownerless medium of mass communication and commerce.

The democratization of knowledge by the print medium brought the Enlightenment. Now, broadband interconnection is supporting decentralized processes that reinvigorate democracy. We can see it happening before our eyes: As a society, we are getting smarter. Networked democracy is taking hold. You can feel it.

Even though America's information ecosystem has radically changed in the past half century, our Founders' insights are just as relevant today as they were more than two hundred years ago. And the key requirement for redeeming the integrity of representative democracy in the age of electronic media is to ensure that citizens are well and fully connected to an open and robust public forum—one that is easily accessible to individuals and that operates according to a meritocracy of ideas.

We the people—as Lincoln put it, "even we here"—are collectively still the key to the survival of America's democracy.

The Rebirth of Democracy

Almost three thousand years ago, Solomon warned that where there is no vision, the people perish. But surely the converse is also true. Where there is leadership with vision and moral courage, the people will flourish and redeem Lincoln's prophecy at Gettysburg that government of the people, by the people, and for the people shall not perish from the earth.

The rule of reason is the true sovereign in the American system. Our self-government is based on the ability of individual citizens to use reason in holding their elected representatives, senators, and presidents accountable for their actions. When reason itself comes under assault, American democracy is put at risk.

Throughout history, those bent on domination have always seen reason as their enemy. Less than a century after the invention of the printing press, Henry VIII was challenged in 1543 by some of his subjects who had taken it upon themselves to question his authority after reading the newly available printed translations of the Bible. His response was to outlaw Bible reading and severely punish transgressors.

Frederick Douglass, a former slave who became the most eloquent American opponent of slavery, wrote about how his owner had forbidden him to learn to read. When he secretly gained literacy, he gained an ability to reason powerfully and to understand the evils of slavery.

One historian who has studied Douglass, François Furstenberg, wrote: "It is striking that Douglass, who had experienced the brutal violence of slavery first hand, believed that illiteracy (as opposed to, say, brute force) explained 'the white man's power to enslave the black man.' This realization was more than intellectual; it was a 'revelation' in all its religious sense. Joining the community of readers would be a new birth, converting Douglass from social death into new life. Suddenly Douglass understood the essential connection between literacy and liberty, ignorance and the 'fitness' to be a slave."

Today, reason is under assault by forces using more sophisticated techniques: propaganda, psychology, electronic mass media. Yet democracy's advocates are beginning to use their own sophisticated techniques: the Internet, online organizing, blogs, and wikis. I feel more confident than ever before that democracy will prevail and that the American people are rising to the challenge of reinvigorating self-government.

We are by nature a courageous and adaptive people. Our forebears overcame great challenges, and so will we. We are already seeing the emergence of new and innovative defenses against the assault on reason. It is my greatest hope that those who read this book will choose to become part of a new movement to rekindle the true spirit of America.

Dr. Martin Luther King once said, "Perhaps a new spirit is rising among us. If it is, let us trace its movements and pray that our own inner being may be sensitive to its guidance, for we are deeply in need of a new way beyond the darkness that seems so close around us."

As John Adams wrote in 1780, ours is a government of laws and not of men. What is at stake today is that defining principle of our nation and thus the very nature of America. As the Supreme Court has written, "Our Constitution is a covenant running from the first generation of Americans to us and then to future generations." The

Constitution includes no wartime exception, though its framers knew well the reality of war. And as Justice Oliver Wendell Holmes reminded us shortly after World War I, the Constitution's principles have value only if we apply them in the difficult times as well as in those when it matters less.

The question before us could be of no greater moment: Will we continue to live as a people under the rule of law as embodied in our Constitution? Or will we fail future generations by leaving them a Constitution far diminished from the charter of liberty we have inherited from our forebears? Our choice is clear.

Acknowledgments

I am very grateful to my wife, Tipper Gore, for helping me so much on this book, and for encouraging me every step of the way.

I also want to thank my children, Karenna Gore Schiff, Kristin Carlson Gore, Sarah LaFon Gore, and Albert Gore III. Special thanks also to Drew Schiff and Paul Cusack and Frank Hunger. All of them have been helpful and patient.

Scott Moyers has been a wonderful editor for this book; it has been a great experience to work with him. The entire team at Penguin has been terrific. Thank you.

Andrew Wylie, as always, guided me to the right editor and in the right direction for this book, and then read the galleys as well and made helpful suggestions. Thank you!

My two research assistants, Elliot Tarloff and Trent Gegax, have done an amazing job of quickly tracking down all the material I needed. I am extremely grateful for their dedication, stamina, commitment to thoroughness and excellence, and good humor. I loved working with them, and we had a lot of fun in spite of the hard work and long hours (including multiple all-nighters; it has been a busy year).

Roy Neel and my office team in Nashville have been incredibly supportive—and Roy also played a crucial role in helping me finish this book on time. Without my Nashville staff, I could never have even considered writing this book this year.

Josh Cherwin and Lisa Berg have helped find me the time and space for writing this book—sometimes during long trips. And Kalee Kreider has helped in multiple ways. Thank you.

Acknowledgments

Special thanks to Dwayne Kemp for all the great meals and for keeping all the supplies up-to-date.

I am also extremely grateful to Lisa Brown and her colleagues, particularly Chris Schroeder and Neil Kinkopf, for the extensive advice and feedback on the constitutional law questions dealt with in the book.

Similarly, I want to thank Dr. V. S. Ramachandran, Dr. Lynn DeLisi, Dr. Joe LeDoux, Dr. Sue Smalley, Anne Peretz, and Dr. Marti Erickson for helping me with the neuroscience and psychology issues in the book. I have learned a great deal from them. Thank you.

Special thanks to the historians who generously spent time helping me to better understand the fascinating historical issues explored in the book: the late Arthur Schlesinger Jr., Graham Allison, Steve Ozment, Frank Turner, Doris Kearns Goodwin and Richard Goodwin, and political scientist Steve Teles.

Thanks to Joel Hyatt, Wes Boyd, Yochai Benkler, and Ben Scott for help and advice—especially on the Internet-related questions.

I am very grateful for the help on environment and energy questions I received from Katie McGinty, Jeannie Nelson, and Will Martin—and for all the other help all three gave to me.

And special thanks to my other longtime friends who took the time to talk with me—and, in many cases, to read hundreds of pages and help me avoid some of the mistakes I otherwise would have made: Marty Peretz, John Seigenthaler, Frank Sutherland, Leon Fuerth, Elaine Kamarck, Peter Knight, Murray Gell-Man, Mike Feldman, Carter Eskew, David Blood, Tom Gegax, Steve Jobs, Tom Downey, Wendell Primus, and Bob Greenstein.

Thanks to T. J. Scaramellino for research on the Frankfurt School of Philosophy.

And finally, for the second book in a row, a very special thanks to my friend Natilee Duning, for her terrific editing advice and help.

Notes

INTRODUCTION

1 **"United States Senate":** Robert C. Byrd, "We Stand Passively Mute," February 12, 2003. http://byrd.senate.gov/speeches/byrd_speeches_2003february/byrd_speeches_2003 march_list/byrd_speeches_2003march_list_1.html.

2 **"Constitution and laws":** Abraham Lincoln, "The Perpetuation of Our Political Institutions," Address Before the Young Men's Lyceum of Springfield, Illinois, January 27, 1838. http://showcase.netins.net/web/creative/lincoln/speeches/lyceum.htm.

3 **September 11:** "Washington Post Poll: Saddam Hussein and the Sept. 11 Attacks," *Washington Post*, September 6, 2003. http://www.washingtonpost.com/wp-srv/politics/polls/vault/stories/data082303.htm.

3 **to the attack:** "Half of Americans Link Hussein and al-Qaeda," *Angus Reid Global Monitor*, January 7, 2007.

4 **"in U.S. history":** Evan Lehman, "Retired General: Iraq Invasion Was 'Strategic Disaster,'" *Lowell Sun*, September 30, 2005.

5 **"be no other":** Thomas Paine, *Common Sense, The Rights of Man and Other Essential Writings of Thomas Paine*, eds. Jack Fruchtman and Sydney Hook (New York: Penguin Books, 2003), p. 38.

6 **from the printed word:** Lawrence K. Grossman, "JFK—Breaking the News," *Columbia Journalism Review*, November/December, 2003.

6 **the world average:** David Bauder, "Average Home Has More TVs Than People," Associated Press, September 21, 2006.

7 **use the Internet:** Joseph J. Pilota et al., "Simultaneous Media Usage: A Critical Consumer Orientation to Media Planning," *Journal of Consumer Behavior* 3 (2004): 285–292.

10 **"dogma of democracy":** Walter Lippmann, *Public Opinion* (New York: Harcourt Brace & Company, 1922), p. 248.

11 **"of opposite opinions":** John Stuart Mill, *On Liberty*, ed. Gertrude Himmelfarb (New York: Penguin Books, 1982), p. 120.

Notes

13 **"mind of man":** Thomas Jefferson, Letter to Benjamin Rush, September 23, 1800.

17 **press in the world:** "Worldwide Press Freedom Index 2006," Reporters Without Borders, October 23, 2006. http://www.rsf.org/rubrique.php3?id_rubrique=639.

17 **the news division:** Paul R. La Monica, "NBC Gets 'Real' in a Virtual World," *CNN Money*, October 19, 2006.

18 **"can be free":** Joy Elmer Morgan, as quoted in Robert McChesney, *Telecommunications, Mass Media, & Democracy* (Oxford:Oxford University Press, 1995), p. 93.

18 **"the public sphere":** Jürgen Habermas, *The Structural Transformation of the Public Sphere* (Cambridge, Mass.: Polity Press, 1992).

19 **the MoveOn ad:** John Nichols, "Bush Helps CBS, CBS Helps Bush," *The Nation,* January 23, 2004.

20 **"is the message' ":** Neil Postman, "Five Things We Need to Know About Technological Change," *Proceedings of the New Tech*, March 27, 1998. http://itrs.scu.edu/tshanks/pages/ Comm12/12Postman.htm.

CHAPTER 1: THE POLITICS OF FEAR

23 **"reasoning as fear":** Edmund Burke, *A Philosophical Inquiry into the Origin of Our Ideas of the Sublime and Beautiful,* ed. Adam Phillips (Oxford: Oxford University Press, 1998), p. 53.

23 **"and burnt women":** Louis D. Brandeis, *Whitney v. California,* 274 U.S. 357 (1927).

24 **"in our power":** Thomas Paine, *Common Sense, The Rights of Man and Other Essential Writings of Thomas Paine,* eds. Jack Fruchtman and Sydney Hook (New York: Penguin Books, 2003), p. 38.

24 **"wisdom cannot be":** John R. Stone, *The Routledge Dictionary of Latin Quotations* (New York: Routledge, 2004), p. 120.

25 **"alien to America":** Dwight Eisenhower, letter to Dr. Robert B. Downs, June 24, 1953.

25 **"age of unreason":** Edward R. Murrow, *See It Now,* CBS broadcast, March 9, 1954.

26 **have been forged:** Mohamed ElBaradei, "The Status of Nuclear Inspections in Iraq: An Update," International Atomic Energy Agency, March 7, 2003. http://www.iaea.org/ NewsCenter/Statements/2003/ebsp2003n006.shtml.

26 **"to combat it":** Thomas Jefferson, "First Inaugural Address," *The Writings of Thomas Jefferson,* ed. Andrew Lipscomb (Washington, D.C.: Thomas Jefferson Memorial Association, 1901), p. 319.

28 **"for other reasons":** Vilayanur S. Ramachandran, *Phantom in the Brain* (New York: Harper Perennial, 1991), p. 156.

28 **"is empirically bankrupt":** Charles Q. Choi, "Voting with the Heart," *Scientific American,* December 2006, p. 34.

28 **"the emotional systems":** Joseph LeDoux, *The Emotional Brain* (New York: Simon and Schuster, 1996), p. 19.

29 **speed and accuracy:** V. S. Ramachandran, personal communication with V. S. Ramachandran, February/March 2007.

29 **making choices carefully:** Melissa L. Finucane et al., "The Affect Heuristic in Judgment of Risks and Benefits, " *Journal of Behavioral Decision Making* 13 (2000): 1–17.

31 *"different brain regions":* Michael S. Fanselow et al., "Why We Think Plasticity

Underlying Pavlovian Fear Conditioning Occurs in the Basolateral Amygdala," *Neuron* 23 (1999): 229–232.

32 "Dalai Lama cells": V. S. Ramachandran, personal communication with V. S. Ramachandran, February/March 2007.

32 "with traumatized persons": L. McCann and L. Pearlman, "Vicarious Traumatization: A Framework for Understanding the Psychological Effects of Working with Victims," *Journal of Traumatic Stress* 3 (1990): 131–149.

34 "the most stress": Judith Mathewson, "The Homeland Security Papers: Stemming the Tide of Terror," ed. Michael W. Ritz et al., USAF Counterproliferation Center, 2004, p. 202.

34 do real memories: Jerry Mander, *Four Arguments for the Elimination of Television* (New York: HarperCollins, 1978), pp. 240–250.

35 So we do: Robert Kubey and Mihaly Csikszentmihalyi, *Television and the Quality of Life* (Hillsdale, Hove and London: Lawrence Erlbaum Associates, 1990), pp. 139–40.

35 once per second: Robert Kubey and Mihaly Csikszentmihalyi, "Television Addiction Is No Mere Metaphor," *Scientific American Mind,* January 2004. http://www.sciam.com/article.cfm?articleID=0005339B-A694-1CC5-B4A8809EC588EEDF&pageNumber=3&catID=2.

36 much more likely: W. R. Klemm, "Identity of Sensory and Motor Systems That Are Critical to the Immobility Reflex ('Animal Hypnosis')," *Journal of Neuroscience Research* 2 (1976): 57–69.

37 discourse and reason: Barry Glassner, "Narrative Techniques of Fear Mongering," *Social Research* 71 (2004): 779–1157.

37 "by any cause": George F. Loewenstein et al., "Risk as Feeling," *Psychological Bulletin* 127 (2001): 267–286.

38 ignore the probability: ibid.

39 *were all wrong:* David Kay, "Transcript: David Kay at Senate Hearing," CNN, January 28, 2004.

39 "distinguish between them": George W. Bush, "Remarks by President Bush and President Alvaro Uribe of Colombia in Photo Opportunity, the Oval Office," September 25, 2002. http://www.whitehouse.gov/news/releases/2002/09/20020925-1.html.

39 "of every wind": Thomas Jefferson, *The Writings of Thomas Jefferson Vol.XV,* ed. Andrew A. Lipscomb (Washington, D.C.: Thomas Jefferson Memorial Association, 1904), p. 409.

40 "new products": Elisabeth Bumiller, "Bush Aides Set Strategy to Sell Policy on Iraq," *New York Times,* September 7, 2002.

40 eight-hour search: Kenneth M. Mead, Inspector General, U.S. Department of Transportation, "Federal Aviation Administration Efforts to Locate Aircraft N711RD," July 15, 2003.

40 to do so: Senator Joseph Lieberman, "Federal Authority Misused by Texas Republicans," press release, August 22, 2003.

40 acknowledge any wrongdoing: Charles Babington, "Delay Draws Third Rebuke," *Washington Post,* October 7, 2004.

41 "a side wind": Winston Churchill, *The Second World War* (Boston: Houghton Mifflin, 1986), p. 148.

42 **"the terrorists win":** Dan Froomkin, "Desperate Times," *Washington Post*, October 31, 2006.

43 **Middle Eastern oil fields:** Glenn Frankel, "U.S. Mulled Seizing Oil Fields in '73," *Washington Post,* January 1, 2004.

CHAPTER 2: BLINDING THE FAITHFUL

45 **"limit of circumstance":** Thomas Browne, *Religio Medici* (London: Henry Washbourne, 1845), p. 19.

45 **"of blind-folded fear":** Thomas Jefferson, *The Writings of Thomas Jefferson Vol. VI*, ed. Andrew A. Lipscomb (Washington, D.C.: Thomas Jefferson Memorial Association, 1904), p. 258.

46 **"by deserving them":** Thomas Jefferson, *The Writings of Thomas Jefferson Vol. XIV,* ed. Andrew A. Lipscomb (Washington, D.C.: Thomas Jefferson Memorial Association, 1904), p. 119.

46 **"grace of God":** Thomas Jefferson, *Jefferson: Political Writings* (Cambridge: Cambridge University Press, 1999), p. 149.

47 **"Faith her right":** John Donne, *John Donne, Selected Poetry,* ed. John Carey (Oxford: Oxford University Press, 1998), p. 262.

49 **"a political faction":** James Madison, Alexander Hamilton, and John Jay, *The Federalist Papers*, ed. Isaac Kramnick (New York: Penguin Books, 1987), p. 128.

49 **"from that source":** ibid.

50 **"matters of opinion":** Robert Jackson, *West Virginia State Board of Education v. Barnette*, 319 U.S. 624 (1943).

50 **"not of men":** John Adams, *Massachusetts Bill of Rights*, 1780.

54 **"or against us":** George W. Bush, "President Welcomes President Chirac to the White House," November 6, 2001. www.whitehouse.gov/news/releases/2001/11/20011106-4.html.

54 **"good will prevail":** George Bush, as quoted in "Bush Vows Monumental Struggle Against Terrorism," National Public Radio, September 13, 2001.

54 **"world of evil":** George W. Bush, "President's Remarks at National Day of Prayer and Rememberance at the National Cathedral," September 14, 2001. www.whitehouse.gov/news/releases/2001/09/20010914-2.html.

55 **"neutral between them":** George W. Bush, "Address to Joint Session of Congress and the American People," September 20, 2001. www.whitehouse.gov/news/releases/2001/09/20010920-8.html.

56 **"for the Democrats":** John Boehner, interview by Michael Medved, *Michael Medved,* November 4, 2006.

57 **before his retirement:** Kevin Drum, "Kerry and Shinseki," Political Animal, *Washington Monthly,* October 9, 2004. http://www.washingtonmonthly.com/archives/individual/2004_10/004888.php.

57 **with being fired:** John R. S. Batiste, "Testimony Before the Senate Democratic Policy Committee," September 25, 2006.

57 **"over his will":** James Madison, Alexander Hamilton, and John Jay, *The Federalist Papers*, ed. Isaac Kramnick (New York: Penguin Books, 1987), p. 417.

58 **"we were in":** William C. Sullivan, as quoted in Select Committee to Study Governmental Operations with Respect to Intelligence Activities, "Supplementary Detailed Staff Reports on Intelligence Activities and the Rights of Americans," Final Report, April 23, 1976.

58 **as a "crusade":** George W. Bush, "Remarks on Arrival at the White House and an Exchange with Reporters," September 16, 2001. http://www.presidency.ucsb.edu/ws/print.php?pid=63346.

58 **"nation battling Satan":** "US Is 'Battling Satan' Says General," *BBC News*, October 17, 2003.

58 **commander in chief:** Michael Moran, "For Once It Flows Uphill," Brave New World, MSNBC, May 14, 2004. http://www.msnbc.msn.com/id/4962140/.

58 **"of the Savior":** David Ingram, "Hayes: Iraq Missionary or Misunderstood?" *Charlotte Observer*, December 23, 2006.

59 **"I am alive":** Scott Higham and Joe Stephens, "New Details of Prison Abuse Emerge," *Washington Post*, May 21, 2004.

59 **" 'piss on himself' ":** Scott Higham and Joe Stephens, "Punishment and Amusement," *Washington Post*, May 22, 2004.

61 **"on a battlefield":** George Orwell, "In Front of Your Nose," *Tribune*, March 22, 1946.

61 **$4 trillion deficit:** Richard Kogan, David Kamin, and Joel Friedman, "Deficit Picture Grimmer Than New CBO Projections Suggest," Center on Budget and Policy Priorities, February 1, 2004. http://www.cbpp.org/1-28-04bud.htm.

62 **"is our due":** Ron Suskind, *The Price of Loyalty* (New York: Simon and Schuster, 2004).

62 **" 'and above reason' ":** John Locke, *John Locke: Resistance, Religion and Responsibility*, ed. John Marshall (Cambridge: Cambridge University Press, 1994), p. 130.

65 **counsel as "quaint":** Alberto Gonzales, "Decision RE: Application of the Geneva Conventions on Prisoners of War to the Conflict with Al Qaeda and the Taliban," January 25, 2002. http://www.msnbc.msn.com/id/4999148/site/newsweek.

65 **used by interrogators:** John Hendren, "Officials Say Rumsfeld OK'd Harsh Interrogation Methods," *Los Angeles Times*, May 21, 2004.

65 **"violating the law":** Richard Nixon, as quoted in interview with David Frost, ABC, May 1977.

65 **"it's not illegal":** ibid.

66 **"be killed, too":** Ann Coulter, "Address to the Conservative Political Action Conference 2002," February 26, 2002. http://www.pfaw.org/pfaw/general/default.aspx?oid=1626.

66 **" 'no man no problem' ":** Dana Milbank, "And the Verdict on Justice Kennedy Is: Guilty," *Washington Post*, April 9, 2005.

67 **"a big way":** Joan Biskupic, "Hill Republicans Target 'Judicial Activism,'" *Washington Post*, September 14, 1997.

67 **"for their behavior":** "Schiavo's Death Steps Up Push for End-of-Life Legislation in U.S.," Seattle Times News Services, April 1, 2005.

68 **"off the taxpayers":** Neal Boortz, *The Neal Boortz Show*, Cox's Radio Syndication, October 24, 2005.

69 **"[terrorist attack] happen":** Jerry Falwell, "Pat Robertson's interview with Jerry Falwell,"

The 700 Club, September 13, 2001.

69 "hates God's people": James Dobson, as quoted in an interview with George Stephanopoulos, *This Week*, November 7, 2004.

70 "would blow then?": Robert Bolt, *A Man for All Seasons* (New York: Vintage Books, 1960).

71 "weapon: Filibuster": Johnny Isakson, "Floor Statement on Iraq Supplemental Remarks as Delivered on Senate Floor," February 15, 2005. http://isakson.senate.gov/floor/2005/021505iraqsupplemental.htm.

CHAPTER 3: THE POLITICS OF WEALTH

74 "the republican standard": Alexander Hamilton, *American History Told by Contemporaries,* ed. Albert Bushnell Hart (New York: The MacMillan Company, 1901), p. 244.

74 "masters of mankind": Adam Smith, *An Inquiry into the Nature and Causes of the Wealth of Nations,* ed. Kathryn Sutheland (Oxford: Oxford University Press, 1993), p. 264.

74 "us against evil": Samuel Johnson, *The Idler # 89*, December 29, 1759.

75 "who enter it": Hannah Arendt, *On Revolution* (New York: Penguin Books, 1963), p. 253.

79 apparatus like the FERC: Lowell Bergman and Jeff Gerth, "Power Trader Tied to Bush Finds Washington All Ears," *New York Times*, May 25, 2001.

80 "as at market": Thomas Jefferson, *The Writings of Thomas Jefferson Vol.XV,* ed. Andrew A. Lipscomb (Washington, D.C.: Thomas Jefferson Memorial Association, 1904), pp. 450–1.

80 "only prejudice you": Niccolò Machiavelli, *The Prince*, trans. N. H. Thompson (New York: P. F. Collier & Son, 1992), p. 51.

82 "my friends' nests": George W. Bush, as quoted by Joe Conason, "Bush Inc.," *Salon*, August 21, 2003.

83 "pursuit of happiness": Samuel Johnson, *Rasselas* (London: Edward Lacey, 1838), p. 78.

83 "No standing army": Thomas Jefferson, *The Writings of Thomas Jefferson,* ed. H. A. Washington (New York: Derby and Jackson, 1859), p. 358.

84 "one common level": John Adams, *The Works of John Adams, Second President of the United States, with a Life of the Author, Vol. II,* ed. Charles Francis Adams (Boston: Little, Brown, and Company, 1865). www.britannica.com/presidents/article-9116850.

86 "in the jackass?": Benjamin Franklin, *The Casket, or Flowers of Literature, Wit and Sentiment*, 1828.

87 "and corrupted instruments": Thomas Jefferson, *The Writings of Thomas Jefferson Vol. XV,* ed. Andrew A. Lipscomb (Washington, D.C.: Thomas Jefferson Memorial Association, 1904), p341.

87 "control their decisions": Andrew Jackson, *State of the Union Addresses* (Whitefish: Kessinger Publishing, 2004), p. 105.

88 "may prove groundless": Abraham Lincoln, "Letter to Col. William F. Elkins, Nov. 21, 1864," *The Lincoln Encyclopedia*, ed. Archer H. Shaw (New York: Macmillan, 1950), p. 40.

88 **Constitution to "persons":** John Marshall Harlan, *Santa Clara County v. Southern Pacific Railroad* 118 U.S. 394 (1886).

90 **"nation toward property":** William McKinley, *Life of William McKinley*, ed. Samuel Fallows (Chicago: Regan Printing House, 1901), p. 389.

90 **"of the day":** Theodore Roosevelt, *The Social and Political Thought of American Progressivism*, ed. Eldon Eisenach (Indianapolis: Hackett Publishing, 2006), p. 274.

91 **in the nation:** Paul Starr, *The Creation of the Media* (New York: Basic Books, 2004), p. 384.

93 **"and the people":** Joseph Goebbels, *The Radio as the Eighth Great Power*, August 18, 1933. http://www.calvin.edu/academic/cas/gpa/goeb56.htm.

94 **"beginning, for propaganda":** Gianni Isola, "Italian Radio: History and Historiography—Special Issue: Italian Media Since World War II," *Historical Journal of Film, Radio and Television*, August 1995.

94 **resistance to cigarettes:** Larry Tye, *The Father of Spin: Edward L. Bernays and the Birth of Public Relations* (New York: Owl Books, 2002).

94 **"overshadow his needs":** Paul Mazur, as quoted in "Century of the Self," *BBC Four*, April–May 2002.

96 **"within certain limits":** Edward Bernays, *Propaganda* (New York: Ig Publishing, 2004), p. 71.

96 **"of economic power":** Walter Lippmann, *Public Opinion* (New York: Harcourt Brace & Company, 1922), p. 158.

CHAPTER 4: CONVENIENT UNTRUTHS

100 **"avenues to truth":** Thomas Jefferson, *The Writings of Thomas Jefferson Vol.XI*, ed. Andrew A. Lipscomb (Washington, D.C.: Thomas Jefferson Memorial Association, 1903), pp. 33.

104 **"to do it":** Ron Suskind, *The Price of Loyalty* (New York: Simon & Schuster, 2004), p. 86.

104 **support an invasion:** Sam Tannenhaus, "Bush's Brain Trust," *Vanity Fair*, July 2003. www.defenselink.mil/transcripts/2003/tr20030509-depsecdef0223.html.

105 **with deadly consequences:** "Top Bush Officials Push Case Against Saddam," CNN, September 8, 2002.

105 **ore in Africa:** George W. Bush, *State of the Union Address*, January 28, 2003. www.white house.gov/news/releases/2003/01/20030128-19.html.

105 **was actually forged:** Mohamed ElBaradei, "The Status of Nuclear Inspections in Iraq: An Update," International Atomic Energy Agency, March 7, 2003. http://www.iaea.org/NewsCenter/Statements/2003/ebsp2003n006.shtml.

107 **"like the answer":** Richard Clarke, interview by Lesley Stahl, *60 Minutes*, CBS, March 2004.

108 **"of catapult the propaganda":** George W. Bush, speech during presidential visit to Greece, N.Y., May 24, 2005. www.whitehouse.gov/news/releases/2005/05/20050524-3.html.

108 **"to that truth":** J. Wright, *The Phaedrus, Lysis, and Protagoras of Plato* (Cambridge: Trinity Press, 1888), p. 78.

109 **"al-Qaeda and Saddam":** George W. Bush, "Remarks by President Bush and President

Alvaro Uribe of Colombia in Photo Opportunity, the Oval Office," September 25, 2002. www.whitehouse.gov/news/releases/2002/09/20020925-1.html.

109 "armed by Saddam": George W. Bush, *State of the Union Address*, January 28, 2003. http://www.whitehouse.gov/news/releases/2003/01/20030128-19.htm.

109 "the Iraqi government": Greg Miller, "Cheney Claims al Qaeda Link to Hussein," *San Francisco Chronicle*, January 23, 2004.

109 "al-Qaeda terrorist network": Colin Powell, Presentation to the United Nations, February 6, 2003. http://www.cnn.com/2003/US/02/05/sprj.irq.powell.transcript.09/index.html.

109 "and al-Qaeda": "Bush Insists Iraq, Al Qaeda had 'Relationship,' " CNN, June 17, 2004.

109 claim was false: Walter Pincus, "Newly Released Data Undercut Prewar Claims," *Washington Post*, November 6, 2005. www.washingtonpost.com/wpdyn/content/article/2005/11/05/AR2005110501267_pf.html.

109 "serious connections whatsoever": Sebastian Rotella, "Allies Find No Links Between Iraq, Al Qaeda," *Los Angeles Times*, November 4, 2004.

110 "with al-Qaeda": Romesh Ratnesar, "Iraq & al Qaeda: Is There a Link?" CNN, August 26, 2002.

110 key intelligence agencies: Peter H. Stone, "Iraq–al Qaeda Links Weak, say Former Bush Officials," *National Journal*, August 8, 2003.

111 "We don't know": Dick Cheney, televised interview with Gloria Borger, CNBC, June 17, 2004.

111 "about the answers": Thomas Pynchon, *Gravity's Rainbow* (New York: Penguin Books, 1995).

111 QAEDA-IRAQ TIE: Philip Shenon and Christopher Marquis, "Panel Finds No Qaeda–Iraq Tie; Describes a Wider Plot for 9/11," *New York Times*, June 17, 2004.

111 "the commission said": David Sanger and Robin Toner, "Bush and Cheney Talk Strongly of Qaeda links with Hussein," *The New York Times*, June 18, 2004.

111 "are on fire": Jon Stewart, *The Daily Show with Jon Stewart*, June 21, 2004.

111 "links the two": "Rumsfeld Questions Saddam–Bin Laden Link," BBC News, October 5, 2004.

112 the U.S. government: Walter Pincus and Karen DeYoung, "Senators Debate Significance of Pentagon Report on Intelligence," *Washington Post*, February 10, 2007.

112 "their own opinions": Leonardo da Vinci, *The Notebooks of Leonardo da Vinci*, ed. Irma Richter (Oxford: Oxford University Press, 1999), p. 283.

113 "they give out": Isidor Feinstein Stone, *In a Time of Torment* (New York: Random House, 1967), p. 317.

113 "any serious weaponry": Elmer Andersen, "Why a Republican Former Governor Will Be Voting for John Kerry," *Minneapolis Star Tribune*, October 13, 2004.

115 government in Baghdad: "Chalabi Is Back in the Political Limelight, Mentioned as a Possible Cabinet Minister," Associated Press, March 1, 2007.

116 did not exist: Warren P. Strobel and John Walcott, "Post-war Planning Non-existent," Knight Ridder Newspapers, October 17, 2004.

116 **more were needed:** Paul Bremer and Malcolm McConnel, *My Year in Iraq* (New York: Simon & Schuster, 2006).

117 **words, "just guessing":** Douglas Jehl and David E. Sanger, "Prewar Assessment on Iraq Saw Chance of Strong Divisions," *New York Times*, September 28, 2004.

117 **"low readiness rates":** Thomas E. Ricks, "General Reported Shortages in Iraq," *Washington Post*, October 18, 2004.

117 **World War II:** David Leonhardt, "What $1.2 Trillion Can Buy," *New York Times*, January 17, 2007.

117 **"and gas fields":** As reported by Jane Mayer, "Contract Sport," *The New Yorker*, February 16, 2004.

118 **by dotted lines:** Judicial Watch press release and maps, "Cheney Energy Task Force Documents Feature Map of Iraqi Oilfields," July 17, 2003. www.judicialwatch.org/ IraqOilMap.pdf.

118 **"prize ultimately lies":** Dick Cheney, Address at the London Institute of Petroleum, August 1999. www.peakoil.net/Publications/Cheney_PeakOil_FCD.pdf.

119 **"international energy policy":** National Energy Policy Development Group, "National Energy Policy Report: Reliable, Affordable, and Environmentally Sound Energy for America's Future," U.S. Department of Energy, May 2001, pp. 8–5. www.white-house.gov/energy/National-Energy-Policy.pdf.

119 **Arabia's oil fields:** Seymour M. Hersh, "Lunch with the Chairman," *The New Yorker*, March 17, 2003. www.newyorker.com/fact/content/articles/030317fa_fact.

119 **reserves of Iraq:** Danny Fortson, Andrew Murray-Watson and Tim Webb, "Future of Iraq: The Spoils of War," *The Independent*, January 7, 2007.

120 **"the United States":** Julian Coman, "Bush's Administration Is Worse Than Nixon's, Says Watergate Aide," *The Telegraph*, April 4, 2004.

120 **"to secret proceedings":** John F. Kennedy, Address to Newspaper Publishers, April 27, 1961. http://www.jfklibrary.org/Historical+Resources/Archives/Reference+Desk/Speeches /JFK/003POF03NewspaperPublishers04271961.html.

120 **"and environmental matters":** Christopher H. Schmitt and Edward T. Pound, "Keeping Secrets," *U.S. News & World Report*, December 22, 2003.

121 **governor of Texas:** John W. Dean, *Worse Than Watergate* (New York: Warner Books, 2005), pp. 56–57.

121 **to run, Halliburton:** ibid., pp. 42–43.

121 **state budget report:** Dana Milbank, "Seek and Ye Shall Not Find," *Washington Post*, March 11, 2003.

121 **receiving for decades:** David Lazarus, "Shooting the Messenger: Report on Layoffs Killed," *San Francisco Chronicle*, January 3, 2003.

121 **"critical infrastructure":** Andrew Card, "Memorandum for the Heads of Executive Departments and Agencies: Action to Safeguard Information Regarding Weapons of Mass Destruction and Other Sensitive Documents Related to Homeland Security," March 19, 2002. www.fas.org/sgp/bush/wh031902.html.

121 **the public domain:** Mathew M. Aid, ed., "Declassification in Reverse," National Security Archive at George Washington University, February 21, 2006. http//www.

gwu.edu/~nsarchiv/NSAEBB/NSAEBB179/#report.

122 **the White House:** "White House Blocks Access to Visitor Logs," Associated Press, January 5, 2007.

122 **"against foreign power":** Thomas Jefferson, *The Writings of Thomas Jefferson Vol.XV,* ed. Andrew A. Lipscomb (Washington, D.C.: Thomas Jefferson Memorial Association, 1904), p. 340.

123 **"a religious issue":** Andrew C. Revkin, "NASA Chief Backs Agency Openness," *New York Times,* February 4, 2006.

123 **"to the last":** Thomas Moore, *Lalla Rookh: The Veiled Prophet of Khorassan* (Halifax: Milner and Sowerby, 1859), p. 70.

124 **numbers given to Congress by the president:** Amy Goldstein, "Foster: White House Had Role in Withholding Medicare Data," *Washington Post,* March 19, 2004.

124 **health care companies:** Jonathan D. Salant, "Medicare Revolving Door Fuels Congress Debate Over Ethics Rules," Bloomberg News, January 30, 2006.

124 **"accused of disloyalty":** As quoted by Ron Suskind, "Faith, Certainty and the Presidency of George W. Bush," *New York Times Magazine,* October 17, 2004.

125 **"what they say":** Ari Fleischer, White House Press Briefing, September 26, 2001. http://www.whitehouse.gov/news/releases/2001/09/20010926-5.html.

126 **"around your neck":** Dan Rather, "Veteran CBS News Anchor Dan Rather Speaks Out on BBC Newsnight Tonight," BBC, May 16, 2002.

126 **"by the administration":** Christiane Amanpour, interview with Tina Brown, "Topic A with Tina Brown," CNBC, September 10, 2003.

126 **"ruin your reputation":** Paul Krugman, "To Tell the Truth," *New York Times,* May 28, 2004.

126 **and unbiased news:** Greg Toppo, "Education Department Paid Commentator to Promote Law," *USA Today,* January 7, 2005.

127 **positive treatment:** Robert Pear, "Dems Attack Videos Promoting Medicare Law," *San Francisco Chronicle,* March 15, 2004.

127 **"deceiving the people":** Hugo Black, *New York Times Co. v. United States,* 403 U.S. 713 (1971).

CHAPTER 5: THE ASSAULT ON THE INDIVIDUAL

129 **tonnage remained the same:** Alan Greenspan, speech to the Conference Board in New York, October 16, 1996.

132 **with their lawyers:** Dahlia Lithwick, "Ashcroft Likes to Listen," *Slate,* November 15, 2001.

133 **"the whole procedure":** Franz Kafka, *The Trial* (London: Gollancz, 1937), first English edition.

133 **"Nazi or Communist":** Winston Churchill, telegram to British Home Secretary Herbert Morrison, November 21, 1943.

134 **down the door:** John Paul Stevens, *Richards v. Wisconsin,* 520 U.S. 385 (1997).

134 **your stuff back:** Anthony Kennedy, *West Covino v. Perkins,* 525 U.S. 234 (1999).

134 **garden-variety crime:** Congressional Research Service, "Report for Congress, Terrorism:

Section by Section Analysis of the USA PATRIOT Act," December 10, 2001. http://www.cdt.org/security/usapatriot/011210crs.pdf, pp.9–10.

134 a foreign power: ibid, pp. 9–11.

134 more than 18,000 filed: Electronic Privacy Information Center, "Foreign Intelligence Surveillance Act Orders 1979–2005." http://www.epic.org/privacy/wiretap/stats/fisa_stats.html.

134 from any court: George W. Bush, "President Discusses Homeland Security at the FBI Academy," White House Release, September 10, 2003. http://www.whitehouse.gov/news/releases/2003/09/20030910-6.html.

135 all your e-mail: Congressional Research Service, "Report for Congress, Terrorism: Section by Section Analysis of the USA PATRIOT Act," December 10, 2001. http://www.cdt.org/security/usapatriot/011210crs.pdf.

135 a massive scale: Attorney General Gonzales, "Memorandum from the United States Department of Justice, Legal Authorities Supporting the Activities of the National Security Agency Described by the President," Department of Justice, January 19, 2006. www.usdoj.gov/opa/whitepaperonnsalegalauthorities.pdf.

136 "and sudden usurpations": James Madison, under the pseudonym "Publius," Federalist Paper No. 45, New York *Independent Journal, New-York Packet,* New York *Daily Advertiser,* January 26, 1788.

136 kinds of companies: Barton Gellman, "The FBI's Secret Scrutiny," *Washington Post,* November 6, 2005.

136 of criminal behavior: Marvin J. Johnson, "Interested Persons Memo: Brief Analysis of Proposed Changes to Attorney General Guidelines," American Civil Liberties Union, May 30, 2002. http://aclu.org/natsec/emergpowers/144141eg20020530.html.

136 a legitimate investigation: Linda E. Fischer, "Guilt by Expressive Association: Political Profiling, Surveillance and the Privacy of Groups," *Arizona Law Review* 46 (2004): 620.

137 "in the country": "Supplementary Detailed Staff Report on Intelligence Activities and the Rights of Americans," United States Senate Select Committee to Study Governmental Operations, April 23, 1976.

137 "off his pedestal": William C. Sullivan, as quoted in Select Committee to Study Governmental Operations with Respect to Intelligence Activities, "Supplementary Detailed Staff Reports on Intelligence Activities and the Rights of Americans," final report, April 23, 1976.

138 still in place: Eric Lichtblau, "Bush Defends Spy Program and Denies Misleading Public," *New York Times,* January 2, 2006.

138 is not reassuring: Eric Lichtblau, "Bush Defends Spy Program and Denies Misleading Public," *The New York Times,* January 2, 2006

138 repeatedly and persistently: Anna Diggs Taylor, *ACLU V. NSA* 06-CV-10204 (2006).

139 on September 11: Alberto Gonzales, "Testimony Before the U.S. Senate Judiciary Committee," published by the *Washington Post,* February 6, 2006. http://www.washingtonpost.com/wp-dyn/content/article/2006/02/06/AR2006020600931.html.

139 not be possible: Alberto Gonzales, "Press Briefing by Attorney General Alberto Gonzales and General Michael Hayden, Principal Deputy Director for National Intelligence,"

December 19, 2005. http://www.whitehouse.gov/news/releases/2005/12/20051219-1.html.

139 not operate domestically: James McGovern, *Congressional Record,* September 14, 2001. Ted Stevens, *Congressional Record,* September 14, 2001.

139 "law is king": Thomas Paine, *Common Sense, The Rights of Man and Other Essential Writings of Thomas Paine,* Jack Fruchtman and Sydney Hook ed. (New York: Penguin Books, 2003), p. 38.

140 of the hijackers: Jim VandeHei and Dan Eggen, "Cheney Cites Justifications for Domestic Eavesdropping," *Washington Post,* January 5, 2006.

141 crashed in Pennsylvania: The Markle Foundation Task Force, "Protecting America's Freedom in the Information Age," The Markle Foundation Task Force publication, October 2002, p. 32.

142 "Dumping more hay": Matthew B. Stannard, "U.S. Phone-Call Database Igniting Privacy Uproar," *San Francisco Chronicle,* May 12, 2006.

142 "liberty and safety": Thomas Jefferson, *The Writings of Thomas Jefferson Vol.III,* Andrew A. Lipscomb, ed. (Washington, D.C.: Thomas Jefferson Memorial Association, 1903), p. 322.

143 "crisis came along": Supreme Court Justice Willam J. Brennan, Jr., "The Quest to Develop a Jurisprudence of Civil Liberties in Times of Security Crises," lecture at Hebrew University in Jerusalem, December 22, 1987.

144 "assertion of authority": Supreme Court Justice Felix Frankfurter, *Youngstown Sheet & Tube Co. v. Sawyer,* 343 U.S. 579 (1952).

144 about their customers: Jon Swartz and Kevin Johnson, "U.S. Asks Internet Firms to Save Data," *USA Today,* June 1, 2006.

147 "after his arrest": Anthony Lewis, "Un-American Activities," *The New York Review of Books* 50 (2003): 16.

147 "do unto me": Matthew 25:34–40.

147 the names secret: American Civil Liberties Union, "Coalition Letter Urging the Senate to Closely Examine Nominee Michael Chertoff's Record," February 1, 2005. http://www.alcu.org/safefree/general/188441eg20050201.html.

148 "its difficulties": Opinion of Court President Aharon Barak, Supreme Court of Israel, September 6, 1999.

150 approved his firing: Dan Eggen, "Fired U.S. Attorney Says Lawmakers Pressured Him," *Washington Post,* March 1, 2007.

150 of any charge: Patrick Quinn, "US War Prisons Legal Vacuum for 14,000," Associated Press, September 16, 2006.

151 them for interrogation: Jackie Spinner, "Soldier: Unit's Role Was to Break Down Prisoners," *Washington Post,* May 8, 2004.

151 "prisoners is concerned": John Barry, Michael Hirsh, Michael Isikoff, "The Roots of Torture," *Newsweek,* May 24, 2004. www.msnbc.msn.com/id/4989481.

152 "and our allies": George W. Bush, *State of the Union Address,* January 28, 2003. http://www. whitehouse.gov/news/releases/2003/01/20030128-19.html.

153 pattern of abuse: Douglas Jehl, Steven Lee Myers, Eric Schmitt, "Abuse of Captives More Widespread, Says Army Survey," *New York Times,* May 26, 2004.

153 **perverted legal memorandum:** Mike Allen and Dana Priest, "Memo on Torture Draws Focus to Bush," *Washington Post,* June 9, 2004.

153 **laws are just wrong:** Neil A. Lewis, "Justice Dept. Toughens Rule on Torture," *New York Times,* January 1, 2005.

154 **Court of Appeals:** ibid.

155 **"blow some steam off":** Jonathan Alter, "The Picture the World Sees," *Newsweek,* May 17, 2004.

155 **"human face—forever":** George Orwell, *1984* (New York: Signet Classic, 1990), p. 267.

156 **"of its provisions":** John Barry, Michael Hirsh, Michael Isikoff, "The Roots of Torture," *Newsweek,* May 24, 2004. www.msnbc.msn.com/id/4989481.

156 **"honest," he said:** Brian Ross and Alexandra Salomon, "Definitely a Cover-Up," ABC News, May 18, 2004.

156 **"going to get":** Laura Ingraham, interview with Bill O'Reilly, *The O'Reilly Factor,* Fox News, September 13, 2006.

157 **"they've just seen":** Jane Mayer, "Whatever It Takes," *The New Yorker,* February 19, 2007. http://www.newyorker.com/fact/content/articles/070219fa_fact_mayer.

157 **any wrongdoing:** Patrick Quinn, "US War Prisons Legal Vacuum for 14,000," Associated Press, September 16, 2006.

159 **"license summary execution":** Adam Liptak, "Legal Scholars Criticize Memos on Torture," *New York Times,* June 25, 2004.

159 **"can long endure":** Abraham Lincoln, the Gettysburg Address, November 19, 1863.

CHAPTER 6: NATIONAL INSECURITY

164 **the greatest magnitude:** Joint United Nations Program on HIV/AIDS, Fact Sheet, 2006.

165 **"moves the world":** Thomas Jefferson, *The Writings of Thomas Jefferson Vol.XIV,* Andrew A. Lipscomb, ed. (Washington, D.C.: Thomas Jefferson Memorial Association, 1903), pp. 222–3.

167 **an imminent threat:** Andrew Buncombe, "CIA Denies Claim That Iraq Posed 'Imminent Danger,' " *The Independent,* February 6, 2004.

167 **with imminent threats:** United Nations, "Charter of the United Nations," June 26, 1945. http://www.un.org/aboutun/charter/.

169 **"adopted in 1996":** Hans Blix, "Address at the Reception to Mark the 50th Anniversary of the UN Scientific Committee on the Effects of Atomic Radiation," May 30, 2006. http://www.unis.unvienna.org/unis/pressrels/2006/unisinf146.html.

170 ***non*-nuclear states:** Amy F. Woolf, "The Nuclear Posture Review: Overview and Emerging Issues," CRS Report for Congress, January 31, 2002.

171 **"no nuclear terrorism":** Graham Allison, "How to Stop Nuclear Terrorism," *Foreign Affairs,* January/February 2004.

171 **to fissile material:** ibid.

171 **"remains inadequately secured":** ibid.

174 **"and degrading treatment":** Geneva Conventions relative to the Treatment of Prisoners of War, Article 3, entered into force 1950. http://www.unhchr.ch/html/menu3/b/91.htm.

175 **"shall know them":** Matthew 7:16.

176 **"lowered the bar":** James Zogby, "Statement Before the United States Senate Committee on the Judiciary," November 18, 2003.

176 **"fact positively harmful":** Craig Murray, "Letter 3. Subject: Receipt of Intelligence Obtained Under Torture," July 2004.

176 **accused of corruption:** Selwyn Raab, "Donovan Cleared of Fraud Charges by Jury in Bronx," *New York Times,* May 26, 1987.

179 **down the discussion:** Lisa Myers, "Did Ashcroft Brush Off Terror Warnings?" NBC News, June 23, 2004.

179 **"radical fundamentalist goals":** The 9/11 Commission, *The 9/11 Commission Report: Final Report of the National Commission on Terrorist Attacks Upon the United States* (New York: W. W. Norton & Company, 2004), p. 273.

179 **was "blinking red":** ibid., p. 259.

179 **was blown off:** Phillip Shelnon and Mark Mazzetti, "Records Show Tenet Briefed Rice on Al Qaeda Threat," *New York Times,* October 2, 2006.

179 **"strike in U.S.":** The 9/11 Commission, *The 9/11 Commission Report: Final Report of the National Commission on Terrorist Attacks Upon the United States* (New York: W. W. Norton & Company, 2004), p. 260.

180 **to journalist Ron Suskind:** Ron Suskind, *The One Percent Doctrine* (New York: Simon & Schuster, 2006), p. 2.

180 **"the United States":** The 9/11 Commission, *The 9/11 Commission Report: Final Report of the National Commission on Terrorist Attacks Upon the United States* (New York: W. W. Norton & Company, 2004), p. 262.

180 **"was not warned":** ibid., p. 265.

181 **fourfold in 2005:** National Counterterrorism Center, "Report on the Incidents of Terrorism 2005," April 11, 2006. wits.nctc.gov/reports/crot2005nctcannexfinal.pdf.

181 **"increasing attacks worldwide":** Office of the Director of the National Intelligence, "Declassified Key Judgments of the National Intelligence Estimate, Trends in Global Terrorism: Implications for the United States," 2006. www.dni.gov/press_releases/Declassified_NIE_Key_Judgments.pdf.

182 **"global counter-terrorism coalition":** "Strategic Survey 2003/2004," The International Institute for Strategic Studies (New York: Routledge, 2004).

182 **corroborated . . . around the world:** "The Middle East Strategic Balance 2003–2004," Shai Feldman and Yiftah Shapir, eds., The Jaffee Center for Strategic Studies, 2004.

183 **of investigative stories:** Steve Vogel and William Branigin, "Army Fires Commander of Walter Reed," *Washington Post,* March 2, 2007.

183 **"into the abyss":** Joseph Hoar, "Testimony to the Senate Committee on Foreign Relations," May 19, 2004.

183 **"over Niagara Falls":** Anthony Zinni interview with Steve Kroft, *60 Minutes* CBS, May 23, 2004, and *Battle Ready* (New York: Putnam Publishing, 2004).

183 **"by Pentagon officials":** Anthony Zinni, *Battle Ready* (New York: Berkley Books, 2004), pp. 426–7.

184 **"to military advice":** Thomas E. Ricks, "US Military Divided on Iraq Occupation," *Washington Post,* May 10, 2004.

184 **"are," he said:** ibid.

184 **"from happening again":** Thomas E. Ricks, "Inside War Room, a Battle Is Raging," *Washington Post,* May 9, 2004.

184 **"think they care":** ibid.

185 **"and foe alike":** Doug Bandow, "Why Conservatives Must Not Vote for Bush," *Salon,* September 10, 2004.

185 **"opposed the war":** David D. Kirkpatrick, "National Review Founder to Leave Stage," *New York Times,* June 29, 2004.

188 **billion and counting:** David Leonhardt, "What $1.2 Trillion Can Buy," *New York Times,* January 17, 2007.

188 **"products in August":** Andrew Card, as quoted by Elisabeth Bumiller, *New York Times,* September 7, 2002.

189 **"on the war":** John King, rushed transcript, "White House Computer Disk Falls in Hands of Democrats; Gore Spokesman Shares Inside Story; Interview with Gov. Bill Owens," CNN.com, June 14, 2002. http://transcripts.cnn.com/TRANSCRIPTS/0206/14/ip.00.html.

189 *Rush Limbaugh Show:* "Rush's interview with Vice President Richard B. Cheney," *The Rush Limbaugh Show,* September 13, 2002. http://www.rushlimbaugh.com/home/weekend_sites/christmas1/content/interview_with_vice_president_richard_b_cheney__transcript.guest.html.

190 **postinvasion stabilization:** Fred Kaplan, "Blow-Back in Baghdad," *Slate,* July 8, 2003.

190 **"America? Absolutely not":** George W. Bush, "The Second Presidential Debate," October 11, 2000. http://www.cbsnews.com/stories/2000/10/11/politics/main 240442.shtml.

CHAPTER 7: THE CARBON CRISIS

192 **it every day:** Timothy Gardner, "World CO_2 Emissions to Rise 75 PCT by 2030," Reuters, June 21, 2006.

192 **largest is Venezuela:** Energy Information Administration, "Crude Oil and Total Petroleum Imports Top 15 Countries," February 2, 2007. http://www.eia.doe.gov/pub/oil_gas/petroleum/data_publications/company_level_imports/current/import.html.

194 **"on a limb":** Quin Shea, as quoted in "Materials Regarding the Clear Skies Act of 2005," transcribed by the National Resource Defense Council (2005), p. 51.

194 **about the report:** "Bush Disses Global Warming Report," CBS News, June 4, 2002.

195 **the earliest opportunity:** Ron Suskind, *The Price of Loyalty* (New York: Simon & Schuster, 2004).

195 **BP, and Shell:** Danny Fortson, Andrew Murray-Watson, and Tim Webb, "Future of Iraq: The Spoils of War," *The Independent,* January 7, 2007.

195 **"Only one had":** "Blood and Oil: How the West Will Profit from Iraq's Most Precious Commodity," *The Independent,* January 7, 2007

195 **of foreign oil:** "Oil Prices and the U.S. Trade Deficit," Federal Reserve Bank of San Francisco, Economic Letter, September 22, 2006.

197 **reduce mercury:** "Information on Power Plant Mercury Emissions Censored," Union of Concerned Scientists, February 18, 2004. http://www.ucsusa.org/scientific_integrity/interference/mercury-emissions.html.

197 of $175 million: Felicity Barringer, "Polluted Sites Could Face Shortage of Cleanup Money," *New York Times,* August 16, 2004.

198 use of parks: Joe Baird, "Ex-Parks Employees Take Aim at Bush, Ex-National Park Bosses Blast Bush," *Salt Lake Tribune,* August 16, 2003.

198 the Bush campaign: "America's Dirtiest Power Plants: Plugged into the Bush Administration," Environmental Integrity Project, Public Citizen's Congress Watch, May 2004. http://www.whitehouseforsale.org/.

199 "pollute with impunity": Richard A. Oppel Jr. and Christopher Drew, "Senators and Attorneys General Seek Investigation into E.P.A. Rules Change," *New York Times,* November 7, 2003.

199 "us," Biondi said: Christopher Drew and Richard A. Oppel Jr., "How Industry Won the Battle of Pollution Control at E.P.A.," *New York Times,* March 6, 2004.

200 the scientific community: Ian Sample, "Scientists Offered Cash to Dispute Climate Study," *The Guardian,* February 2, 2007.

200 "in the debate": Frank Luntz, as quoted in "Frontline Interview," PBS, November 13, 2006.

201 "anthropogenic climate change": Bob Ward, "Letter to Nick Thomas," September 4, 2006. http://www.climatesciencewatch.org/index.php/csw/details/royal-society-exxon-letter/.

201 "global warming science": "Smoke, Mirrors & Hot Air," Union of Concerned Scientists, January 2007. http://www.ucsusa.org/news/press_release/ExxonMobil-GlobalWarming-tobacco.html.

201 "over forty years": "Scientists' Report Documents ExxonMobil's Tobacco-like Disinformation Campaign on Global Warming Science," Union of Concerned Scientists, January 2007. http://www.ucsusa.org/news/press_release/ExxonMobil-GlobalWarming-tobacco.html.

202 "non-peer-reviewed pseudoscience": John D. Rockefeller and Olympia Snowe, "Letter to Rex Tilson," October 27, 2006. http://snowe.senate.gov/public/index.cfm?FuseAction=PressRoom.PressReleases&ContentRecord_id=9acba744-802a-23ad-47be-2683985c724e&Region_id=&Issue_id=.

202 worth $400 million: "Exxon Chairman's $400 Million Parachute," ABC News, April 14, 2006.

203 of the planet: "Stratospheric Ozone," The National Center for Atmospheric Research, Accessed 2007. http://www.ucar.edu/learn/1_6_1.html.

204 little as thirty-four years: Marika Holland et al., "Future Abrupt Reductions in the Summer Arctic Sea Ice," *Geophysical Research Letters* 33 (2006).

205 the Richter scale: Ken Kostel and Steve Bradt, "Glacial Earthquakes Point to Rising Temperatures in Greenland," *Earth Institute News,* March 23, 2006.

205 "warming is over": Gary Stix, "A Climate Repair Manual," *Scientific American,* September 2006.

209 for global warming: Elisabeth Rosenthal and Andrew Revkin, "Panel Issues Bleak Report on Climate Change," *New York Times,* February 2, 2007.

210 "period of consequences": Winston Churchill, *Never Give In, The Best of Winston*

Churchill's Speeches, Winston Churchill, ed. (New York: Hyperion, 2003), p. 153.

210 **"stand for freedom":** Winston Churchill, *The Second World War* (Boston: Houghton Mifflin Company, 1986), p. 294.

211 **"his not understanding":** Upton Sinclair, *I, Candidate for Governor: And How I Got Licked* (Berkeley: University of California Press, 1994), p. 108.

211 **about 50 percent:** Emanuel A. Kerry, "Increasing Destructiveness of Tropical Cyclones over the Past 30 Years," *Nature* 436 (2005): 686–688.

212 **"save our country":** Abraham Lincoln, "Second Annual Message," December 1, 1862. http://www.presidency.ucsb.edu/ws/index.php?pid=29503.

CHAPTER 8: DEMOCRACY IN THE BALANCE

215 **"will attach themselves":** James Madison, Alexander Hamilton, and John Jay, *The Federalist Papers,* Isaac Kramnick, ed. (New York: Penguin Books, 2003), p. 73.

216 **"auxiliary precautions":** James Madison, Alexander Hamilton, John Jay, *The Federalist Papers,* Isaac Kramnick, ed. (New York: Penguin Books, 2003), p. 319.

217 **"in the Legislature":** James Madison, "Letter to Thomas Jefferson, April 2, 1798," *The Writings of James Madison,* Gaillard Hunt, ed. (New York: G. P. Putnam's Sons, 1906), vol. 6, pp. 312–313.

217 **"his military role":** Supreme Court Justice Robert H. Jackson, *Youngstown Sheet & Tube Co. v. Sawyer,* 103 F.Supp. 569 (1952).

218 **"President and Congress":** Supreme Court Justice Felix Frankfurter, *Youngstown Sheet & Tube Co. v. Sawyer,* 103 F.Supp. 569 (1952).

221 **"describe as totalitarian":** Supreme Court Justice Robert H. Jackson, *Youngstown Sheet & Tube Co. v. Sawyer* 103 F.Supp. 569 (1952).

221 **"not of men":** John Adams, Massachusetts Bill of Rights, 1780.

221 **"can keep it":** Benjamin Franklin, at the 1787 Constitutional Convention in Philadelphia, *The American Historical Review,* vol. 11, 1906, p. 618.

221 **enforce the law:** Anna Diggs Taylor, *ACLU V. NSA* 06-CV-10204 (2006).

222 **"definition of tyranny":** James Madison, under the pseudonym "Publius," Federalist Paper No. 47, New York *Independent Journal, New-York Packet,* New York *Daily Advertiser,* January 30, 1788.

224 **as it is:** Constitution of the United States, Article I, Section 7, September 23, 1788.

224 **four years in office:** Editorial board of *The New York Times,* "Veto? Who Needs a Veto?" *New York Times,* May 5, 2006.

225 **"rule of law":** Charlie Savage, "Bush Challenges Hundreds of Laws," *Boston Globe,* April 30, 2006.

225 **"unlimited executive power":** ibid.

227 **"the Mayberry Machiavellis":** Ron Suskind, "Why Are These Men Laughing?" *Esquire,* January 2003.

228 **"its co-ordinate branches":** Alexander Hamilton, under the pseudonym "Publius," Federalist Paper No. 78, New York *Independent Journal, New-York Packet,* New York *Daily Advertiser,* May 28, 1788.

228 **"everything to fear":** ibid.

228 **"legislative and executive powers":** Charles de Secondat, baron de Montesquieu, *The Spirit of the Laws,* vol. 1, Thomas Nugent, trans. (London: J. Nourse, 1777), pp. 221–237, passim.

229 **"legislature or executive":** *The Annals of Congress,* House of Representatives, First Congress, 1st Session, pp. 448–460 (compiled between 1834 and 1856).

229 **"completely independent judiciary":** Carl Hulse and David D. Kirkpatrick, "DeLay Says Federal Judiciary Has 'Run Amok,' Adding Congress Is Partly to Blame," *New York Times,* April 8, 2005.

230 **"for their behavior":** Charles Babington, "Senator Links Violence to 'Political' Decisions," *Washington Post,* April 5, 2005.

230 **"power of the purse":** Rick Klein, "DeLay Apologizes for Blaming Federal Judges in Schiavo Case," *Boston Globe,* April 14, 2005.

230 **"them in line":** Debbie Elliott, "Congressional Republicans Target 'Activist' Judiciary," *All Things Considered,* National Public Radio, March 26, 2005.

230 **"engage in violence":** Senator John Cornyn (R-Tex.), floor speech in the U.S. Senate, April 4, 2005; cornyn.senate.gov/record.cfm?id=236007.

231 **"to an end":** Ruth Marcus, "Booting the Bench," *Washington Post,* April 11, 2005.

231 **"nothing to do":** Peter Wallsten, "Evangelical Groups Seek 'Defunding' of Judges," *Los Angeles Times,* April 23, 2005.

231 **"and it's gone":** ibid.

232 **"in the community":** Alexander Hamilton, under the pseudonym "Publius," Federalist Paper No. 78, New York *Independent Journal, New-York Packet,* New York *Daily Advertiser,* May 28, 1788.

233 **judge in attendance:** Doug Kendall and Eric Sorkin, "Nothing for Free: How Private Judicial Seminars Are Undermining Environmental Protections and Breaking the Public's Trust," Community Rights Council, July 2000. www.tripsforjudges.org/crc.pdf.

234 **also increased dramatically:** ibid.

234 **Republican-appointed judges:** ibid.

234 **"'involving economic issues'":** ibid.

241 **"us reason together":** Isaiah 1:18.

242 **"a systemic crisis":** Orrin Hatch, "Crisis, What Crisis?" *USA Today,* September 5, 1997.

242 **"and the Constitution":** Orrin Hatch, "Crisis Mode," *National Review* Online, January 12, 2005. http://www.nationalreview.com/comment/hatch200501120729.asp.

242 **"always received a vote":** Bill Frist, "It's Time for Up-or-Down Vote," *USA Today,* May 15, 2005.

242 **"not always right":** Charles Babington, "Filibuster Precedent? Democrats Point to '68 and Fortas," *Washington Post,* March 18, 2005.

242 **"mischief of factions":** James Madison, under the pseudonym "Publius," Federalist Paper No. 10, New York *Independent Journal, New-York Packet,* New York *Daily Advertiser,* November 22, 1787.

243 **"this blocking mechanism":** George Will, "Shock and Awe in the Senate," *Newsweek,* December 6, 2004.

243 **to eliminate it:** John McCain, interview with Chris Matthews, *Hardball,* MSNBC,

April 14, 2005.

244 "it with you": As quoted by Ron Suskind, "Faith, Certainty and the Presidency of George W. Bush," *New York Times Magazine,* October 17, 2004.

CHAPTER 9: A WELL-CONNECTED CITIZENRY

245 "of the people": Abraham Lincoln, "The Perpetuation of Our Political Institutions," address before the Young Men's Lyceum of Springfield, Illinois, January 27, 1838. http://showcase.netins.net/web/creative/lincoln/speeches/lyceum.htm.

248 category as infants: L. Alan Sroufe, Byron Egeland, and Terri Kreutzer, "The Fate of Early Experience Following Developmental Change: Longitudinal Approaches to Individual Adaptation in Childhood," *Child Development* 61 (1990): 1363–1373.

248 the communication environment: Marti Erickson, personal communication with Marti Erickson, January/February 2007.

250 "reason and information": Thomas Jefferson, *The Writings of Thomas Jefferson Vol.III,* Andrew A. Lipscomb, ed. (Washington, D.C.: Thomas Jefferson Memorial Association, 1903), p. 37.

252 "all is safe": Thomas Jefferson, *The Writings of Thomas Jefferson Vol.XIV,* ed. Andrew A. Lipscomb, (Washington, D.C.: Thomas Jefferson Memorial Association, 1903), p. 384.

252 "to the slaughter": George Washington, *The Writings of George Washington Vol.III,* Jared Sparks, ed. (Boston: Ferdinand Andrews, 1838), p. 562.

254 name two candidates: American National Election Study, 2000.

255 from television news: James Snyder and David Stromberg, "Media Markets' Impact on Politics," 2004. americandemocracy.nd.edu/speaker_series/files/SnyderPaper.pdf.

255 on the courts: FindLaw, "Most Americans Can't Name Any Supreme Court Justices," January 10, 2006. http://company.findlaw.com/pr/2006/011006.supremes.html.

255 by William Rehnquist: American National Election Study, 2000.

255 of Congress unconstitutional: Annenberg Public Policy Center, "Constitution Day: For Many Americans, It's Time for the Basics," September 14, 2006. www.annenberg publicpolicycenter.org.

255 to declare war: Ilya Somin, "When Ignorance Isn't Bliss," Cato Institute Policy Analysis No. 525, September 22, 2004.

255 "the United States": Quoted in the Intercollegiate Studies Institute, "The Coming Crisis in Citizenship," 2006. http://www.americancivicliteracy.org/report/summary.html.

256 "church and state": ibid.

256 "it for granted": John S. and James L. Knight Foundation, "The Future of the First Amendment," 2005, p. 3. http://www.knightfdn.org/default.asp?story=news_at_knight/ releases/2005/2005_01_31_firstamend.html.

256 "set them right": Thomas Jefferson, *The Writings of Thomas Jefferson Vol.VII,* Andrew A. Lipscomb, ed. (Washington, D.C.: Thomas Jefferson Memorial Association, 1904), p. 253.

256 "never will be": Thomas Jefferson, *The Writings of Thomas Jefferson Vol.XIV,* ed. Andrew A. Lipscomb, (Washington, D.C.: Thomas Jefferson Memorial Association, 1903), p. 384.

258 on the proposition: Katherine Hunt, "Prop. 87 Divides Californians Along Party Lines," MarketWatch, November 3, 2006. http://www.marketwatch.com/news/story/

Story.aspx?guid=%7BBBBD63BEC-B0EA-45BF-B78E-62140B829168%7D&siteid=&
print=true&dist=printTop.

262 **"nourished and promoted":** Vinton G. Cerf, "Prepared Statement to the U.S. Senate Committee on Commerce, Science and Transportation," February 7, 2006, p. 2.

263 **"single public place":** Larry Lessig, *Free Culture* (New York: Penguin Press, 2004), p. 42.

267 **"tiered Internet":** Ben Scott, "Testimony Before the United States Senate Committee on Commerce, Science and Transportation," May 25, 2006. www.freepress.net/docs/senate_nn_commerce_testimony.doc.

269 **joined the movement:** Ben Scott, "Beyond Net Neutrality: Internet Freedom," *TomPaine.commonsense*, January 26, 2007. http://www.tompaine.com/articles/2007/01/26/beyond_net_neutrality_internet_freedom.php.

CONCLUSION: THE REBIRTH OF DEMOCRACY

271 **severely punish transgressors:** François Furstenberg, *In the Name of the Father* (New York: Penguin Press, 2006) pp. 170–1.

272 **evils of slavery:** ibid pp.147–50.

272 **"be a slave":** ibid p.148.

272 **"close around us":** Martin Luther King Jr., "Beyond Vietnam: A Time to Break Silence," address at a meeting of clergy and laity concerned at Riverside Church in New York City, April 4, 1967. http://www.hartford-hwp.com/archives/45a/058.html.

272 **"to future generations":** Sandra Day O'Connor, Anthony Kennedy, and David Souter, *Planned Parenthood of Southeastern PA v. Casey*, 505 U.S. 833 (1992).

273 **it matters less:** Oliver Wendell Holmes, dissent in *Abrams v. US*, 250 U.S. 616 (1919).

Index

Index

Index

McLuhan, Marshall, 20

Madison, James
  on abridgment of freedoms, 136
  on factions, 49, 61, 68, 242
  on judicial branch, 229
  on reason, 215
  on tyrannical power, 222
  on war-making and president, 217

Mail, opening without warrant, 135, 136, 225–26

Manichaeism, 55

Marshall, John, 228

Mass media. *See* Media

Material witness statute, 149

Mayer, Jane, 157

Mazur, Paul, 94

Media
  news coverage, deficiencies of, 3–4, 5, 16–18
  one-way media, dangers of, 16, 91–94, 97,
    102–3, 246
  phony video press releases, 126, 127
  press, muzzling of, 125–26
  right-wing propagandists, 66–69
  wealth-power coupling, 77–78, 98–99
  See also Internet; Printing press and democ-
    racy; Propaganda; Radio; Television

Medicare drug benefit, 81, 124, 150

Meese, Edwin, 225

Mehmood, Anser, 146–47

Mercury pollution, 197

Meyer, Alden, 201

Military, U.S.
  Geneva Conventions protection of, 149–74
  Iraq War, lack of preparedness, 113–15,
    182–83
  leaders on Iraq War fiasco, 183–84
  military candor, suppression of, 57, 113–14,
    184
  on prisoner torture, 151

Mill, John Stuart, 11

Milošević, Slobodan, 33

Monopolies
  and mass media, 98–99
  wealth-power coupling, 83–84

Montesquieu, Baron de, 228

Moqed, Majed, 141

More, Thomas, 70

Morgan, Joy Elmer, 18

Moussaoui, Zacarias, 179

MoveOn.org, 18–19, 262–63

Muckrakers, 89

Murrow, Edward R., 7, 25

Muskie, Ed, 43

Mussolini, Benito, 92, 93

Muttitt, Greg, 195

National Intelligence Estimate, 116–17, 181

National parks, 198

National security
  global security approach, 162–65
  preemption doctrine, 166–68

Nazism
  intelligence of leaders, 251–53
  and media/propaganda, 92–93, 253

New Deal, 68, 97, 150, 229

Nixon, Richard
  Bush compared to, 42–43, 65, 120
  Congress and, 212

No-bid contracts, 80–81

Nuclear Non-Proliferation Treaty, 170

Nuclear Posture Review, 170

Nuclear weapons, 169–73
  agreements/treaties, rejected by Bush, 169–71
  nuclear preemption doctrine, 170, 172
  space-based, 172–73

Nunn, Sam, 171

Odom, William, 4

Oil
  Arctic Refuge drilling, 198
  and climate crisis, 191–94
  and Iraq War, 117–18, 119, 193–94, 195
  suppliers to U.S., 192
  U.S. dependence, dangers of, 191–93,
    195–96

Oil companies
  Bush's favoritism, 119, 195, 200–202, 204
  climate change pseudostudies, 199–201
  Iraq oil, access to, 119, 195